LECTURES

ON THE

DRAMATIC LITERATURE

OF THE

AGE OF ELIZABETH.

BY

WILLIAM HAZLITT.

PHILADELPHIA:
J. B. LIPPINCOTT COMPANY.

AS A TRIBUTE

TO PUBLIC VIRTUE AND PRIVATE WORTH

AND AS A MEMORIAL OF LONG AND TRIED FRIENDSHIP

THIS VOLUME IS INSCRIBED,

IN THE NAME OF ITS AUTHOR

TO

BASIL MONTAGU

CONTENTS.

ADVERTISEMENT TO THE LAST LONDON EDITION,

BY THE AUTHOR'S SON.

The former editions of the Lectures, originally delivered by the author at the Surrey Institution in 1818, and published in the same year, having become exhausted, the present reprint has been undertaken, for the purpose of supplying the constant and increasing demand which is made for it.

There is no feature in the retrospect of the last few years, more important and more delightful than the steady advance of an improved taste in literature: and both as a cause and as a consequence of this, the works of William Hazlitt, which heretofore have been duly appreciated only by the few, are now having ample justice done them by the many. With reference to the present work, the Edinburgh Review eloquently observes, "Mr. Hazlitt possesses one noble quality at least for the office which he has chosen, in the intense admiration and love which he feels for the great authors on whose excellencies he chiefly dwells. His relish for their beauties is so keen, that while he describes them, the pleasures which they impart become almost palpable to the sense, and we seem, scarcely in a figure, to feast and banquet on their 'nectared sweets.' He introduces us almost corporally into the divine presence of the great of old time—enables us to hear the living oracles of wisdom drop from their lips—and makes us partakers, not only of those joys which they diffused, but of those which they felt in the inmost recesses of their souls. He draws aside the veil of time with a hand tremulous with mingled delight and reverence ; and descants with kindling enthusiasm, on all the delicacies of that picture of genius which he discloses. His intense admiration of intellectual beauty seems always to sharpen his critical faculties. He perceives it, by a kind of intuitive power, how deeply soever it may be buried in rubbish ; and separates it in a moment from all that would encumber or deface it. At the same time, he exhibits to us those hidden sources of beauty, not like an anatomist, but like a lover. He does not coolly dissect the form to show the springs whence the blood flows all eloquent, and the divine expression is kindled ; but makes us feel in the sparkling or softened eye, the wreathed smile, and the tender bloom. In a word, he at once analyzes and describes—so that our enjoyments of loveliness are not chilled, but brightened by our acquaintance with their inward sources. The knowledge communicated in his lectures breaks no sweet enchantment, nor chills one feeling of youthful joy. His criticisms, while they extend our insight into the causes of poetical excellence, teach us, at the same time, more keenly to enjoy, and more fondly to revere it."

LECTURES

ON THE

AGE OF ELIZABETH, &c.

LECTURE I.—INTRODUCTORY.

General View of the Subject.

The age of Elizabeth was distinguished, beyond, perhaps, any other in our history, by a number of great men, famous in different ways, and whose names have come down to us with unblemished honours; statesmen, warriors, divines, scholars, poets, and philosophers, Raleigh, Drake, Coke, Hooker, and higher and more sounding still, and still more frequent in our mouths, Shakspeare, Spenser, Sidney, Bacon, Jonson, Beaumont and Fletcher, men whom fame has eternized in her long and lasting scroll, and who by their words and acts were benefactors of their country, and ornaments of human nature. Their attainments of different kinds bore the same general stamp, and was sterling: what they did had the mark of their age and country upon it. Perhaps the genius of Great Britain (if I may so speak without offence or flattery) never shone out fuller or brighter, or looked more like itself, than at this period. Our writers and great men had something in them that savoured of the soil from which they grew: they were not French, they were not Dutch, or German, or Greek, or Latin; they were truly English. They did not look out of themselves to see what they should be; they sought for truth and nature, and found it in themselves. There was no tinsel, and but little art; they were not the spoiled children of affectation and refinement, but a bold, vigorous, independent race of thinkers, with prodigious strength and energy, with none but natural grace, and heartfelt, unobtrusive delicacy. They were not at all sophisticated. The mind of their country was great in them, and it prevailed. With their learning and unexampled acquirement they did not forget that they were men: with all their endeavours after excellence, they did not lay aside the strong original bent and character of their minds. What they performed was chiefly nature's handiwork; and time has claimed it for his own.—To these, however, might be added others not less learned, nor with a scarce less happy vein, but less fortunate in the event, who, though as renowned in their day, have sunk into "mere oblivion," and of whom the only record (but that the noblest) is to be found in their works. Their works and their names, "poor, poor, dumb names," are all that remains of such men as Webster, Decker, Marston, Marlowe, Chapman, Heywood, Middleton, and Rowley! "How lov'd, how honour'd once avails them not:" though they were the friends and fellow-labourers of Shakspeare, sharing his fame and fortunes with him, the rivals of Jonson, and the masters of Beaumont and Fletcher's well-sung woes! They went out one by one unnoticed, like evening lights; or were swallowed up in the headlong torrent of puritanic zeal which succeeded, and swept away everything in its unsparing course, throwing up the wrecks of taste and genius at random, and at long fitful intervals, amidst the painted gew-gaws and foreign frippery of the reign of Charles II., and from which we are only now recovering the scattered fragments and broken images to erect a temple to true Fame! How long before it will be completed?

If I can do anything to rescue some of these writers from hopeless obscurity, and to do them right, without prejudice to well deserved reputation, I shall have succeeded in what I chiefly propose. I shall not attempt, indeed, to adjust the spelling, or restore the pointing, as if the genius of poetry lay hid in errors of the press, but leaving these weightier matters of criticism to those who are more able and willing to bear the burden, try to bring out their real beauties to the eager sight, "draw the curtain of Time, and show the picture of Genius," restraining my own admiration within reasonable bounds.

There is not a lower ambition, a poorer way of thought, than that which would confine all excellence, or arrogate its final ac complishment to the present, or modern times. We ordinarily speak and think of those who had the misfortune to write or live before us, as labouring under very singular privations and disad vantages in not having the benefit of those improvements which we have made, as buried in the grossest ignorance, or the slaves "of poring pedantry;" and we make a cheap and infallible estimate of their progress in civilization upon a graduated scale of perfectibility, calculated from the meridian of our own times. If we have pretty well got rid of the narrow bigotry that would limit all sense or virtue to our own country, and have fraternized, like true cosmopolites, with our neighbours and contemporaries, we have made our self-love amends by letting the generation we live in engross nearly all our admiration, and by pronouncing a sweeping sentence of barbarism and ignorance on our ancestry backwards, from the commencement (as near as can be) of the nineteenth, or the latter end of the eighteenth century. From thence we date a new era, the dawn of our own intellect, and that of the world, like "the sacred influence of light" glimmering on the confines of "Chaos and old night;" new manners rise, and all the cumbrous "pomp of elder days" vanishes, and is lost in worse than Gothic darkness. Pavilioned in the glittering pride of our superficial accomplishments and upstart pretensions, we fancy that everything beyond that magic circle is prejudice and error; and all, before the present enlightened period, but a dull and useless blank in the great map of time. We are so dazzled with the gloss and novelty of modern discoveries, that we cannot take into our mind's eye the vast expanse, the lengthened perspective of human intellect, and a cloud hangs over and conceals its loftiest monuments, if they are removed to a little distance from us—the cloud of our vanity and short-sightedness. The modern sciolist stultifies all understanding but his own, and that which he conceives like his own. We think, in this age of reason and consummation of philosophy, because we knew nothing twenty or thirty years ago, and began then to think for the first time in our lives, that the rest of mankind were in the same predicament, and never knew anything till we did; that the world had grown old in sloth and ignorance, had dreamt out its lon minority of five thousand years in a dozing state, and that it first began to wake out of sleep, to rouse itself, and look about it, startled by the light of our unexpected discoveries, and the noise we made about them. Strange error of our infatuated self-love. Because the clothes we remember to have seen worn when we were children are now out of fashion, and our grandmothers were then old women, we conceive, with magnanimous continuity of reasoning, that it must have been much worse three hundred years before, and that grace, youth, and beauty are things of modern date—as if nature had ever been old, or the sun had first shone on our folly and presumption. Because, in a word, the last generation, when tottering off the stage, were not so active, so sprightly, and so promising as we were, we begin to imagine that people formerly must have crawled about in a feeble, torpid state, like flies in winter, in a sort of dim twilight of the understanding; "nor can we think what thoughts they could conceive," in the absence of all those topics that so agreeably enliven and diversify our conversation and literature, mistaking the imperfection of our knowledge for the defect of their organs, as if it was necessary for us to have a register and certificate of their thoughts, or as if, because they did not see with our eyes, hear with our ears, and understand with our understandings, they could hear, see, and understand nothing. A falser inference could not be drawn, nor one more contrary to the maxims and cautions of a wise humanity. "Think," says Shakspeare, the prompter of good and true feelings, "there's livers out of Britain." So there have been thinkers, and great and sound ones, before our time. They had the same capacities that we have, sometimes greater motives for their exertion, and for the most part, the same subject-matter to work upon. What we learn from nature, we may hope to do as well as they; what we learn from them we may in general expect to do worse.—What is, I think, as likely as anything to cure us of this overweening admiration of the present, and unmingled contempt for past times, is the looking at the finest old pictures; at Raphael's heads, at Titian's faces, at Claude's landscapes. We have there the evidence of the senses, without the alterations of opinion or disguise of language. We there see the blood circulate through the veins (long before it was known that t did so), the same red and white "by nature's own sweet and cunning hand laid on," the same thoughts passing through the mind and seated on the lips, the same blue sky, and glittering sunny vales, "where Pan, knit with the Graces and the Hours in dance, leads on the eternal spring." And we begin to feel that nature and the mind of man are not a thing of yesterday, as we had been led to suppose; and that "there are more things between heaven and earth than were ever dreamt of in our philosophy."—Or grant that we improve, in some respects, in a uniformly progressive ratio, and build, Babel-high, on the foundation of other men's knowledge, as in matters of science and speculative inquiry, where, by going often over the same general ground, certain general conclusions have been arrived at, and in the number of persons reasoning on a given subject, truth has at last been hit upon, and long-established error exploded; yet this does not apply to cases of individual power and knowledge, to a million of things besides, in which we are still to seek as much as ever, and in which we can only hope to find, by going to the fountain-head of thought and experience. We are quite wrong in supposing (as we are apt to do), that we can plead an exclusive title to wit and wisdom, to taste and genius, as the net produce and clear reversion of the age we live in, and that all we have to do to be great is to despise those who have gone before us as nothing.

Or even if we admit a saving clause in this sweeping proscription, and do not make the rule absolute, the very nature of the exception shows the spirit in which they are made. We single out one or two striking instances, say Shakspeare or Lord Bacon, which we would fain treat as prodigies, and as a marked contrast to the rudeness and barbarism that surrounded them. These we delight to dwell upon and magnify; the praise and wonder we heap upon their shrines are at the expense of the time in which they lived, and would leave it poor indeed. We make them out something more than human, "matchless, divine, what we will," so to make them no rule for their age, and no infringement of the abstract claim to superiority which we set up. Instead of letting them reflect any lustre, or add any credit to the period of history to which they rightfully belong, we only make use of their example to insult and degrade it still more beneath our own level.

It is the present fashion to speak with veneration of old English literature; but the homage we pay to it is more akin to the rites of superstition than to the worship of true religion. Our faith is doubtful; our love cold; our knowledge little or none. We now and then repeat the names of some of the old writers by rote, but we are shy of looking into their works. Though we seem disposed to think highly of them, and to give them every credit for a masculine and original vein of thought, as a matter of literary courtesy and enlargement of taste, we are afraid of coming to the proof, as too great a trial of our candour and patience. We regard the enthusiastic admiration of these obsolete authors, or a desire to make proselytes to a belief in their extraordinary merits, as an amiable weakness, a pleasing delusion; and prepare to listen to some favourite passage, that may be referred to in support of this singular taste, with an incredulous smile; and are in no small pain for the result of the hazardous experiment; feeling much the same awkward condescending disposition to patronize these first crude attempts at poetry and lispings of the Muse, as when a fond parent brings forward a bashful child to make a display of its wit or learning. We hope the best, put a good face on the matter, but are sadly afraid the thing cannot answer.—Dr. Johnson said of these writers generally, that "they were sought after because they were scarce, and would not have been scarce had they been much esteemed." His decision is neither true history nor sound criticism. They were esteemed, and they deserved to be so.

One cause that might be pointed out here, as having contributed to the long-continued neglect of our earlier writers, lies in the very nature of our academic institutions, which unavoidably neutralizes a taste for the productions of native genius, estranges the mind from the history of our own literature, and makes it in each successive age like a book sealed. The Greek and Roman classics are a sort of privileged text-books, the standing order of the day, in a University education, and leave little leisure for a competent acquaintance with, or due admiration of, a whole host of able writers of our own, who are suffered to moulder in obscurity on the shelves of our libraries, with a decent reservation of one or two top-names, that are cried up for form's sake, and to save the national character. Thus we keep a few of these always ready in capitals, and strike off the rest to prevent the tendency to a superfluous population in the republic of letters; in other words, to prevent the writers from becoming more numerous than the readers. The ancients are become effete in this respect, they no longer increase and multiply; or if they have imitators among us, no one is expected to read, and still less to admire them. It is not possible that the learned professors and the reading public should clash in this way, or necessary for them to use any precautions against each other. But it is not the same with the living languages, where there is danger of being overwhelmed by the crowd of competitors, and pedantry has combined with ignorance to cancel their unsatisfied claims.

We affect to wonder at Shakspeare, and one or two more of that period, as solitary instances upon record; whereas it is our own dearth of information that makes the waste; for there is no time more populous of intellect, or more prolific of intellectual wealth, than the one we are speaking of. Shakspeare did not look upon himself in this light, as a sort of monster of poetical genius, or on his contemporaries as "less than smallest dwarfs," when he speaks with true, not false modesty, of himself and them, and of his wayward thoughts, "desiring this man's art, and that man's scope." We fancy that there were no such men, that could either add to or take anything away from him, but such there were. He indeed overlooks and commands the admiration of posterity, but he does it from the *table-land* of the age in which he lived. He towered above his fellows, "in shape and gesture proudly eminent," but he was one of a race of giants, the tallest, the strongest, the most graceful, and beautiful of them; but it was a common and a noble brood. He was not something sacred and aloof from the vulgar herd of men, but shook hands with nature and the circumstances of the time, and is distinguished from his immediate contemporaries, not in kind, but in degree and greater variety of excellence. He did not form a class or species by himself, but belonged to a class or species. His age was necessary to him; nor could he have been wrenched from his place in the edifice of which he was so conspicuous a part, without equal injury to himself and it. Mr. Wordsworth says of Milton, that "his soul was like a star, and dwelt apart." This cannot be said with any propriety of Shakspeare, who certainly moved in a constellation of bright luminaries, and "drew after him a third part of the heavens." If we allow, for argument's sake (or for truth's, which is better), that he was in himself equal to all his competitors put together; yet there was more dramatic excellence in that age than in the whole of the period that has elapsed since. If his contemporaries, with their united strength, would hardly make one Shakspeare, certain it is that all his successors would not make half a one. With the exception of a single writer, Otway, and of a single play of his ('Venice Preserved'), there is nobody in tragedy and dramatic poetry (I do not here speak of comedy), to be compared to the great men of the age of Shakspeare, and immediately after. They are a mighty phalanx of kindred spirits closing him round, moving in the same orbit, and impelled by the same causes in their whirling and eccentric career. They had the same faults and the same excellences; the same strength, and depth, and richness, the same truth of character, passion, imagination, thought and language, thrown, heaped, massed together without careful polishing or exact method, but poured out in unconcerned profusion from the lap of nature and genius in boundless and unrivalled magnificence. The sweetness of Decker, the thought of Marston, the gravity of Chapman, the grace of Fletcher and his young-eyed wit, Jonson's learned sock, the flowing vein of Middleton, Heywood's ease, the pathos of Webster, and Marlowe's deep designs, add a double lustre to the sweetness, thought, gravity, grace, wit, artless nature, copiousness, ease, pathos, and sublime conceptions of Shakspeare's Muse. They are indeed the scale by which we can best ascend to the true knowledge and love of him. Our admiration of them does not lessen our relish for him: but, on the contrary, increases and confirms it. For such an extraordinary combination and development of fancy and genius many causes may be assigned, and we seek for the chief of them in religion, in politics, in the circumstances of the time, the recent diffusion of letters, in local situation, and in the character of the men who adorned that period, and availed themselves so nobly of the advantages placed within their reach.

I shall here attempt to give a general sketch of these causes, and of the manner in which they operated to mould and stamp the poetry of the country at the period of which I have to treat; independently of incidental and fortuitous causes, for which there is no accounting, but which, after all, have often the greatest share in determining the most important results.

The first cause I shall mention, as contributing to this general effect, was the Reformation, which had just then taken place. This event gave a mighty impulse, and increased activity to thought and inquiry, and agitated the inert mass of accumulated prejudices throughout Europe. The effect of the concussion was general, but the shock was greatest in this country. It toppled down the full-grown, intolerable abuses of centuries at a blow; heaved the ground from under the feet of bigoted faith and slavish obedience; and the roar and dashing of opinions, loosened from their accustomed hold, might be heard like the noise of an angry sea, and has never yet subsided. Germany first broke the spell of misbegotten fear, and gave the watchword; but England joined the shout, and echoed it back with her island voice from her thousand cliffs and craggy shores, in a longer and a louder strain. With that cry the genius of Great Britain rose and threw down the gauntlet to the nations. There was a mighty fermentation: the waters were out; public opinion was in a state of projection. Liberty was held out to all to think and speak the truth. Men's brains were busy; their spirits stirring; their hearts full; and their hands not idle. Their eyes were open to expect the greatest things, and their ears burned with curiosity and zeal to know the truth, that the truth might make them free. The death-blow which had been struck at scarlet vice and bloated hypocrisy loosened their tongues, and made the talismans and love-tokens of Popish superstition, with which she had beguiled her followers and committed abominations with the people, fall harmless from their necks.

The translation of the Bible was the chief engine in the great work. It threw open, by a secret spring, the rich treasures of religion and morality, which had been there locked up as in a shrine. It revealed the visions of the prophets, and conveyed the lessons of inspired teachers (such they were thought) to the meanest of the people. It gave them a common interest in the common cause. Their hearts burnt within them as they read. It gave a *mind* to the people, by giving them common subjects of thought and feeling. It cemented their union of character and sentiment: it created endless diversity and collision of opinion. They found objects to employ their faculties, and a motive in the magnitude of the consequences attached to them, to exert the utmost eagerness in the pursuit of truth, and the most daring intrepidity in maintaining it. Religious controversy sharpens the understanding by the subtlety and remoteness of the topics it discusses, and braces the will by their infinite importance. We perceive in the history of this period a nervous masculine intellect. No levity, no feebleness, no indifference; or if there were, it is a relaxation from the intense activity which gives a tone to its general character. But there is a gravity approaching to piety a seriousness of impression, a conscientious severity of argument, an habitual fervour and enthusiasm in their mode of handling almost every subject. The debates of the schoolmen were sharp and subtle enough; but they wanted interest and grandeur, and were, besides, confined to a few: they did not affect the general mass of the community. But the Bible was thrown open to all ranks and conditions "to run and read," with its wonderful table of contents from Genesis to the Revelations. Every village in England would present the scene so well described in Burns's Cotter's Saturday Night. I cannot think that all this variety and weight of knowledge could be thrown in all at once upon the mind of a people, and not make some impression upon it, the traces of which might be discerned in the manners and literature of the age. For, to leave more disputable points, and take only the historical parts of the Old Testament, or the moral sentiments of the New, there is nothing like them in the power of exciting awe and admiration, or of rivetting sympathy. We see what Milton has made of the account of the Creation, from the manner in which he has treated it, imbued and impregnated with the spirit of the time of which we speak. Or what is there equal (in that romantic interest and patriarchal simplicity which goes to the heart of a country, and rouses it, as it were, from its lair in wastes and wildnesses) to the story of Joseph and his Brethren, of Rachael and Laban, of Jacob's Dream, of Ruth and Boaz, the descriptions in the book of Job, the deliverance of the Jews out of Egypt, or the account of their captivity and return from Babylon? There is in all these parts of the Scripture, and numberless more of the same kind, to pass over the Orphic hymns of David, the prophetic denunciations of Isaiah, or the gorgeous visions of Ezekiel, an originality, a vastness of conception, a depth and tenderness of feeling, and a touching simplicity in the mode of narration, which he who does not feel must be made of no "penetrable stuff." There is something in the character of Christ too (leaving religious faith quite out of the question) of more sweetness and majesty, and more likely to work a change in the mind of man, by the contemplation of its idea alone, than any to be found in history, whether actual or feigned. This character is that of a sublime humanity, such as was never seen on earth before nor since. This shone manifestly both in his words and actions. We see it in his washing the disciples' feet the night before his death, that unspeakable instance of humility and love, "above all art, all meanness, and all pride;" and in the leave he took of them on that occasion, "My peace I give unto you: that peace which the world cannot give, give I unto you;" and in his last commandment, that "they should love one another." Who can read the account of his behaviour on the cross, when turning to his mother he said, "Woman, behold thy son," and to the disciple John, "Behold thy mother," and "from that hour that disciple took her to his own home," without having his heart smote within him? We see it in his treatment of the woman taken in adultery, and in his excuse for the woman who poured precious ointment on his garment as an offering of devotion and love, which is here all in all. His religion was the religion of the heart. We see it in his discourse with the disciples as they walked together towards Emmaus, when their hearts burned within them; in his sermon from the Mount, in his parable of the good Samaritan, and in that of the Prodigal Son—in every act and word of his life, a grace, a mildness, a dignity of love, a patience and wisdom worthy of the Son of God. His whole life and being were imbued, steeped in this word, *charity;* it was the spring, the well-head from which every thought and feeling gushed into act; and it was this that breathed a mild glory from his face in that last agony upon the cross, "when the meek Saviour bowed his head and died," praying for his enemies. He was the first true teacher of morality; for he alone conceived the idea of a pure humanity. He redeemed man from the worship of that idol, self, and instructed him by precept and example to love his neighbour as himself, to forgive our enemies, to do good to those that curse us and despitefully use us. He taught the love of good for the sake of good, without regard to personal or sinister views, and made the affections of the heart the sole seat of morality, instead of the pride of the understanding or the sternness of the will. In answering the question, "who is our neighbour?" as one who stands in need of our assistance, and whose wounds we can bind up, he has done more to humanize the thoughts and tame the unruly passions, than all who have tried to reform and benefit mankind. The very idea of abstract benevolence, of the desire to do good because another wants our services, and of regarding the human race as one family, the offspring of one common parent, is hardly to be found in any other code or system. It was "to the Jews a stumbling block, and to the Greeks foolishness." The Greeks and Romans never thought of considering others, but as they were Greeks or Romans, as they were bound to them by certain positive ties, or, on the other hand, as separated from them by fiercer antipathies. Their virtues were the virtues of political machines, their vices were the vices of demons, ready to inflict or endure pain with obdurate and remorseless inflexibility of purpose. But in the Christian religion, "we perceive a softness coming over the heart of a nation, and the iron scales that fence and harden it, melt and drop off." It becomes malleable, capable of pity, of forgiveness, of relaxing in its claims, and remitting its power. We strike it, and it does not hurt us: it is not steel or marble, but flesh and blood, clay tempered with tears, and "soft as sinews of the new-born babe." The gospel was first preached to the poor, for it consulted their wants and interests, not its own pride and arrogance. It first promulgated the equality of mankind in the community of duties and benefits. It denounced the iniquities of the chief priests and pharisees, and declared itself at variance with principalities and powers, for it sympathizes not with the oppressor, but the oppressed. It first abolished slavery, for it did not consider the power of the will to inflict injury, as clothing it with a right to do so. Its law is good, not power. It at the same time tended to wean the mind from the grossness of sense, and a particle of its divine flame was lent to brighten and purify the lamp of love!

There have been persons who, being sceptics as to the divine mission of Christ, have taken an accountable prejudice to his doctrines, and have been disposed to deny the merit of his character; but this was not the feeling of the great men in the age of Elizabeth (whatever might be their belief,) one of whom says of him, with a boldness equal to its piety:

> "The best of men
> That e'er wore earth about him, was a sufferer;
> A soft, meek, patient, humble, tranquil spirit;
> The first true gentleman that ever breathed."

This was old honest Decker, and the lines ought to embalm his memory to every one who has a sense either of religion, or philosophy, or humanity, or true genius. Nor can I help thinking, that we may discern the traces of the influence exerted by religious faith in the spirit of the poetry of the age of Elizabeth, in the means of exciting terror and pity, in the delineation of the passions of grief, remorse, love, sympathy, the sense of shame, in the fond desires, the longings after immortality, in the heaven of hope, and the abyss of despair it lays open before us.*

The literature of this age, then, I would say, was strongly influenced (among other causes,) first by the spirit of Christianity, and secondly, by the spirit of Protestantism.

The effects of the Reformation on politics and philosophy may

* In some Roman Catholic countries, pictures in part supplied the place of the translation of the Bible: and this dumb art arose in the silence of the written oracles

be seen in the writings and history of the next and of the following ages. They are still at work, and will continue to be so. The effects on the poetry of the time were chiefly confined to the moulding of the character, and giving a powerful impulse to the intellect of the country. The immediate use or application that was made of religion to subjects of imagination and fiction was not (from an obvious ground of separation) so direct or frequent, as that which was made of the classical and romantic literature.

For, much about the same time, the rich and fascinating stores of the Greek and Roman mythology, and those of the romantic poetry of Spain and Italy, were eagerly explored by the curious, and thrown open in translations to the admiring gaze of the vulgar. This last circumstance could hardly have afforded so much advantage to the poets of that day, who were themselves, in fact, the translators, as it shows the general curiosity and increasing interest in such subjects, as a prevailing feature of the times. There were translations of Tasso by Fairfax, and of Ariosto by Harrington, of Homer and Hesiod by Chapman, and of Virgil long before, and Ovid soon after; there was Sir Thomas North's translation of Plutarch, of which Shakspeare has made such admirable use in his Coriolanus and Julius Cæsar; and Ben Jonson's tragedies of Catiline and Sejanus may themselves be considered as almost literal translations into verse, of Tacitus, Sallust, and Cicero's Orations in his consulship. Boccacio, the divine Boccacio, Petrarch, Dante, the satirist Aretine, Machiavel, Castiglione, and others, were familiar to our writers, and they make occasional mention of some few French authors, as Ronsard and Du Bartas; for the French literature had not at this stage arrived at its Augustan period, and it was the imitation of their literature a century afterwards, when it had arrived at its greatest height (itself copied from the Greek and Latin,) that enfeebled and impoverished our own. But of the time that we are considering, it might be said, without much extravagance that every breath that blew, every wave that rolled to our shores, brought with it some accession to our knowledge, which was engrafted on the national genius. In fact, all the disposable materials that had been accumulating for a long period of time, either in our own or in foreign countries, were now brought together, and required nothing more than to be wrought up, polished, or arranged in striking forms, for ornament and use. To this every inducement prompted; the novelty of the acquisition of knowledge in many cases, the emulation of foreign wits, and of immortal works, the want and the expectation of such works among ourselves, the opportunity and encouragement afforded for their production by leisure and affluence; and, above all, the insatiable desire of the mind to beget its own image, and to construct out of itself, and for the delight and admiration of the world and posterity, that excellence of which the idea exists hitherto only in its own breast, and the impression of which it would make as universal as the eye of heaven, the benefit as common as the air we breathe. The first impulse of genius is to create what never existed before: the contemplation of that which is so created, is sufficient to satisfy the demands of taste; and it is the habitual study and imitation of the original models that takes away the power, and even wish to do the like. Taste limps after genius, and from copying the artificial models, we lose sight of the living principle of nature. It is the effort we make, and the impulse we acquire, in overcoming the first obstacles, that projects us forward; it is the necessity for exertion that makes us conscious of our strength; but this necessity and this impulse once removed, the tide of fancy and enthusiasm, which is at first a running stream, soon settles and crusts into the standing pool of dulness, criticism, and *virtu*.

What also gave an unusual *impetus* to the mind of man at this period, was the discovery of the New World, and the reading of voyages and travels. Green islands and golden sands seemed to arise, as by enchantment, out of the bosom of the watery waste, and invite the cupidity, or wing the imagination of the dreaming speculator. Fairy land was realized in new and unknown worlds. "Fortunate fields and groves and flowery vales, thrice happy isles," were found floating "like those Hesperian gardens famed of old," beyond Atlantic seas, as dropt from the zenith. The people, the soil, the clime, every thing gave unlimited scope to the curiosity of the traveller and reader. Other manners might be said to enlarge the bounds of knowledge, and new mines of wealth were tumbled at our feet It is from a voyage to the Straits of Magellan that Shakspeare has taken the hint of Prospero's Enchanted Island, and of the savage Caliban with his god Setebos.* Spenser seems to have had the same feeling in his mind in the production of his Faery Queen, and vindicates his poetic fiction on this very ground of analogy.

" Right well I wote, most mighty sovereign,
That all this famous antique history
Of some the abundance of an idle brain
Will judged be, and painted forgery,
Rather than matter of just memory:
Since none that breatheth living air, doth know
Where is that happy land of faery
Which I so much do vaunt, but nowhere show,
But vouch antiquities which nobody can know.

But let that man with better sense avise,
That of the world least part to us is read:
And daily how through hardy enterprize
Many great regions are discovered,
Which to late age were never mentioned.
Who ever heard of the Indian Peru?
Or who in venturous vessel measured
The Amazon's huge river, now found true?
Or fruitfullest Virginia who did ever view?

Yet all these where when no man did them know,
Yet have from wisest ages hidden been:
And later times things more unknown shall show.
Why then should witless man so much misween
That nothing is but that which he hath seen?
What, if within the moon's fair shining sphere,
What, if in every other star unseen,
Of other worlds he happily should hear?
He wonder would much more; yet such to some appear.

Fancy's air-drawn pictures after history's waking dream showed like clouds over mountains; and from the romance of real life to the idlest fiction, the transition seemed easy. Shakspeare, as well as others of his time, availed himself of the old Chronicles, and of the traditions or fabulous inventions contained in them in such ample measure, and which had not yet been appropriated to the purposes of poetry or the drama. The stage

* See a Voyage to the Straits of Magellan, 1594.

was a new thing; and those who had to supply its demands laid their hands upon whatever came within their reach: they were not particular as to the means, so that they gained the end. Lear is founded upon an old ballad; Othello on an Italian novel; Hamlet on a Danish, and Macbeth on a Scotch tradition: one of which is to be found in Saxo-Grammaticus, and the last in Hollingshed. The Ghost-scenes and the Witches in each, are authenticated in the old Gothic history. There was also this connecting link between the poetry of this age and the supernatural traditions of a former one, that the belief in them was still extant, and in full force and visible operation among the vulgar (to say no more, in the time of our authors. The appalling and wild chimeras of superstition and ignorance, "those bodiless creations that ecstacy is very cunning in," were inwoven with existing manners and opinions, and all their effects on the passions of terror or pity might be gathered from common and actual observation—might be discerned in the workings of the face, the expressions of the tongue, the writhings of a troubled conscience. "Your face, my Thane, is as a book where men may read strange matters." Midnight and secret murders, too, from the imperfect state of the police, were more common; and the ferocious and brutal manners that would stamp the brow of the hardened ruffian or hired assassin, more incorrigible and undisguised. The portraits of Tyrrel and Forrest were, no doubt, done from the life. We find that the ravages of the plague, the destructive rage of fire, the poisoned chalice, lean famine, the serpent's mortal sting, and the fury of wild beasts, were the common topics of their poetry, as they were common occurrences in more remote periods of history. They were the strong ingredients thrown into the cauldron of tragedy to make it "thick and slab." Man's life was (as it appears to me) more full of traps and pit-falls; of hair-breadth accidents by flood and field; more way-laid by sudden and startling evils; it trod on the brink of hope and fear; stumbled upon fate unawares; while the imagination, close behind it, caught at and clung to the shape of danger, or "snatched a wild and fearful joy" from its escape. The accidents of nature were less provided against; the excesses of the passions and of lawless power were less regulated, and produced more strange and desperate catastrophes. The tales of Boccacio are founded on the great pestilence of Florence; Fletcher the poet died of the plague, and Marlowe was stabbed in a tavern quarrel. The strict authority of parents, the inequality of ranks, or the hereditary feuds between different families, made more unhappy loves or matches.

"The course of true love never did run smooth."

Again, the heroic and martial spirit which breathes in our elder writers, was yet in considerable activity in the reign of Elizabeth. "The age of chivalry was not then quite gone, nor the glory of Europe extinguished for ever." Jousts and tournaments were still common with the nobility in England and in foreign countries. Sir Philip Sidney was particularly distinguished for his proficiency in these exercises (and indeed fell a martyr to his ambition as a soldier)—and the gentle Surrey was still more famous, on the same account, just before him. It is true, the general use of fire-arms gradually superseded the necessity of skill in the sword, or bravery in the person: and we find many symptoms of the rapid degeneracy in this respect. It was comparatively an age of peace,

"Like strength reposing on his own right arm;"

but the sound of civil combat might still be heard in the distance, the spear glittered to the eye of memory, or the clashing of armour struck on the imagination of the ardent and the young. They were borderers on the savage state, on the times of war and bigotry, though in the lap of arts, of luxury, and knowledge. They stood on the shore and saw the billows rolling after the storm: "they heard the tumult, and were still." The manners and out-of-door amusements were more tinctured with a spirit of adventure and romance. The war with wild beasts, &c., was more strenuously kept up in country sports. I do not think we could get from sedentary poets, who had never mingled in the vicissitudes, the dangers, or excitements of the chase, such descriptions of hunting and other athletic games, as are to be found in Shakspeare's Midsummer Night's Dream, or Fletcher's Noble Kinsmen.

With respect to the good cheer and hospitable living of those times, I cannot agree with an ingenious and agreeable writer of the present day, that it was general or frequent. The very stress laid upon certain holidays and festivals, shows that they did not keep up the same Saturnalian license and open-house all the year round. They reserved themselves for great occasions, and made the best amends they could for a year of abstinence and toil by a week of merriment and convivial indulgence. Persons in middle life at this day, who can afford a good dinner every day, do not look forward to it as any particular subject of exultation: the poor peasant, who can only contrive to treat himself to a joint of meat on a Sunday, considers it as an event in the week. So, in the old Cambridge comedy of the Returne from Parnassus, we find this indignant description of the progress of luxury in those days, put into the mouth of one of the speakers:

> " Why is't not strange to see a ragged clerke,
> Some stammell weaver, or some butcher's sonne,
> That scrubb'd a late within a sleeveless gowne,
> When the commencement, like a morrice dance,
> Hath put a bell or two about his legges,
> Created him a sweet cleane gentleman:
> How then he 'gins to follow fashions.
> He whose thin sire dwelt in a smokye roofe,
> Must take tobacco, and must wear a locke.
> His thirsty dad drinks in a wooden bowle,
> But his sweet self is served in silver plate.
> His hungry sire will scrape you twenty legges
> For one good Christmas meal on new-year's day,
> But his mawe must be capon cramm'd each day."
>
> *Act III, Scene* 2.

This does not look as if in those days "it snowed of meat and think," as a matter of course throughout the year! The distinctions of dress, the badges of different professions, the very signs of the shops, which we have set aside for written inscriptions over the doors, were, as Mr. Lamb observes, a sort of visible language to the imagination, and hints for thought. Like the costumes of different foreign nations, they had an immediate striking and picturesque effect, giving scope to the fancy. The surface of society was embossed with hieroglyphics, and poetry existed "in act and complement extern." The poetry of former times might be directly taken from real life, as our poetry is taken from the poetry of former times. Finally, the face of nature, which was the same glorious object then that it is now, was open to them; and coming first, they gathered her fairest flowers to live for ever in their verse—the movements of the human heart were not hid from them, for they had the same passions as we, only less disguised, and less subject to control. Decker has given an admirable description of a mad-house in one of his plays. But it might be perhaps objected, that it was only a literal account taken from Bedlam at that time: and it might be answered, that the old poets took the same methods of describing the passions and fancies of men whom they met at large, which forms the point of communion between us; for the title of the old play, 'A Mad World, my Masters,' is hardly yet obsolete; and we are pretty much the same Bedlam still, perhaps a little better managed, like the real one, and with more care and humanity shown to the patients!

Lastly, to conclude this account; what gave a unity and common direction to all these causes, was the natural genius of the country, which was strong in these writers in proportion to their strength. We are a nation of islanders, and we cannot help it; nor mend ourselves if we would. We are something in ourselves, nothing when we try to ape others. Music and painting are not our *forte*: for what we have done in that way has been little, and that borrowed from others with great difficulty. But we may boast of our poets and philosophers. That's something. We have had strong heads and sound hearts among us. Thrown on one side of the world, and left to bustle for ourselves, we have fought out many a battle for truth and freedom. That is our natural style; and it were to be wished we had in no instance departed from it. Our situation has given us a certain cast of thought and character; and our liberty has enabled us to make the most of it. We are of a stiff clay, not moulded into every fashion, with stubborn joints not easily bent. We are slow to think, and therefore impressions do not work upon us till they act in masses. We are not forward to express our feelings, and therefore they do not come from us till they force their way in the most impetuous eloquence. Our language is, as it were, to begin anew, and we make use of the most singular and boldest combinations to explain ourselves. Our wit comes from us, "like birdlime, brains and all." We pay too little attention to form and method, leave our works in an unfinished state, but still the materials we work in are solid and of nature's mint; we do not deal in counterfeits. We both under and over-do, but we keep an eye to the prominent features, the main chance. We are more for weight than show; care only about what interests ourselves, instead of trying to impose upon others by plausible appearances, and are obstinate and intractable in not conforming to common rules, by which many arrive at their ends with half the real waste of thought and trouble. We neglect all but the principal object, gather our force to make a great blow, bring it down, and relapse into sluggishness and indifference again. *Materiam superabat opus*, cannot be said of us. We may be accused of grossness, but not of flimsiness; of extravagance, but not of affectation; of want of art and refinement, but not of a want of truth and nature. Our literature, in a word, is Gothic and grotesque; unequal and irregular; not cast in a previous mould, nor of one uniform texture, but of great weight in the whole, and of incomparable value in the best parts. It aims at an excess of beauty or power, hits or misses, and is either very good indeed, or absolutely good for nothing. This character applies in particular to our literature in the age of Elizabeth, which is its best period, before the introduction of a rage for French rules and French models; for whatever may be the value of our own original style of composition, there can be neither offence nor presumption in saying, that it is at least better than our second-hand imitations of others. Our understanding (such as it is and must remain, to be good for anything) is not a thoroughfare for common places, smooth as the palm of one's hand, but full of knotty points and jutting excrescences, rough, uneven, overgrown with brambles; and I like this aspect of the mind (as some one said of the country), where nature keeps a good deal of the soil in her own hands. Perhaps the genius of our poetry has more of Pan than of Apollo; "but Pan is a God, Apollo is no more!"

LECTURE II.

On the Dramatic Writers contemporary with Shakspeare, Lyly, Marlowe, Heywood, Middleton, and Rowley.

The period of which I shall have to treat (from the Reformation to the middle of Charles I.) was prolific in dramatic excellence even more than in any other. In approaching it, we seem to be approaching the RICH STROND described in Spenser, where treasures of all kinds lay scattered, or rather crowded together on the shore in inexhaustible but unregarded profusion, "rich as the oozy bottom of the deep in sunken wrack and sumless treasuries." We are confounded with the variety, and dazzled with he dusky splendour of names sacred in their obscurity, and works gorgeous in their decay, "majestic, though in ruin," like Guyon when he entered the Cave of Mammon, and was shown the massy pillars and huge unwieldy fragments of gold, covered with dust and cobwebs, and shedding a faint shadow of uncertain light,

> "Such as a lamp whose light doth fade away
> Or as the moon clothed with cloudy night
> Doth show to him that walks in fear and sad affright."

The dramatic literature of this period only wants exploring, to fill the inquiring mind with wonder and delight, and to convince us that we have been wrong in lavishing all our praise on "new-born gauds, though they are made and moulded of things past;" and in "giving to dust, that is a little gilt, more laud than gilt o'er-dusted." In short, the discovery of such an unsuspected and forgotten mine of wealth will be found amply to repay the labour of the search, and it will be hard if in most cases curiosity does not end in admiration, and modesty teach us wisdom. A few of the most singular productions of these times remain unclaimed; of others, the authors are uncertain; many of them are joint productions of different pens; but of the best the writers' names are in general known, and obviously stamped on the productions themselves. The names of Ben Jonson, for instance, Massinger, Beaumont and Fletcher, are almost, though not quite, as familiar to us as that of Shakspeare; and their works still keep regular possession of the stage. Another set of writers included in the same general period (the end of the sixteenth and the beginning of the seventeenth century,) who are next, or equal, or sometimes superior to these in power, but whose names are now little known, and their writings nearly obsolete, are Lyly, Marlowe, Marston, Chapman, Middleton, and Rowley, Heywood, Webster, Decker, and Ford. I shall devote the present and two following Lectures to the best account I can give of these, and shall begin with some of the least known.

The earliest tragedy of which I shall take notice (I believe the earliest that we have) is that of Ferrex and Porrex, or Gorboduc (as it has been generally called,) the production of Thomas Sackville, Lord Buckhurst, afterwards created Earl of Dorset, assisted by one Thomas Norton. This was first acted with applause before the Queen in 1561, the noble author being then quite a young man. This tragedy being considered as the first in our language, is certainly a curiosity, and in other respects it is also remarkable; though, perhaps, enough has been said about it. As a work of genius, it may be set down as nothing, for it contains hardly a memorable line or passage; as a work of art, and the first of its kind attempted in the language, it may be considered as a monument of the taste and skill of the authors. Its merit is confined to the regularity of the plot and metre, to its general good sense, and strict attention to common decorum. If the poet has not stamped the peculiar genius of his age upon this first attempt, it is no inconsiderable proof of strength of mind and conception sustained by its own sense of propriety alone, to have so far anticipated the taste of succeeding times as to have avoided any glaring offence against rules and models, which had no existence in his day. Or perhaps a truer solution might be, that there were as yet no examples of a more ambiguous and irregular kind to tempt him to err, and as he had not the impulse or resources within himself to strike out a new path, he merely adhered with modesty and caution to the classical models with which, as a scholar, he was well acquainted. The language of the dialogue is clear, unaffected, and intelligible without the smallest difficulty, even to this day; it has "no figures nor no fantasies," to which the most fastidious critic can object, but the dramatic power is nearly none at all. It is written expressly to set forth the dangers and mischiefs that arise from the division of sovereign power; and the several speakers dilate upon the different views of the subject in turn, like clever school-boys set to compose a thesis, or declaim upon the fatal consequences of ambition, and the uncertainty of human affairs. The author, in the end, declares for the doctrine of passive obedience and non-resistance; a doctrine which indeed was seldom questioned at that time of day. Eubulus, one of the old king's counsellors thus gives his opinion—

"Eke fully with the duke my mind agrees,
That no cause serves, whereby the subject may
Call to account the doings of his prince;
Much less in blood by sword to work revenge:
No more than may the hand cut off the head.
In act nor speech, no nor in secret thought,
The subject may rebel against his lord,
Or judge of him that sits in Cæsar's seat,
With grudging mind to damn those he mislikes.
Though kings forget to govern as they ought,
Yet subjects must obey as they are bound."

Yet how little he was borne out in this inference by the unbiassed dictates of his own mind, may appear from the freedom and unguarded boldness of such lines as the following, addressed by a favourite to a prince, as courtly advice:

"Know ye that lust of kingdoms hath no law:
The gods do bear and will allow in kings
The things that they abhor in rascal routs.
When kings on slender quarrels run to wars,
And then in cruel and unkindly wise
Command thefts, rapes, murder of innocents,
The spoil of towns, ruins of mighty realms;
Think you such princes do suppose themselves

Subject to laws of kind and fear of gods?
Murders and violent thefts in private men
Are heinous crimes, and full of foul reproach;
Yet none offence, but deck'd with noble name
Of glorious conquests in the hands of kings."

The principal characters make as many invocations to the names of their children, their country, and their friends, as Cicero in his Orations, and all the topics insisted upon are open, direct, urged in the face of day, with no more attention to time or place, to an enemy who overhears, or an accomplice to whom they are addressed; in a word, with no more dramatic insinuations or bye-play than the pleadings in a court of law. Almost the only passage that I can instance, as rising above this didactic tone of mediocrity into the pathos of poetry, is one where Marcella laments the untimely death of her lover, Ferrex:

"Ah! noble prince, how oft have I beheld
Thee mounted on thy fierce and trampling steed,
Shining in armour bright before the tilt
And with thy mistress' sleeve tied on thy helm,
And charge thy staff to please thy lady's eye.
That bowed the head-piece of thy friendly foe!
How oft in arms on horse to bend the mace,
How oft in arms on foot to break the sword,
Which never now these eyes may see again!"

There seems a reference to Chaucer in the wording of the following lines—

"Then saw I how he smiled with slaying knife
Wrapp'd under cloke, then saw I deep deceit
Lurk in his face, and death prepared for me."*

Sir Philip Sidney says of this tragedy: "Gorboduc is full of stately speeches, and well-sounding phrases, climbing to the height of Seneca his style, and as full of notable morality; which it doth most delightfully teach, and thereby obtain the very end of poetry." And Mr. Pope, whose taste in such matters was very different from Sir Philip Sidney's, says in still

* "The smiler with the knife under his cloke."—*Knight's Tale.*

stronger terms: "That the writers of the succeeding age might have improved as much in other respects, by copying from him a propriety in the sentiments, an unaffected perspicuity of style, and an easy flow in the numbers. In a word, that chastity, correctness, and gravity of style, which are so essential to tragedy, and which all the tragic poets who followed, not excepting Shakspeare himself, either little understood, or perpetually neglected." It was well for us and them that they did so!

The Induction to the Mirrour for Magistrates does his muse more credit. It sometimes reminds one of Chaucer, and at others seems like an anticipation, in some degree, both of the measure and manner of Spenser. The following stanzas may give the reader an idea of the merit of this old poem, which was published in 1563:

"By him lay heauie Sleepe cosin of Death
Flat on the ground, and still as any stone,
A very corps, saue yeelding forth a breath.
Small keepe tooke he whom Fortune frowned on,
Or whom she lifted vp into the throne
Of high renowne, but as a liuing death,
So dead aliue, of life he drew the breath.

The bodies rest, the quiet of the hart,
The trauiles ease, the still nights feere was he.
And of our life in earth the better part,
Reuer of sight, and in whom we see
Things oft that tide, and oft that neuer bee.
Without respect esteeming equally
King *Crœsus* pompe, and *Irus* pouertie.

And next in order sad Old Age we found,
His beard all hoare, his eyes hollow and blind,
With drouping cheere still poring on the ground,
As on the place where nature him assign'd
To rest, when that the sister's had vntwin'd
His vitall thred, and ended with their knife
The fleeting course of fast declining life.

There heard we him with broke and hollow plaint
Rew with himselfe his end approaching fast,
And all for nought his wretched mind torment,
With sweete remembrance of his pleasures past,
And fresh delites of lustie youth forewast.

Recounting which, how would he sob and shreek?
And to be young againe of *Ioue* besecke.

But and the cruell fates so fixed be,
That time forepast cannot returne againe,
This one request of *Ioue* yet prayed he:
That in such withred plight, and wretched paine,
As *Eld* (accompanied with lothsome traine)
Had brought on him, all were it woe and griefe,
He might a while yet linger forth his life.

And not so soone descend into the pit;
Where Death, when he the mortall corps hath slaine,
With wretchlesse hand in graue doth couer it,
Thereafter neuer to enjoy againe
The gladsome light, but in the ground ylaine,
In depth of darknesse waste and weare to nought,
As he had nere into the world been brought.

But who had seene him, sobbing how he stood
Vnto himselfe, and how he would bemone
His youth forepast, as though it wrought him good
To talk of youth, all were his youth forgone,
He would haue mused and maruail'd much whereon
This wretched Age should life desire so faine,
And knowes ful wel life doth but length his paine.

Crookebackt he was, toothshaken, and blere eyed,
Went on three feete, and sometime crept on foure,
With old lame bones, that ratled by his side,
His scalpe all pil'd, and he with eld forelore:
His withred first still knocking at Death's dore,
Fumbling and drivueling as he draws his breath,
For briefe, the shape and messenger of Death."

John Lyly (born in the Weald of Kent about the year 1553), was the author of Midas and Endymion, of Alexander and Campaspe, and of the comedy of Mother Bombie. Of the last it may be said, that it is very much what its name would import, old, quaint, and vulgar.—I may here observe, once for all, that I would not be understood to say, that the age of Elizabeth was all of gold without any alloy. there was both gold and lead in it, and often in one and the same writer. In our impatience to form an opinion, we conclude, when we first meet with a good thing, that it is owing to the age; or, if we meet with a bad one it is characteristic of the age, when, in fact, it is neither; for there are good and bad in almost all ages, and one age excels in one thing, another in another—only one age may excel more and in higher things than another, but none can excel equally and completely in all. The writers of Elizabeth, as poets, soared to the height they did by indulging their own unrestrained enthusiasm; as comic writers they chiefly copied the manners of the age, which did not give them the same advantages over their successors. Lyly's comedy, for instance, is "poor, unfledged, has never winged from view o' th' nest," and tries in vain to rise above the ground with crude conceits and clumsy levity. Lydia, the heroine of the piece, is silly enough, if the rest were but as witty. But the author has shown no partiality in the distribution of his gifts. To say the truth, it was a very common fault of the old comedy, that its humours were too low, and the weaknesses exposed too great to be credible, or an object of ridicule, even if they were. The affectation of their courtiers is passable, and diverting as a contrast to present manners; but the eccentricities of their clowns are "very tolerable, and not to be endured." Any kind of activity of mind might seem to the writers better than none: any nonsense served to amuse their hearers; any cant phrase, any coarse allusion, any pompous absurdity, was taken for wit and drollery. Nothing could be too mean, too foolish, too improbable, or too offensive, to be a proper subject for laughter. Any one (looking hastily at this side of the question only) might be tempted to suppose the youngest children of Thespis a very callow brood, chirping their slender notes, or silly swains "grating their lean and flashy jests on scrannel pipes of wretched straw." The genius of comedy looked too often like a lean and hectic pantaloon; love was a slip-shod shepherdess; wit a parti-coloured fool like harlequin, and the plot came hobbling like a clown after all. A string of impertinent and farcical jests (or rather blunders), was with great formality ushered into the world as "a right pleasant and conceited comedy." Comedy could not descend lower than it sometimes did, without glancing at physical imperfections and deformity. The two young persons in the play before us, on whom the event of the plot chiefly hinges, do in fact turn out to be no better than changelings and natural idiots. This is carrying innocence and simplicity too far. So again, the character of Sir Tophas in Endymion, an affected, blustering, talkative, cowardly pretender, treads too near upon blank stupidity and downright want of common sense to be admissible as a butt for satire. Shakspeare has contrived to clothe the lamentable nakedness of the same sort of character with a motley garb from the wardrobe of his imagination, and has redeemed it from insipidity by a certain plausibility of speech and playful extravagance of humour. But the undertaking was nearly desperate. Ben Jonson tried to overcome the difficulty by the force of learning and study; and thought to gain his end by persisting in error; but he only made matters worse, for his clowns and coxcombs (if we except Bobadil) are the most incorrigible and insufferable of all others.—The story of Mother Bomdie is little else than a tissue of absurd mistakes, arising from the confusion of the different characters one with another, like another Comedy of Errors, and ends in their being (most of them) married in a game at cross-purposes to the persons they particularly dislike.

To leave this, and proceed to something pleasanter, Midas and Endymion, which are worthy of their names and of the subject. The story in both is classical, and the execution is for the most part elegant and simple. There is often something that reminds one of the graceful communicativeness of Lucian or of Apuleius, from whom one of the stories is borrowed. Lyly made a more attractive picture of Grecian manners at second-hand, than of English characters from his own observation. The poet (which is the great merit of a poet in such a subject) has transported himself to the scene of action, to ancient Greece or Asia Minor; the manners, the images, the traditions are preserved with truth and delicacy, and the dialogue (to my fancy) glides and sparkles like a clear stream from the Muses' spring. I know few things more perfect in characteristic painting, than the exclamation of the Phrygian shepherds, who, afraid of betraying the secret of Midas's ears, fancy that "the very reeds bow down, as though they listened to their talk;" nor more affecting in sentiment than the apostrophe addressed by his friend Eumenides to Endymion, on waking from his long sleep: "Behold, the twig to which thou laidest down thy head is now become a tree." The narrative is sometimes a little wandering and desultory; but if it had been ten times as tedious, this thought would have redeemed it; for I cannot conceive of anything more beautiful, more simple, or touching, than this exquisitely chosen image and dumb proof of the manner in which he passed his life, from youth to old age, in a dream, a dream of love. Happy Endymion! Faithful Eumenides! Divine Cynthia! Who would not wish to pass his life in such a sleep, a long, long sleep, dreaming of some fair heavenly Goddess, with the moon shining upon his face and the trees growing silently over his head!—There is something in this story which has taken a strange hold of my fancy, perhaps "out of my weakness and my melancholy;" but for the satisfaction of the reader I will quote the whole passage:—"It is silly sooth, and dallies with the innocence of love like the old age."

"*Cynthia.* Well, let us to Endymion. I will not be so stately (good Endymion) not to stoop to do thee good; and if thy liberty consist in a kiss from me, thou shalt have it. And although my mouth hath been heretofore as untouched as my thoughts, yet now to recover thy life (though to restore thy youth it be impossible) I will do that to Endymion which yet never mortal man could boast of heretofore, nor shall ever hope for hereafter. (*She kisses him.*)

Eumenides. Madam, he beginneth to stir.

Cynthia. Soft, Eumenides, stand still.

Eumenides. Ah! I see his eyes almost open.

Cynthia. I command thee once again, stir not: I will stand behind him.

Panelion. What do I see? Endymion almost awake?

Eumenides. Endymion, Endymion, art thou deaf or dumb? Or hath this long sleep taken away thy memory? Ah! my sweet Endymion, seest thou not Eumenides, thy faithful friend; thy faithful Eumenides, who for thy sake hath been careless of his own content? Speak, Endymion! Endymion! Endymion!

Endymion. Endymion! I call to mind such a name.

Eumenides. Hast thou forgotten thyself, Endymion? Then do I not marvel thou rememberest not thy friend. I tell thee thou art Endymion, and I Eumenides. Behold also, Cynthia, by whose favour thou art awaked, and by whose virtue thou shalt continue thy natural course.

Cynthia. Endymion! Speak, sweet Endymion! knowest thou not Cynthia!

Endymion. Oh heavens! whom do I behold? Fair Cynthia, divine Cynthia?

Cynthia. I am Cynthia, and thou Endymion.

Endymion. Endymion! What do I hear? What! a grey-beard, hollow eyes, withered body, decayed limbs, and all in one night?

Eumenides. One night! Thou hast slept here forty years, by what enchantress, as yet it is not known: and behold the twig to which thou laidest thy head, is now become a tree. Callest thou not Eumenides to remembrance?

Endymion. Thy name I do remember by the sound, but thy favour I do not yet call to mind: only divine Cynthia, to whom time, fortune, death, and destiny are subject, I see and remember; and in all humility, I regard and reverence.

Cynthia. You shall have good cause to remember Eumenides, who hath for thy safety forsaken his own solace.

Endymion. Am I that Endymion, who was wont in court to lead my life, and in jousts, tourneys, and arms, to exercise my youth? Am I that Endymion?

Eumenides. Thou art that Endymion, and I Eumenides: wilt thou not yet call me to remembrance?

Endymion. Ah! sweet Eumenides, I now perceive thou art he, and that myself have the name of Endymion; but that this should be my body, I doubt: for how could my curled locks be turned to grey hair, and my strong body to a dying weakness, having waxed old, and not knowing it.

Cynthia. Well, Endymion, arise: awhile sit down, for that thy limbs are stiff and not able to stay thee, and tell what thou hast seen in thy sleep all this while. What dreams, visions, thoughts, and fortunes: for it is impossible but in so long a time thou shouldst see strange things."

Act V. Scene 1.

It does not take away from the pathos of this poetical allegory on the chances of love and the progress of human life, that it may be supposed to glance indirectly at the conduct of Queen Elizabeth to our author, who, after fourteen years' expectation of the place of Master of the Revels, was at last disappointed. This princess took no small delight in keeping her poets in a sort of Fool's Paradise. The wit of Lyly, in parts of this romantic drama, seems to have grown spirited and classical with his subject. He puts this fine hyperbolical irony in praise of Dipsas, (a most unamiable personage, as it will appear,) into the mouth of Sir Tophas:

"Oh, what fine thin hair hath Dipsas! What a pretty low forehead! What a tall and stately nose! What little hollow eyes! What great and goodly lips! How harmless is she, being toothless! Her fingers fat and short, adorned with long nails like a bittern! What a low stature she is, and yet what a great foot she carrieth! How thrifty must she be, in whom there is no waist; how virtuous she is like to be over whom no man can be jealous!"

Act III. Scene 3.

It is singular that the style of this author, which is extremely sweet and flowing, should have been the butt of ridicule to his contemporaries, particularly Drayton, who compliments Sydney as the author that

"Did first reduce
Our tongue from Lyly's writing, then in use;
Talking of stones, stars, plants, of fishes, flies,
Playing with words and idle similes,
As the English apes and very zanies be
Of every thing that they do hear and see."

Which must apply to the prose style of his work, called "Euphues and his England," and is much more like Sir Philip Sydney's own manner, than the dramatic style of our poet. Besides the passages above quoted, I might refer to the opening speeches of Midas, and again to the admirable contention between Pan and Apollo for the palm of music.—His Alexander and Campaspe is another sufficient answer to the charge. This play is a very pleasing transcript of old manners and sentiment. It is full of sweetness and point, of Attic salt and the honey of Hymettus. The following song given to Apelles, would not disgrace the mouth of the prince of painters:

"Cupid and my Campaspe play'd
At cards for kisses, Cupid paid;
He stakes his quiver, bow, and arrows:
His mother's doves and team of sparrows;
Loses them too, then down he throws
The coral of his lip, the rose
Growing on 's cheek (but none knows how)
With these the crystal of his brow
And then the dimple of his chin;
All these did my Campaspe win.
At last he set her both his eyes,
She won, and Cupid blind did rise.
O, Love! has she done this to thee?
What shall, alas! become of me?"

The conclusion of this drama is as follows. Alexander addressing himself to Apelles, says,

"Well, enjoy one another: I give her thee frankly, Apelles. Thou shalt see that Alexander maketh but a toy of love, and leadeth affection in fetters: using fancy as a fool to make him sport, or a minstrel to make him merry. It is not the amorous glance of an eye can settle an idle thought in the heart: no, no, it is children's game, a life for sempsters and scholars; the one, pricking in clouts, have nothing else to think on; the other picking fancies out of books, have little else to marvel at. Go, Apelles, take with you your Campaspe; Alexander is cloyed with looking on at that, which thou wonderest at.

Apelles. Thanks to your majesty on bended knee; you have honoured Apelles.

Campaspe. Thanks with bowed heart; you have blessed Campaspe.

[*Exeunt*

Alexander. Page, go warn Clytus and Parmenio, and the other lords, to be in readiness; let the trumpet sound, strike up the drum, and I will presently into Persia. How now, Hephistion, is Alexander able to resist love as he list?

Hephistion. The conquering of Thebes was not so honourable as the subduing of these thoughts.

Alexander. It were a shame Alexander should desire to command the world, if he could not command himself. But come, let us go. And, good Hephistion, when all the world is won, and every country is thine and mine, either find me out another to subdue, or on my word, I will fall in love."

Marlowe is a name that stands high, and almost first in this list of dramatic worthies. He was a little before Shakspeare's time,* and has a marked character both from him and the rest. There is a lust of power in his writings, a hunger and thirst after unrighteousness, a glow of the imagination, unhallowed by any thing but its own energies. His thoughts burn within him like a furnace with bickering flames: or throwing out black smoke and mists, that hide the dawn of genius, or like a poison ous mineral, corrode the heart. His "Life and Death of Doctor Faustus," though an imperfect and unequal performance, is his greatest work. Faustus himself is a rude sketch, but it is a gigantic one. This character may be considered as a personification of the pride of will and eagerness of curiosity, sublimed beyond the reach of fear and remorse. He is hurried away, and, as it were, devoured by a tormenting desire to enlarge his knowledge to the utmost bounds of nature and art, and to extend his power with his knowledge. He would realize all the fictions of a lawless imagination, would solve the most subtle speculations of abstract reason; and for this purpose sets at defiance all mortal

* He died about 1594.

consequences, and leagues himself with demoniacal power, with "fate and metaphysical aid." The idea of witchcraft and necromancy, once the dread of the vulgar and the darling of the visionary recluse, seems to have had its origin in the restless tendency of the human mind, to conceive of and aspire to more than it can achieve by natural means, and in the obscure apprehension that the gratification of this extravagant and unauthorized desire can only be attained by the sacrifice of all our ordinary hopes and better prospects, to the infernal agents that lend themselves to its accomplishment. Such is the foundation of the present story. Faustus, in his impatience to fulfil at once and for a moment, for a few short years, all the desires and conceptions of his soul, is willing to give in exchange his soul and body to the great enemy of mankind. Whatever he fancies, becomes by this means present to his sense: whatever he commands is done. He calls back time past, and anticipates the future: the visions of antiquity pass before him, Babylon in all its glory, Paris and Œnone: all the projects of philosophers, or creations of the poet, pay tribute at his feet: all the delights of fortune, of ambition, of pleasure, and of learning are centred in his person; and from a short-lived dream of supreme felicity and drunken power, he sinks into an abyss of darkness and perdition. This is the alternative to which he submits; the bond which he signs with his blood! As the outline of the character is grand and daring, the execution is abrupt and fearful. The thoughts are vast and irregular; and the style halts and staggers under them, "with uneasy steps;"— "such footing found the sole of unblest feet." There is a little fustian and incongruity of metaphor now and then, which is not very injurious to the subject. It is time to give a few passages in illustration of this account. He thus opens his mind at the beginning:

"How am I glutted with conceit of this!
Shall I make spirits fetch me what I please?
Resolve me of all ambiguities?
Perform what desperate enterprize I will?
I'll have them fly to India for gold,
Ransack the ocean for orient pearl,
And search all corners of the new-found world
For pleasant fruits and princely delicates.

I'll have them read me strange philosophy,
And tell the secrets of all foreign kings:
I'll have them wall all Germany with brass,
And make swift Rhine circle fair Wittenberg;
I'll have them fill the public schools with skill,
Wherewith the students shall be bravely clad;
I'll levy soldiers with the coin they bring,
And chase the Prince of Parma from our land,
And reign sole king of all the provinces:
Yea, stranger engines for the brunt of war
Than was the fiery keel at Antwerp bridge,
I'll make my servile spirit to invent.

Enter VALDES *and* CORNELIUS.

Come, German Valdes and Cornelius,
And make me blest with your sage conference.
Valdes, sweet Valdes, and Cornelius,
Know that your words have won me at the last
To practise magic and concealed arts.
Philosophy is odious and obscure;
Both Law and Physic are for petty wits;
'Tis magic, magic, that hath ravish'd me.
Then, gentle friends, aid me in this attempt;
And I, that have with subtle syllogisms
Gravell'd the pastors of the German church,
And made the flow'ring pride of Wittenberg
Swarm to my problems, as th' infernal spirits
On sweet Musæus when he came to hell;
Will be as cunning as Agrippa was,
Whose shadow made all Europe honour him.

Valdes. These books, thy wit, and our experience
Shall make all nations to canonize us.
As Indian Moors obey their Spanish lords,
So shall the spirits of every element
Be always serviceable to us three.
Like Lions shall they guard us when we please;
Like Almain Rutters with their horseman's staves,
Or Lapland giants trotting by our sides:
Sometimes like women, or unwedded maids,
Shadowing more beauty in their airy brows
Than have the white breasts of the Queen of Love.
From Venice they shall drag whole argosies,
And from America the golden fleece,
That yearly stuffs old Philip's treasury*;
If learned Faustus will be resolute.

* An anachronism.

Faustus. As resolute am I in this
As thou to live, therefore object it not."

In his colloquy with the fallen angel, he shows the fixedness of his determination:—

"What! is great Mephostophilis so passionate
For being deprived of the joys of heaven?
Learn thou of Faustus manly fortitude,
And scorn those joys thou never shalt possess."

Yet we afterwards find him faltering in his resolution, and struggling with the extremity of his fate:

"My heart is harden'd, I cannot repent:
Scarce can I name salvation, faith, or heaven;
Swords, poisons, halters, and envenom'd steel
Are laid before me to dispatch myself;
And long ere this I should have done the deed,
Had not sweet pleasure conquer'd deep despair.
Have I not made blind Homer sing to me
Of Alexander's love and Œnon's death?
And hath not he that built the walls of Thebes
With ravishing sounds of his melodious harp,
Made music with my Mephostophilis?
Why should I die then or basely despair?
I am resolv'd, Faustus shall not repent.
Come, Mephostophilis, let us dispute again,
And reason of divine astrology."

There is one passage more of this kind, which is so striking and beautiful, so like a rapturous and deeply passionate dream, that I cannot help quoting it here: it is the address to the Appa rition of Helen.

Enter HELEN *again, passing over between two Cupids.*

Faustus. Was this the face that launch'd a thousand ships,
And burnt the topless tow'rs of Ilium?
Sweet Helen, make me immortal with a kiss.
Her lips suck forth my soul! See where it flies.
Come, Helen, come, give me my soul again.
Here will I dwell, for Heav'n is in these lips,
And all is dross that is not Helena.
I will be Paris, and for love of thee,
Instead of Troy shall Wittenberg be sack'd;
And I will combat with weak Menelaus,

And wear thy colours on my plumed crest;
Yea, I will wound Achilles in the heel,
And then return to Helen for a kiss.
—Oh! thou art fairer than the evening air,
Clad in the beauty of a thousand stars:
Brighter art thou than flaming Jupiter,
When he appeared to hapless Semele;
More lovely than the monarch of the sky
In wanton Arethusa's azure arms;
And none but thou shalt be my paramour."

The ending of the play is terrible, and his last exclamations betray an anguish of mind and vehemence of passion not to be contemplated without shuddering:

—"Oh, Faustus!
Now hast thou but one bare hour to live,
And then thou must be damn'd perpetually.
Stand still, you ever-moving spheres of heav'n,
That time may cease, and midnight never come.
Fair nature's eye, rise, rise again, and make
Perpetual day; or let this hour be but a year,
A month, a week, a natural day,
That Faustus may repent, and save his soul.
(*The Clock strikes twelve.*)
It strikes! it strikes! Now, body, turn to air,
Or Lucifer will bear thee quick to hell.
Oh soul! be changed into small water-drops,
And fall into the ocean; ne'er to be found.
(*Thunder. Enter the* Devils.)
Oh! mercy, Heav'n! Look not so fierce on me!
Adders and serpents, let me breathe awhile!—
Ugly hell, gape not! Come not, Lucifer!
I'll burn my books! Oh! Mephostophilis."

Perhaps the finest *trait* in the whole play, and that which softens and subdues the horror of it, is the interest taken by the two scholars in the fate of their master, and their unavailing attempts to dissuade him from his relentless career. The regard to learning is the ruling passion of this drama, and its indications are as mild and amiable in them as its ungoverned pursuit has been fatal to Faustus.

"Yet, for he was a scholar once admir'd

For wondrous knowledge in our German schools,
We'll give his mangled limbs due burial;
And all the students, clothed in mourning black,
Shall wait upon his heavy funeral."

So the Chorus:

"Cut is the branch that might have grown full strait,
And burned is Apollo's laurel bough,
That sometime grew within this learned man."

And still more affecting are his own conflicts of mind and agonizing doubts on this subject just before, when he exclaims to his friends: "Oh, gentlemen! Hear me with patience, and tremble not at my speeches. Though my heart pant and quiver to remember that I have been a student here these thirty years; oh! would I had never seen Wittenberg, never read book!" A finer compliment was never paid, nor a finer lesson ever read to the pride of learning. The intermediate comic parts, in which Faustus is not directly concerned, are mean and grovelling to the last degree. One of the Clowns says to another, "Snails! what hast got there? A book? Why thou can'st not tell ne'er a word on't." Indeed, the ignorance and barbarism of the time, as here described, might almost justify Faustus's overstrained admiration of learning, and turn the heads of those who possessed it from novelty and unaccustomed excitement, as the Indians are made drunk with wine! Goëthe, the German poet, has written a drama on this tradition of his country, which is considered a master-piece. I cannot find in Marlowe's play, any proofs of the atheism or impiety attributed to him, unless the belief in witchcraft and the Devil can be regarded as such; and at the time he wrote, not to have believed in both would have been construed into the rankest atheism and irreligion. There is a delight, as Mr. Lamb says, "in dallying with interdicted subjects;" but that does not, by any means, imply either a practical or speculative disbelief of them.

'Lust's Dominion, or The Lascivious Queen,' is referable to the same general style of writing; and is a striking picture, or rather caricature of the unrestrained love of power, not as connected with learning, but with regal ambition and external sway. There is a good deal of the same intense passion, the same recklessness of purpose, the same smouldering fire within: but there is not any of the same relief to the mind in the lofty imaginative nature of the subject, and the continual repetition of plain practical villainy and undigested horrors disgusts the sense and blunts the interest. The mind is hardened into obduracy, not melted into sympathy, by such barefaced and barbarous cruelty. Eleazar, the Moor, is such another character as Aaron in 'Titus Andronicus;' and this play might be set down without injustice as "pew-fellow" to that. I should think Marlowe has a much fairer claim to be the author of 'Titus Andronicus' than Shakspeare, at least from internal evidence; and the argument of Schlegel, that it must have been Shakspeare's, because there was no one else capable of producing either its faults or beauties, fails in each particular. The Queen is the same character in both these plays, and the business of the plot is carried on in much the same revolting manner, by making the nearest friends and relatives of the wretched victims the instruments of their sufferings and persecution by an arch-villain. To show, however, that the same strong-braced tone of passionate declamation is kept up, take the speech of Eleazer on refusing the proffered crown:

"What, do none rise?
No, no, for kings indeed are deities.
And who'd not (as the sun) in brightness shine?
To be the greatest is to be divine.
Who among millions would not be the mightiest?
To sit in godlike state; to have all eyes
Dazzled with admiration, and all tongues
Shouting loud prayers; to rob every heart
Of love; to have the strength of every arm;
A sovereign's name, why 'tis a sovereign charm.
This glory round about me hath thrown beams:
I have stood upon the top of fortune's wheel,
And backwards turned the iron screw of fate.
The destinies have spun a silken thread
About my life; yet thus I cast aside
The shape of Majesty, and on my knee
To this Imperial state lowly resign

> This usurpation; wiping off your fears
> Which struck so hard upon me."

This is enough to show the unabated vigour of the author's style. This strain is certainly doing justice to the pride of ambition, and the imputed majesty of kings.

We have heard much of "Marlowe's mighty line," and this play furnishes frequent instances of it. There are a number of single lines that seem struck out in the heat of a glowing fancy, and leave a track of golden fire behind them. The following are a few that might be given.

> "I know he is not dead; I know proud death
> Durst not behold such sacred majesty."
> * * * * *
> "Hang both your greedy ears upon my lips,
> Let them devour my speech, suck in my breath."
> * * * * *
> —"From discontent grows treason,
> And on the stalk of treason death."
> * * * * *
> "Tyrants swim safest in a crimson flood."
> * * * * *

The two following lines—

> "Oh! I grow dull, and the cold hand of sleep
> Hath thrust his icy fingers in my breast"-

are the same as those in King John—

> "And none of you will bid the winter come
> To thrust his icy fingers in my maw."

And again the Moor's exclamation:

> "Now by the proud complexion of my cheeks,
> Ta'en from the kisses of the amorous sun"

is the same as Cleopatra's—

> "But I that am with Phœbus' amorous pinches black," &c.

Eleazer's sarcasm,

—— "These dignities,
Like poison, make men swell; this rat's-bane honour,
Oh, 'tis so sweet! they'll lick it till they burst"—

shows the utmost virulence of smothered spleen; and his concluding strain of malignant exultation has been but tamely imitated by Young's Zanga:

"Now, tragedy, thou minion of the night,
Rhamnusia's pew-fellow,* to thee I'll sing,
Upon a harp made of dead Spanish bones,
The proudest instrument the world affords:
To thee that never blushest, though thy cheeks
Are full of blood, O Saint Revenge, to thee
I consecrate my murders, all my stabs," &c.

It may be worth while to observe, for the sake of the curious, that many of Marlowe's most sounding lines consist of monosyllables, or nearly so. The repetition of Eleazer's taunt to the Cardinal, retorting his own words upon him, "Spaniard or Moor, the saucy slave shall die"—may perhaps have suggested Falconbridge's spirited reiteration of the phrase, "And hang a calf's skin on those recreant limbs."

I do not think 'The Rich Jew of Malta' so characteristic a specimen of this writer's powers. It has not the same fierce glow of passion or expression. It is extreme in act, and outrageous in plot and catastrophe; but it has not the same vigorous filling up. The author seems to have relied on the horror inspired by the subject, and the national disgust excited against the principal character, to rouse the feelings of the audience: for the rest, it is a tissue of gratuitous, unprovoked, and incredible atrocities, which are committed, one upon the back of the other, by the parties concerned, without motive, passion or object. There are, notwithstanding, some striking passages in it, as Barabbas's description of the bravo, Philia Borzo†; the relation of

* This expression seems to be ridiculed by Falstaff.

† "He sent a shaggy, tattered, staring slave,
That when he speaks draws out his grisly beard,
And winds it twice or thrice about his ear;
Whose face has been a grindstone for men's swords:

his own unaccountable villanies to Ithamore; his rejoicing over his recovered jewels "as the morning lark sings over her young;" and the backwardness he declares in himself to forgive the Christian injuries that are offered him,* which may have given the idea of one of Shylock's speeches, where he ironically disclaims any enmity to the merchants on the same account. It is perhaps hardly fair to compare the Jew of Malta with the Merchant of Venice; for it is evident that Shakspeare's genius shows to as much advantage in knowledge of character, in variety, and stage-effect, as it does in point of general humanity.

Edward II. is, according to the modern standard of composi-

His hands are hack'd, some fingers cut quite off,
Who when he speaks, grunts like a hog, and looks
Like one that is employed in catzerie,
And cross-biting; such a rogue
As is the husband to a hundred whores;
And I by him must send three hundred crowns."

Act IV.

"In spite of these swine-eating Christians
(Unchosen nation, never circumcised;
Such poor villains as were ne'er thought upon,
Till Titus and Vespasian conquer'd us)
Am I become as wealthy as I am.
They hoped my daughter would have been a nun;
But she's at home, and I have bought a house
As great and fair as is the Governor's:
And there, in spite of Malta, will I dwell,
Having Ferneze's hand; whose heart I'll have,
Ay, and his son's too, or it shall go hard.

"I am not of the tribe of Levi, I,
That can so soon forget an injury.
We Jews can fawn like spaniels when we please;
And when we grin we bite; yet are our looks
As innocent and harmless as a lamb's.
I learn'd in Florence how to kiss my hand,
Heave up my shoulders when they call me dog,
And duck as low as any bare-foot Friar:
Hoping to see them starve upon a stall,
Or else be gather'd for in our synagogue,
That when the offering bason comes to me,
Even for charity I may spit into it"

tion, Marlowe's best play. It is written with few offences against the common rules, and in a succession of smooth and flowing lines. The poet however succeeds less in the voluptuous and effeminate descriptions which he here attempts, than in the more dreadful and violent bursts of passion. Edward II. is drawn with historic truth, but without much dramatic effect. The management of the plot is feeble and desultory; little interest is excited in the various turns of fate; the characters are too worthless, have too little energy, and their punishment is, in general, too well deserved to excite our commiseration; so that this play will bear, on the whole, but a distant comparison with Shakspeare's Richard II. in conduct, power, or effect. But the death of Edward II., in Marlowe's tragedy, is certainly superior to that of Shakspeare's King; and in heart-breaking distress, and the sense of human weakness, claiming pity from utter helplessness and conscious misery, is not surpassed by any writer whatever.

> " *Edward.* Weep'st thou already? List awhile to me,
> And then thy heart, were it as Gurney's is,
> Or as Matrevis, hewn from the Caucasus,
> Yet will it melt ere I have done my tale.
> This dungeon where they keep me, is the sink
> Wherein the filth of all the castle falls.
> *Lightborn.* Oh villains.
> *Edward.* And here in mire and puddle have I stood
> This ten days' space; and lest that I should sleep,
> One plays continually upon a drum.
> They give me bread and water, being a king;
> So that, for want of sleep and sustenance,
> My mind's distemper'd, and my body's numb'd:
> And whether I have limbs or no, I know not.
> Oh! would my blood drop out from every vein,
> As doth this water from my tatter'd robes!
> Tell Isabel, the Queen, I look'd not thus,
> When for her sake I ran at tilt in France,
> And there unhors'd the Duke of Cleremont."

There are some excellent passages scattered up and down. The description of the King and Gaveston looking out of the palace window, and laughing at the courtiers as they pass, and that of the different spirit shown by the lion and the forest deer, when wounded, are among the best. The song "Come live with me and be my love," to which Sir Walter Raleigh wrote an answer, is Marlowe's.

Heywood I shall mention next, as a direct contrast to Marlowe in everything but the smoothness of his verse. As Marlowe's imagination glows like a furnace, Heywood's is a gentle lambent flame, that purifies without consuming. His manner is simplicity itself. There is nothing supernatural, nothing startling, or terrific. He makes use of the commonest circumstances of every-day life, and of the easiest tempers, to show the workings, or rather the inefficacy of the passions, the *vis inertiæ* of tragedy. His incidents strike from their very familiarity, and the distresses he paints invite our sympathy from the calmness and resignation with which they are borne. The pathos might be deemed purer from its having no mixture of turbulence or vindictiveness in it; and in proportion as the sufferers are made to deserve a better fate. In the midst of the most untoward reverses and cutting injuries, good nature and good sense keep their accustomed sway. He describes men's errors with tenderness, and their duties only with zeal, and the heightenings of a poetic fancy. His style is equally natural, simple, and unconstrained. The dialogue (bating the verse) is such as might be uttered in ordinary conversation. It is beautiful prose put into heroic measure. It is not so much that he uses the common English idiom for everything (for that I think the most poetical and impassioned of our elder dramatists do equally), but the simplicity of the characters and the equable flow of the sentiments do not require or suffer it to be warped from the tone of level speaking, by figurative expressions, or hyperbolical allusions. A few scattered exceptions occur now and then, where the hectic flush of passion forces them from the lips, and they are not the worse for being rare. Thus, in the play called 'A Woman Killed with Kindness,' Wendoll, when reproached by Mrs. Frankford with his obligations to her husband, interrupts her hastily, by saying

—— "Oh speak no more!
For more than this I know, and have recorded
Within the *red-leaved table* of my heart."

And further on, Frankford, when doubting his wife's fidelity, says, with less feeling indeed, but with much elegance of fancy,

> "Cold drops of sweat sit dangling on my hairs,
> Like morning dew upon the golden flow'rs."

So also, when returning to his house at midnight to make the fatal discovery, he exclaims,

> ——"Astonishment,
> Fear, and amazement, beat upon my heart,
> Even as a madman beats upon a drum."

It is the reality of things present to their imaginations that makes these writers so fine, so bold, and yet so true in what they describe. Nature lies open to them like a book, and was not to them "invisible, or dimly seen" through a veil of words and filmy abstractions. Such poetical ornaments are however to be met with at considerable intervals in this play, and do not disturb the calm serenity and domestic simplicity of the author's style. The conclusion of Wendoll's declaration of love to Mrs. Frankford may serve as an illustration of its general merits, both as to purity of thought and diction:

> "Fair, and of all beloved, I was not fearful
> Bluntly to give my life into your hand,
> And at one hazard, all my earthly means.
> Go, tell your husband: he will turn me off,
> And I am then undone. I care not, I;
> 'Twas for your sake. Perchance in rage he'll kill me;
> I care not; 'twas for you. Say I incur
> The general name of villain through the world,
> Of traitor to my friend: I care not, I;
> Poverty, shame, death, scandal, and reproach,
> For you I'll hazard all: why what care I?
> For you I love, and for your love I'll die."

The affecting remonstrance of Frankford to his wife, and her repentant agony at parting with him, are already before the public, in Mr. Lamb's Specimens. The winding up of this play is rather awkwardly managed, and the moral is, according to established usage, equivocal. It required only Frankford's reconciliation to his wife, as well as his forgiveness of her, for the highest breach of matrimonial duty, to have made a 'Woman Killed with Kindness,' a complete anticipation of the 'Stranger.' Heywood, however, was in that respect but half a Kotzebue!—The view here given of country manners is truly edifying. As to the higher walk of tragedy, we see the manners and moral sentiments of kings and nobles of former times, here we have the feuds and amiable qualities of country 'squires and their relatives; and such as were the rulers, such were their subjects. The frequent quarrels and ferocious habits of private life are well exposed in the fatal rencounter between Sir Francis Acton and Sir Charles Mountford about a hawking match, in the ruin and rancorous persecution of the latter in consequence, and in the hard, unfeeling, cold-blooded treatment he receives in his distress from his own relations, and from a fellow of the name of Shafton. After reading the sketch of this last character, who is introduced as a mere ordinary personage, the representative of a class, without any preface or apology, no one can doubt the credibility of that of Sir Giles Overreach, who is professedly held up (I should think almost unjustly) as a prodigy of grasping and hardened selfishness. The influence of philosophy and prevalence of abstract reasoning, if it has done nothing for our poetry, has done, I should hope, something for our manners. The callous declaration of one of these unconscionable churls,

"This is no world in which to pity men,"

might have been taken as a motto for the good old times in general, and with a very few reservations, if Heywood has not grossly libelled them.—Heywood's plots have little of artifice or regularity of design to recommend them. He writes on carelessly, as it happens, and trusts to Nature, and a certain happy tranquillity of spirit, for gaining the favour of the audience. He is said, besides attending to his duties as an actor, to have composed regularly a sheet a day. This may account in some measure for the unembarrassed facility of his style. His own account makes the number of his writings for the stage, or those in which he had a main hand, upwards of two hundred. In fact, I do not wonder at any quantity that an author is said to have written; for the more a man writes, the more he can write.

The same remarks will apply, with certain modifications, to other remaining works of this writer, the 'Royal King and Loyal Subject,' 'A Challenge for Beauty,' and 'The English Traveller.' The barb of misfortune is sheathed in the mildness of the writer's temperament, and the story jogs on very comfortably, without effort or resistance, to the *euthanasia* of the catastrophe. In two of these the person principally aggrieved survives, and feels himself none the worse for it. The most splendid passage in Heywood's comedies is the account of Shipwreck by Drink, in 'The English Traveller,' which was the foundation of Cowley's Latin poem, *Naufragium Joculare.*

The names of Middleton and Rowley, with which I shall conclude this Lecture, generally appear together as two writers who frequently combined their talents in the production of joint pieces. Middleton (judging from their separate works) was "the more potent spirit" of the two; but they were neither of them equal to some others. Rowley appears to have excelled in describing a certain amiable quietness of disposition and disinterested tone of morality, carried almost to a paradoxical excess, as in his 'Fair Quarrel,' and in the comedy of 'A Woman never Vexed,' which is written in many parts, with a pleasing simplicity and *naiveté* equal to the novelty of the conception. Middleton's style was not marked by any peculiar quality of his own, but was made up, in equal proportions, of the faults and excellences common to his contemporaries. In his 'Women beware Women,' there is a rich marrowy vein of internal sentiment, with fine occasional insight into human nature, and cool cutting irony of expression. He is lamentably deficient in the plot and denouement of the story. It is like the rough draught of a tragedy, with a number of fine things thrown in, and the best made use of first; but it tends to no fixed goal, and the interest decreases, instead of increasing as we read on, for want of previous arrangement and an eye to the whole. We have fine studies of heads, a piece of richly coloured drapery, "a foot, an hand, an eye from Nature drawn, that's worth a history;" but the groups are ill disposed, nor are the figures proportioned to each other or the size of the canvas. The author's power is *in* the subject, not *over* it; or he is in possession of excellent materials, which he husbands very ill. This character, though it applies more particularly to Middleton, might be applied generally to the age. Shakspeare alone seemed to stand over his work, and to do what he pleased with it. He saw to the end of what he was about, and with the same faculty of lending himself to the impulses of Nature and the impression of the moment, never forgot that he himself had a task to perform, nor the place which each figure ought to occupy in his general design.—The characters of Livia, of Brancha, of Leantio and his mother, in the play of which I am speaking, are all admirably drawn. The art and malice of Livia show equal want of principle and acquaintance with the world; and the scene in which she holds the mother in suspense, while she betrays the daughter into the power of the profligate duke, is a master-piece of dramatic skill. The proneness of Brancha to tread the primrose path of pleasure, after she has made the first false step, and her sudden transition from unblemished virtue to the most abandoned vice, in which she is notably seconded by her mother-in-law's ready submission to the temptations of wealth and power, form a true and striking picture. The first intimation of the intrigue that follows, is given in a way that is not a little remarkable for simplicity and acuteness. Brancha says,

"Did not the duke look up? Methought he saw us."

To which the more experienced mother answers,

"That's every one's conceit that sees a duke;
If he look stedfastly, he looks straight at them,
When he, perhaps, good careful gentleman,
Never minds any, but the look he casts
Is at his own intentions, and his object
Only the public good."

It turns out, however, that he had been looking at them, and not "at the public good." The moral of this tragedy is rendered more impressive from the manly, independent character of Leantio in the first instance, and the manner in which he dwells, in a sort of doting abstraction, on his own comforts, of being possessed of a beautiful and faithful wife. As he approaches his own house, and already treads on the brink of perdition, he exclaims with an exuberance of satisfaction not to be restrained—

" How near am I to a happiness
That earth exceeds not! not another like it:
The treasures of the deep are not so precious,
As are the concealed comforts of a man
Lock'd up in woman's love. I scent the air
Of blessings when I come but near the house:
What a delicious breath marriage sends forth!
The violet bed's not sweeter. Honest wedlock
Is like a banqueting house built in a garden,
On which the spring's chaste flowers take delight
To cast their modest odours; when base lust,
With all her powders, paintings, and best pride,
Is but a fair house built by a ditch side.
When I behold a glorious dangerous strumpet,
Sparkling in beauty and destruction too,
Both at a twinkling, I do liken straight
Her beautified body to a goodly temple
That's built on vaults where carcases lie rotting;
And so by little and little I shrink back again,
And quench desire with a cool meditation;
And I'm as well, methinks. Now for a welcome
Able to draw men's envies upon man:
A kiss now that will hang upon my lip,
As sweet as morning dew upon a rose,
And full as long; after a five days' fast
She'll be so greedy now and cling about me:
I take care how I shall be rid of her:
And here 't begins."

This dream is dissipated by the entrance of Brancha and his Mother.

" *Bran.* Oh, sir, you're welcome home.
Moth. Oh, is he come? I am glad on't.
Lean. (*Aside.*) Is that all?
Why this is dreadful now as sudden death
To some rich man that flatters all his sins
With promise of repentance when he's old,
And dies in the midway before he comes to 't.
Sure you're not well, Brancha! how dost, prithee?
Bran. I have been better than I am at this time.
Lean. Alas, I thought so.

Bran. Nay, I have been worse too,
Than now you see me, sir.
Lean. I'm glad thou mend'st yet,
I feel my heart mend too. How came it to thee?
Has any thing dislik'd thee in my absence?
Bran. No, certain, I have had the best content
That Florence can afford.
Lean. Thou makest the best on't:
Speak, mother, what's the cause? you must needs know.
Moth. Troth, I know none, son; let her speak herself;
Unless it be the same gave Lucifer a tumbling cast; that's pride.
Bran. Methinks this house stands nothing to my mind;
I'd have some pleasant lodging i' th' high street, sir;
Or if 'twere near the court, sir, that were much better;
'Tis a sweet recreation for a gentlewoman
To stand in a bay-window, and see gallants.
Lean. Now I have another temper, a mere stranger
To that of yours, it seems; I should delight
To see none but yourself.
Bran. I praise not that;
Too fond is as unseemly as too churlish;
I would not have a husband of that proneness,
To kiss me before company, for a world;
Besides, 'tis tedious to see one thing still, sir,
Be it the best that ever heart affected;
Nay, wer't yourself, whose love had power you know
To bring me from my friends, I would not stand thus,
And gaze upon you always; troth, I could not, sir;
As good be blind, and have no use of sight,
As look on one thing still: what's the eye's treasure,
But change of objects? You are learned, sir,
And know I speak not ill; 'tis full as virtuous
For woman's eye to look on several men,
As for her heart, sir, to be fixed on one.
Lean. Now, thou com'st home to me; a kiss for that word.
Bran. No matter for a kiss, sir; let it pass;
'Tis but a toy, we'll not so much as mind it;
Let's talk of other business, and forget it.
What news now of the pirates? any stirring?
Prithee discourse a little.
Moth. (*Aside.*) I'm glad he's here yet,
To see her tricks himself; I had lied monstrously
If I had told 'em first.
Lean. Speak, what's the humour, sweet,
You make your lips so strange? This was not wont.
Bran. Is there no kindness betwixt man and wife,
Unless they make a pigeon-house of friendship,

And be still billing? 'Tis the idlest fondness
That ever was invented; and 'tis pity
It's grown a fashion for poor gentlewomen;
There's many a disease kiss'd in a year by't,
And a French court'sy made to't. Alas, sir,
Think of the world, how we shall live, grow serious;
We have been married a whole fortnight now.
Lean. How? a whole fortnight! why, is that so long?
Bran. 'Tis time to leave off dalliance; 'tis a doctrine
Of your own teaching, if you be remember'd,
And I was bound to obey it.
Moth. (*Aside.*) Here's one fits him;
This was well catch'd i' faith, son, like a fellow
That rids another country of a plague,
And brings it home with him to his own house.
[*A messenger from the Duke knocks within.*
Who knocks?
Lean. Who's there now? Withdraw you, Brancha;
Thou art a gem no stranger's eye must see,
Howe'er thou'rt pleas'd now to look dull on me. [*Exit Brancha.*"

The Witch of Middleton is his most remarkable performance; both on its own account, and from the use that Shakspeare has made of some of the characters and speeches in his 'Macbeth.' Though the employment which Middleton has given to Hecate and the rest, in thwarting the purposes and perplexing the business of familiar and domestic life, is not so grand or appalling as the more stupendous agency which Shakspeare has assigned them, yet it is not easy to deny the merit of the first invention to Middleton, who has embodied the existing superstitions of the time, respecting that anomalous class of beings, with a high spirit of poetry, of the most grotesque and fanciful kind. The songs and incantations made use of are very nearly the same. The other parts of this play are not so good; and the solution of the principal difficulty, by Antonio's falling down a trap-door, most lame and impotent. As a specimen of the similarity of the preternatural machinery, I shall here give one entire scene.

"*The Witches' Habitation.*

Enter HECCAT, STADLIN, HOPPO, *and other Witches.*

Hec. The moon's a gallant: see how brisk she rides.
Stad. Here's a rich evening, Heccat.
Hec. Aye, is 't not, wenches,
To take a journey of five thousand miles?

Hop. Ours will be more to-night.

Hec. Oh, 't will be precious. Heard you the owl yet?

Stad. Briefly, in the copse,
As we came through now.

Hec. 'Tis high time for us then.

Stad. There was a bat hung at my lips three times
As we came through the woods, and drank her fill:
Old Puckle saw her.

Hec. You are fortunate still,
The very scritch-owl lights upon your shoulder,
And woos you like a pigeon. Are you furnish'd?
Have you your ointments?

Stad. All.

Hec. Prepare to flight then.
I'll overtake you swiftly.

Stad. Hie then, Heccat!
We shall be up betimes.

Hec. I'll reach you quickly. [*They ascend.*

Enter FIRESTONE.

Fire. They are all going a-birding to-night. They talk of fowls i' th' air, that fly by day, I'm sure ther'll be a company of foul sluts there to-night. If we have not mortality affeared, I'll be hang'd, for they are able to putrify it, to infect a whole region. She spies me now

Hec. What, Firestone, our sweet son?

Fire. A little sweeter than some of you; or a dunghill were too good for me.

Hec. How much hast there?

Fire. Nineteen, and all brave plump ones; besides six lizards, and three serpentine eggs.

Hec. Dear and sweet boy! What herbs hast thou?

Fire. I have some mar-martin and man-dragon.

Hec. Marmarittin, and mandragora, thou would'st say.

Fire. Here's pannax, too. I thank thee; my pan akes, I am sure, with kneeling down to cut 'em

Hec. And selago,
Hedge-hissop, too! How near he goes my cuttings!
Were they all cropt by moon-light?

Fire. Every blade of 'em, or I am a moon-calf, mother.

Hec. Hie thee home with 'em.
Look well to th' house to-night: I'm for aloft.

Fire. Aloft, quoth you? I would you would break your neck once, that I might have all quickly (*Aside.*)—Hark, hark, mother! They are above the steeple already, flying over your head with a noise of musicians.

Hec. They are indeed. Help me! Help me! I'm too late else.

SONG (*in the air above.*)

Come away, come away!
Heccat, Heccat, come away!

Hec. I come, I come, I come, I come,
With all the speed I may,
With all the speed I may.
Where's Stadlin?
(*Above.*) Here.
Hec. Where's Puckle?
(*Above.*) Here:
And Hoppo too, and Hellwain too;
We lack but you, we lack but you.
Come away, make up the count
Hec. I will but 'noint, and then I mount.
(*A Spirit descends in the shape of a cat.*)
(*Above.*) There's one come down to fetch his dues;
A kiss, a coll, a sip of blood;
And why thou stay'st so long, I muse, I muse,
Since th' air's so sweet and good?
Hec. Oh, art thou come,
What news, what news?
Spirit. All goes still to our delight,
Either come, or else
Refuse, refuse.
Hec. Now I am furnish'd for the flight.
Fire. Hark, hark! The cat sings a brave treble in her own language.
Hec. (*Ascending with the Spirit.*)
Now I go, now I fly,
Malkin, my sweet spirit, and I.
Oh, what a dainty pleasure 'tis
To ride in the air
When the moon shines fair,
And sing, and dance, and toy, and kiss!
Over woods, high rocks, and mountains,
Over seas our mistress' fountains,
Over steep towers and turrets
We fly by night, 'mongst troops of spirits.
No ring of bells to our ears sounds,
No howls of wolves, no yelps of hounds;
No, not the noise of water's breach,
Or cannon's roar our height can reach.
(*Above.*) No ring of bells, &c.

Fire. Well, mother, I thank your kindness. You must be gamboling i' the air, and leave me to walk here like a fool and a mortal. [*Exit.*

The incantation scene at the cauldron is also the original of that in Macbeth, and is in like manner introduced by the Duchess's visiting the Witches' habitation.

"*The Witches' Habitation.*

Enter DUCHESS, HECCAT, FIRESTONE.

Hec. What death is 't you desire for Almachildes?
Duch. A sudden and a subtle.
Hec. Then I've fitted you.
Here lie the gifts of both; sudden and subtle;
His picture made in wax and gently molten
By a blue fire kindled with dead men's eyes,
Will waste him by degrees.
Duch. In what time, pr'ythee?
Hec. Perhaps in a month's progress.
Duch. What! A month?
Out upon pictures, if they be so tedious;
Give me things with some life.
Hec. Then seek no farther.
Duch. This must be done with speed, dispatched this night,
If it may possibly.
Hec. I have it for you:
Here's that will do't. Stay but perfection's time,
And that's not five hours hence.
Duch. Can'st thou do this?
Hec. Can I?
Duch. I mean, so closely.
Hec. So closely do you mean too?
Duch. So artfully, so cunningly.
Hec. Worse and worse; doubts and incredulities,
They make me mad. Let scrupulous creatures know,
Cum volui, ripis ipsis mirantibus, amnes
In fontes rediere suos: concussaque sisto,
Stantia concutio cantu freta; nubila pello,
Nubilaque induco: ventos abigoque vocoque.
Vipereas rumpo verbis et carmine fauces;
Et silvas moveo, jubeoque tremiscere montes,
Et mugire solum, manesque exire sepulchris.
Te quoque, Luna, traho.
Can you doubt me then, daughter?
That can make mountains tremble, miles of woods walk;
Whole earth's foundations bellow, and the spirits
Of the entomb'd to burst out from their marbles;
Nay, draw yon moon to my involv'd designs?

Fire. I know as well as can be when my mother's mad, and our great cat angry; for the one spits French then, and the other spits Latin.

Duch. I did not doubt you, mother.
Hec. No? what did you?
My power's so firm, it is not to be question'd.
Duch. Forgive what's past: and now I know th' offensiveness
That vexes art, I'll shun the occasion ever

Hec. Leave all to me and my five sisters, daughter.
It shall be conveyed in at howlet-time.
Take you no care My spirits know their moments;
Raven or scritch-owl never fly by th' door,
But they call in (I thank 'em), and they lose not by 't.
I give 'em barley soak'd in infants' blood:
They shall have *semina cum sanguine*,
Their gorge cramm'd full, if they come once to our house:
We are no niggard. [*Exit* DUCHESS.

Fire. They fare but too well when they come hither. They ate up as much t' other night as would have made me a good conscionable pudding.

Hec. Give me some lizard's brain: quickly, Firestone!
Where's grannam Stadlin, and all the rest o' th' sisters?

Fire. All at hand, forsooth. [*The other Witches appear*

Hec. Give me marmaritin; some bear-breech. When?

Fire. Here's bear-breech and lizard's brain, forsooth.

Hec. Into the vessel;
And fetch three ounces of the red-hair'd girl
I kill'd last midnight.

Fire. Whereabout, sweet mother?

Hec. Hip; hip or flank. Where is the acopus?

Fire. You shall have acopus, forsooth.

Hec. Stir, stir about, whilst I begin the charm.

A CHARM SONG.

(*The Witches going about the cauldron.*)

Black spirits, and white; red spirits, and grey
Mingle, mingle, mingle, you that mingle may
  Titty, Tiffin, keep it stiff in;
  Firedrake, Puckey, make it lucky;
  Liard, Robin, you must bob in.
Round, around, around, about, about;
All ill come running in; all good keep out!

1st Witch. Here's the blood of a bat.
Hec. Put in that; oh, put in that.
2nd Witch. Here's libbard's-bane.
Hec. Put in again.
1st Witch. The juice of toad; the oil of adder.
2nd Witch. Those will make the younker madder.
Hec. Put in; there's all, and rid the stench.
Fire. Nay, here's three ounces of the red-hair'd wench.
All. Round, around, around, &c.
Hec. So, so, enough: into the vessel with it.
There; 't hath the true perfection. I'm so light
At any mischief: there's no villony
But is a tune, methinks.

Fire. A tune! 'Tis to the tune of damnation then, I warrant you, and that song hath a villanous burthen.

Hec. Come, my sweet sisters; let the air strike our tune
Whilst we show reverence to yon peeping moon.

[*The Witches dance and then exeunt.*"

I will conclude this account with Mr. Lamb's observations on the distinctive characters of these extraordinary and formidable personages, as they are described by Middleton or Shakspeare:

"Though some resemblance may be traced between the Charms in Macbeth and the Incantations in this play, which is supposed to have preceded it, this coincidence will not detract much from the originality of Shakspeare. His witches are distinguished from the witches of Middleton by essential differences. These are creatures to whom man or woman, plotting some dire mischief, might resort for occasional consultation. Those originate deeds of blood, and begin bad impulses to men. From the moment that their eyes first meet Macbeth's, he is spell-bound. That meeting sways his destiny. He can never break the fascination. These Witches can hurt the body; those have power over the soul. Hecate, in Middleton, has a son, a low buffoon: the Hags of Shakspeare have neither child of their own, nor seem to be descended from any parent. They are foul anomalies, of whom we know not whence they sprung, nor whether they have beginning or ending. As they are without human passions, so they seem to be without human relations. They come with thunder and lightning, and vanish to airy music. This is all we know of them. Except Hecate, they have no names, which heightens their mysteriousness. The names, and some of the properties which Middleton has given to his Hags, excite smiles. The Weird Sisters are serious things. Their presence cannot co-exist with mirth. But in a lesser degree, the Witches of Middleton are fine creations. Their power too is, in some measure, over the mind. They 'raise jars, jealousies, strifes, like a thick scurf o'er life.' "*

* Lamb's 'Specimens of English Dramatic Poets.' Vol. I. p. 187. Moxon, London.

LECTURE III.

On Marston, Chapman, Decker, and Webster.

THE writers of whom I have already treated may be said to have been "no mean men;" those of whom I have yet to speak are certainly no whit inferior. Would that I could do them anything like justice! It is not difficult to give at least their seeming due to great and well-known names; for the sentiments of the reader meet the descriptions of the critic more than half way, and clothe what is perhaps vague and extravagant praise with a substantial form and distinct meaning. But in attempting to extol the merits of an obscure work of genius, our words are either lost in empty air, or are "blown stifling back" upon the mouth that utters them. The greater those merits are, and the truer the praise, the more suspicious and disproportionate does it almost necessarily appear; for it has no relation to any image previously existing in the public mind, and therefore looks like an imposition fabricated out of nothing. In this case, the only way that I know of is, to make these old writers (as much as can be) vouchers for their own pretensions, which they are well able to make good. I shall in the present lecture give some account of Marston and Chapman, and afterwards of Decker and Webster.

Marston is a writer of great merit, who rose to tragedy from the ground of comedy, and whose *forte* was not sympathy, either with the stronger or softer emotions, but an impatient scorn and bitter indignation against the vices and follies of men, which vented itself either in comic irony or in lofty invective. He was properly a satirist. He was not a favourite with his contemporaries nor they with him. He was first on terms of great intimacy, and afterwards at open war, with Ben Jonson; and he is most unfairly criticized in The Return from Parnassus, under the name of Monsieur Kinsayder, as a mere libeller and buffoon. Writers in their life-time do all they can to degrade and vilify one another, and expect posterity to have a very tender care of their reputations! The writers of this age, in general, cannot however be reproached with this infirmity. The number of plays that they wrote in conjunction is a proof of the contrary; and a circumstance no less curious, as to the division of intellectual labour, than the cordial union of sentiment it implied. Unlike most poets, the love of their art surmounted their hatred of one another. Genius was not become a vile and vulgar pretence, and they respected in others what they knew to be true inspiration in themselves. They courted the applause of the multitude, but came to one another for judgment and assistance. When we see these writers working together on the same admirable productions, year after year, as was the case with Beaumont and Fletcher, Middleton and Rowley, with Chapman, Decker, and Jonson, it reminds one of Ariosto's eloquent apostrophe to the Spirit of Ancient Chivalry, when he has seated his rival knights, Renaldo and Ferraw, on the same horse:

> "Oh ancient knights of true and noble heart,
> They rivals were, one faith they liv'd not under
> Besides, they felt their bodies shrewdly smart
> Of blows late given, and yet (behold a wonder)
> Thro' thick and thin, suspicion set apart,
> Like friends they ride, and parted not asunder,
> Until the horse with double spurring drived
> Unto a way parted in two, arrived."*

Marston's Antonio and Mellida is a tragedy of considerable force and pathos; but in the most critical parts, the author frequently breaks off or flags without any apparent reason but want of interest in his subject; and farther, the best and most affecting situations and bursts of feeling are too evidently imitations of Shakspeare. Thus the unexpected meeting between Andrugio and Lucio, in the beginning of the third act, is a direct counterpart of that between Lear and Kent, only much weakened: and the interview between Antonio and Mellida has a strong resemblance to the still more affecting one between Lear and Cordelia, and is most wantonly disfigured by the sudden introduction

* Sir John Harrington's translation.

of half a page of Italian rhymes, which gives the whole an air of burlesque. The conversation of Lucio and Andrugio, again, after his defeat, seems to invite, but will not bear a comparison with Richard the Second's remonstrance with his courtiers, who offered him consolation in his misfortunes; and no one can be at a loss to trace the allusion to Romeo's conduct on being apprized of his banishment, in the termination of the following speech·

"*Antonio.* Each man takes hence life, but no man death;
He's a good fellow, and keeps open house;
A thousand thousand ways lead to his gate,
To his wide-mouthed porch: when niggard life
Hath but one little, little wicket through.
We wring ourselves into this wretched world
To pule and weep, exclaim, to curse and rail,
To fret and ban the fates, *to strike the earth*
As I do now. Antonio, curse thy birth,
And die."

The following short passage might be quoted as one of exquisite beauty and originality—

—"As having clasp'd a rose
Within my palm, the rose being ta'en away,
My hand retains a little breath of sweet;
So may man's trunk, his spirit slipp'd away,
Hold still a faint perfume of his sweet guest."
Act IV, Scene 1.

The character of Felice in this play is an admirable satirical accompaniment, and is the favourite character of this author (in all probability his own), that of a shrewd, contemplative cynic, and sarcastic spectator in the drama of human life. It runs through all his plays, is shared by Quadratus and Lampatho in 'What you Will,' (it is into the mouth of the last of these that he has put that fine invective against the uses of philosophy, in the account of himself and his spaniel, "who still slept while he baus'd leaves, tossed o'er the dunces, por'd on the old print"), and is at its height in the Fawn and Malevole, in his 'Parasitaster' and 'Malcontent.' These two comedies are his *chef-d'œuvres.* The character of the Duke Hercules of Ferrara, disguised as the Parasite, in the first of these, is well sustained throughout, with great sense, dignity, and spirit. He is a wise censurer of men and things, and rails at the world with charitable bitterness. He may put in a claim to a sort of family likeness to the Duke, in 'Measure for Measure,' only the latter descends from his elevation to watch in secret over serious crimes; the other is only a spy on private follies. There is something in this cast of character (at least in comedy—perhaps it neutralizes the tone and interest in tragedy), that finds a wonderful reciprocity in the breast of the reader or audience. It forms a kind of middle term or point of union between the busy actors in the scene and the indifferent bystander, insinuates the plot, and suggests a number of good wholesome reflections, for the sagacity and honesty of which we do not fail to take credit to ourselves. We are let into its confidence, and have a perfect reliance on its sincerity. Our sympathy with it is without any drawback; for it has no part to perform itself, and "is nothing, if not critical." It is a sure card to play. We may doubt the motives of heroic actions, or differ about the just limits and extreme workings of the passions; but the professed misanthrope is a character that no one need feel any scruples in trusting, since the dislike of folly and knavery in the abstract is common to knaves and fools with the wise and honest! Besides the instructive moral vein of Hercules as the Fawn or Parasitaster, which contains a world of excellent matter most aptly and wittily delivered, there are two other characters perfectly hit off, Gonzago, the old prince of Urbino, and Granuffo, one of his lords in waiting. The loquacious, good-humoured, undisguised vanity of the one is excellently relieved by the silent gravity of the other. The wit of this last character (Granuffo) consists in his not speaking a word through the whole play; he never contradicts what is said, and only assents by implication. He is a most infallible courtier, and follows the prince like his shadow, who thus graces his pretensions.

"We would be private, only Faunus stay; he is a wise fellow, daughter, a very wise fellow, for he is still just of my opinion; my Lord Granuffo, you may likewise stay, for I know you'll say nothing."

And again, a little farther on, he says—

"Faunus, this Granuffo is a right wise good lord, a man of excellent discourse, and never speaks; his signs to me and men of profound reach instruct abundantly; he begs suits with signs, gives thanks with signs, puts off his hat leisurely, maintains his beard learnedly, keeps his lust privately, makes a nodding leg courtly, and lives happily."—"Silence," [replies Hercules,] "is an excellent modest grace; but especially before so instructing a wisdom as that of your Excellency."

The garrulous self-complacency of this old lord is kept up in a vein of pleasant humour; an instance of which might be given in his owning of some learned man, that "though he was no duke, yet he was wise;" and the manner in which the others play upon this foible, and make him contribute to his own discomfiture, without his having the least suspicion of the plot against him, is full of ingenuity and counterpoint. In the last scene he says, very characteristically,

"Of all creatures breathing, I do hate those things that struggle to seem wise, and yet are indeed very fools. I remember when I was a young man, in my father's days, there were four gallant spirits for resolution, as proper for body, as witty in discourse, as any were in Europe; nay, Europe had not such. I was one of them. We four did all love one lady; a most chaste virgin she was: we all enjoyed her, and so enjoyed her, that, despite the strictest guard was set upon her, we had her at our pleasure. I speak it for her honour, and my credit. Where shall you find such witty fellows now-a-days? Alas! how easy is it in these weaker times to cross love-tricks! Ha! ha! ha! Alas, alas! I smile to think (I must confess with some glory to mine own wisdom), to think how I found out, and crossed, and curbed, and in the end made desperate Tiberio's love. Alas! good silly youth, that dared to cope with age and such a beard!

Hercules. But what yet might your well-known wisdom think,
If such a one, as being most severe,
A most protested opposite to the match
Of two young lovers; who having barr'd them speech,
All interviews, all messages, all means
To plot their wished ends; even he himself
Was by their cunning made the go-between,
The only messenger, the token-carrier;
Told them the times when they might fitly meet,
Nay, show'd the way to one another's bed?"

To which Gonzago replies, in a strain of exulting dotage

"May one have the sight of such a fellow for nothing? Doth there breathe such an egregious ass? Is there such a foolish animal in *rerum natura?* How is it possible such a simplicity can exist? Let us not lose our laughing at him, for God's sake; let folly's sceptre light upon him, and to the Ship of Fools with him instantly.

Dondolo. Of all these follies I arrest your grace."

Molière has built a play on nearly the same foundation, which is not much superior to the present. Marston, among other topics of satire, has a fling at the pseudo-critics and philosophers of his time, who were "full of wise saws and modern instances." Thus he freights his Ship of Fools.

" *Dondolo.* Yes, yes; but they got a supersedeas; all of them proved themselves either knaves or madmen, and so were let go: there's none left now in our ship but a few citizens that let their wives keep their shop-books, some philosophers, and a few critics; one of which critics has lost his flesh with fishing at the measure of Plautus' verses; another has vowed to get the consumption of the lungs, or to leave to posterity the true orthography and pronunciation of laughing.

Hercules. But what philosophers ha' ye?

Dondolo. Oh, very strange fellows; one knows nothing, dares not aver he lives, goes, sees, feels.

Nymphadoro. A most insensible philosopher.

Dondolo. Another, that there is no present time; and that one man to-day and to-morrow, is not the same man; so that he that yesterday owed money, to-day owes none; because he is not the same man.

Herod. Would that philosophy hold good in law?

Hercules. But why has the Duke thus laboured to have all the fools shipped out of his dominions?

Dondolo. Marry, because he would play the fool alone without any rival.

Act IV.

Molière has enlarged upon the same topic in his *Mariage Forcé*, but not with more point or effect. Nymphadoro's reasons for devoting himself to the sex generally, and Hercules's description of the different qualifications of different men, will also be found to contain excellent specimens, both of style and matter. The disguise of Hercules as the Fawn is assumed voluntarily, and he is comparatively a calm and dispassionate observer of the times. Malevole's disguise in the Malcontent has been forced upon him by usurpation and injustice, and his invectives are accordingly more impassioned and virulent. His satire does not "like a wild goose fly, unclaimed of any man," but has a bitter and personal application. Take him in the words of the usurping Duke's account of him:

"This Malevole is one of the most prodigious affections that ever conversed with Nature; a man, or rather a monster, more discontent than Lucifer when he was thrust out of the presence. His appetite is unsatiable as the grave, as far from any content as from heaven. His highest delight is to procure others vexation, and therein he thinks he truly serves heaven; for 'tis his position, whosoever in this earth can be contented is a slave, and damned; therefore does he afflict all, in that to which they are most affected. The elements struggle with him; his own soul is at variance with herself; his speech is halter-worthy at all hours. I like him, 'faith; he gives good intelligence to my spirit, makes me understand those weaknesses which others' flattery palliates. Hark! they sing.

Enter MALEVOLE, *after the song.*

Pietro Jacomo. See he comes! Now shall you hear the extremity of a Malcontent; he is as free as air; he blows over every man. And—Sir, whence come you now?

Malevole. From the public place of much dissimulation, the church.

Pietro Jacomo. What didst there?

Malevole. Talk with a usurer; take up at interest.

Pietro Jacomo. I wonder what religion thou art of?

Malevole. Of a soldier's religion.

Pietro Jacomo. And what dost think makes most infidels now?

Malevole. Sects, sects. I am weary; would I were one of the Duke's hounds.

Pietro Jacomo. But what's the common news abroad? Thou dogg'st rumour still.

Malevole. Common news? Why, common words are, God save ye, Fare ye well: common actions, flattery and cozenage: common things, women and cuckolds."

Act I. Scene 3.

In reading all this, one is somehow reminded perpetually of Mr. Kean's acting: in Shakspeare we do not often think of him, except in those parts which he constantly acts, and in those one cannot forget him. I might observe on the above passage, in excuse for some bluntness of style, that the ideal barrier between names and things seems to have been greater then than now. Words have become instruments of more importance than formerly. To mention certain actions, is almost to participate in them, as if consciousness were the same as guilt. The standard of delicacy varies at different periods, as it does in different countries, and is not a general test of superiority. The French, who pique themselves (and justly, in some particulars) on their quickness of tact and refinement of breeding, say and do things which we, a plainer and coarser people, could not think of without a blush. What would seem gross allusions to us at present, were without offence to our ancestors, and many things passed for jests with them, or matters of indifference, which would not now be endured. Refinement of language, however, does not keep pace with simplicity of manners. The severity of criticism exercised in our theatres towards some unfortunate straggling phrases in the old comedies, is but an ambiguous compliment to the immaculate purity of modern times. Marston's style was by no means more guarded than that of his contemporaries. He was also much more of a free-thinker than Marlowe, and there is a frequent and not unfavourable allusion, in his works, to later sceptical opinions. In the play of the 'Malcontent' we meet with an occasional mixture of comic gaiety, to relieve the more serious and painful business of the scene, as in the easy loquacious effrontery of the old *intriguante* Maquerella, and in the ludicrous facility with which the idle courtiers avoid or seek the notice of Malevole, as he is in or out of favour; but the general tone and import of the piece is severe and moral. The plot is somewhat too intricate and too often changed (like the shifting of a scene,) so as to break and fritter away the interest at the end; but the part of Aurelia, the Duchess of Pietro Jacomo, a dissolute and proud-spirited woman, is the highest strain of Marston's pen. The scene in particular, in which she receives and exults in the supposed news of her husband's death, is nearly unequalled in boldness of conception and in the unrestrained force of passion, taking away not only the consciousness of guilt, but overcoming the sense of shame.*

Next to Marston, I must put Chapman, whose name is better known as the translator of Homer than as a dramatic writer. He is, like Marston, a philosophic observer, a didactic reasoner: but he has both more gravity in his tragic style, and more levity in his comic vein. His 'Bussy d'Ambois,' though not without interest or some fancy, is rather a collection of apophthegms or pointed sayings in the form of a dialogue, than a poem or a tragedy. In his verses the oracles have not ceased. Every other line is an axiom in morals—a libel on mankind, if truth is

* See conclusion of Lecture IV

a libel. He is too stately for a wit, in his serious writings—too formal for a poet. 'Bussy d'Ambois' is founded on a French plot and French manners. The character, from which it derives its name, is arrogant and ostentatious to an unheard-of degree, but full of nobleness and lofty spirit. His pride and unmeasured pretensions alone take away from his real merit; and by the quarrels and intrigues in which they involve him, bring about the catastrophe, which has considerable grandeur and imposing effect, in the manner of Seneca. Our author aims at the highest things in poetry, and tries in vain, wanting imagination and passion, to fill up the epic moulds of tragedy with sense and reason alone, so that he often runs into bombast and turgidity—is extravagant and pedantic at one and the same time. From the nature of the plot, which turns upon a love intrigue, much of the philosophy of this piece relates to the character of the sex. Milton says

> "The way of woman's will is hard to hit."

But old Chapman professes to have found the clue to it, and winds his uncouth way through all the labyrinth of love. Its deepest recesses "hide nothing from his view." The close intrigues of court policy, the subtle workings of the human soul, move before him like a sea, dark, deep, and glittering with wrinkles for the smile of beauty. Fulke Greville alone could go beyond him in gravity and mystery. The plays of the latter (Mustapha and Alaham) are abstruse as the mysteries of old, and his style inexplicable as the riddles of the Sphinx. As an instance of his love for the obscure, the marvellous, and impossible, he calls up "the ghost of one of the old kings of Ormus," as a prologue to one of his tragedies; a very reverend and inscrutable personage, who, we may be sure, blabs no living secrets. Chapman, in his other pieces, where he lays aside the gravity of the philosopher and poet, discovers an unexpected comic vein, distinguished by equal truth of nature and lively good humour. I cannot say that this character pervades any one of his entire comedies; but the introductory sketch of Monsieur D'Olive is the undoubted prototype of that light, flippant, gay, and infinitely delightful class of character, of the professed men of wit and pleasure about town, which we have in such perfection in Wycherly and Congreve, such as Sparkish, Witwoud, and Petulant, &c., both in the sentiments and in the style of writing. For example, take the last scene of the first act.

Enter D'OLIVE.

Rhoderique. What, Monsieur D'Olive, the only admirer of wit and good words.

D'Olive. Morrow, wits: morrow, good wits: my little parcels of wit, I have rods in pickle for you. How dost, Jack; may I call thee, sir, Jack yet?

Mugeron. You may, sir; sir's as commendable an addition as Jack, for aught I know.

D'Ol. I know it, Jack, and as common too.

Rhod. Go to, you may cover; we have taken notice of your embroidered beaver.

D'Ol. Look you: by heaven thou'rt one of the maddest bitter slaves in Europe: I do but wonder how I made shift to love thee all this while

Rhod. Go to, what might such a parcel-gilt cover be worth?

Mug. Perhaps more than the whole piece beside.

D'Ol. Good i'faith, but bitter. Oh, you mad slaves, I think you had Satyrs to your sires, yet I must love you, I must take pleasure in you, and i'faith tell me, how is't? live I see you do, but how? but how, wits?

Rhod. 'Faith, as you see, like poor younger brothers.

D'Ol. By your wits?

Mug. Nay, not turned poets, neither.

D'Ol. Good in sooth! But indeed, to say truth, time was when the sons of the Muses had the privilege to live only by their wits, but times are altered: monopolies are now called in, and wit's become a free trade for all sorts to live by: lawyers live by wit, and they live worshipfully: soldiers live by wit, and they live honourably: panders live by wit, and they live honestly: in a word, there are but few trades but live by wit, only bawds and midwives by woman's labours, as fools and fiddlers do making mirth, pages and parasites by making legs, painters and players by making mouths and faces: ha, does't well, wits?

Rhod. 'Faith, thou followest a figure in thy jests, as country gentlemen follow fashions, when they be worn threadbare.

D'Ol. Well, well, let's leave these wit skirmishes, and say when shall we meet?

Mug. How think you, are we not met now?

D'Ol. Tush, man! I mean at my chamber, where we may make free use of ourselves; that is, drink sack, and talk satire, and let our wits run the wild-goose chase over court and country. I will have my chamber the rendezvous of all good wits, the shop of good words, the mint of good jests, an ordinary of fine discourse; critics, essayists, linguists, poets, and other professors of that faculty of wit, shall at certain hours i' th' day, resort thither; it shall be a second Sorbonne, where all doubts or differences of learning, honour, duelism, criticism, and poetry, shall be disputed: and how, wits, do ye follow the court still?

Rhod. Close at heels, sir; and I can tell you, you have much to answer to your stars, that you do not so too.

D'Ol. As why, wits? as why?

Rhod. Why, sir, the court's as 'twere the stage: and they that have a good suit of parts and qualities ought to press thither to grace them, and receive their due merit.

D'Ol. Tush, let the court follow me: he that soars too near the sun, melts his wings many times; as I am, I possess myself, I enjoy my liberty, my learning, my wit: as for wealth and honour, let 'em go; I'll not lose my learning to be a lord, nor my wit to be an alderman.

Mug. Admirable D'Olive!

D'Ol. And what! you stand gazing at this comet here, and admire it, I dare say.

Rhod. And do not you?

D'Ol. Not I, I admire nothing but wit.

Rhod. But I wonder how she entertains time in that solitary cell: does she not take tobacco, think you?

D'Ol. She does, she does: others make it their physic, she makes it her food: her sister and she take it by turn, first one, then the other, and Vandome ministers to them both.

Mug. How sayest thou by that Helen of Greece the Countess's sister? here were a paragon, Monsieur D'Olive, to admire and marry too.

D'Ol. Not for me.

Rhod. No! what exceptions lie against the choice?

D'Ol. Tush, tell me not of choice; if I stood affected that way, I would choose my wife as men do valentines, blindfold or draw cuts for them, for so I shall be sure not to be deceived in choosing; for take this of me, there's ten times more deceit in women than in horse flesh; and I say still, that a pretty well-paced chamber-maid is the only fashion; if she grows full or fulsome, give her but sixpence to buy her a hand-basket, and send her the way of all flesh, there's no more but so.

Mug. Indeed that's the savingest way.

D'Ol. O me! what a hell 'tis for a man to be tied to the continual charge of a coach, with the appurtenances, horses, men, and so forth: and then to have a man's house pestered with a whole country of guests, grooms, panders, waiting maids, &c. I careful to please my wife, she careless to displease me; shrewish if she be honest; intolerable if she be wise; imperious as an empress; all she does must be law, all she says gospel: oh, what a penance 'tis to endure her! I glad to forbear still, all to keep her loyal, and yet perhaps when all's done my heir shall be like my horse-keeper: Fie on't! the very thought of marriage were able to cool the hottest liver in France.

Rhod. Well, I durst venture twice the price of your gilt coney's wool, we shall have you change your copy ere a twelvemonth's day.

Mug. We must have you dubb'd o' th' order; there's no remedy: you that have, unmarried, done such honourable service in the commonwealth, must needs receive the honour due to 't in marriage.

Rhod. That he may do, and never marry.

D'Ol. As how, wits ? I'faith as how ?

Rhod. For if he can prove his father was free o' th' order, and that he was his father's son, then, by the laudable custom of the city, he may be a cuckold by his father's copy, and never serve for 't.

D'Ol. Ever good, i'faith!

Mug. Nay, how can he plead that, when 'tis as well known his father died a bachelor ?

D'Ol. Bitter, in verity, bitter! But good still in its kind.

Rhod. Go to, we must have you follow the lantern of your forefathers.

Mug. His forefathers ? 'Sbody, had he more fathers than one ?

D'Ol. Why, this is right: here's wit canvast out on 's coat, into 's jacket: the string sounds ever well, that rubs not too much o' th' frets: I must love you, wits, I must take pleasure in you. Farewell, good wits: you know my lodging, make an errand thither now and then, and save your ordinary; do, wits, do.

Mug. We shall be troublesome t' ye.

D'Ol. O God, sir, you wrong me, to think I can be troubled with wit: I love a good wit as I love myself: if you need a brace or two of crowns at any time, address but your sonnet, it shall be as sufficient as your bond at all times: I carry half a score birds in a cage, shall ever remain at your call. Farewell, wits; farewell, good wits. [*Exit.*

Rhod. Farewell, the true map of a gull: by heaven he shall to th' court! 'tis the perfect model of an impudent upstart; the compound of a poet and a lawyer; he shall sure to th' court.

Mug. Nay, for God's sake, let's have no fools at court.

Rhod. He shall to 't, that 's certain. The duke had a purpose to dispatch some one or other to the French king, to entreat him to send for the body of his niece, which the melancholy Earl of St. Anne, her husband, hath kept so long unburied, as meaning one grave should entomb himself and her together.

Mug. A very worthy subject for an embassage, as D'Olive is for an ambassador agent; and 'tis as suitable to his brain, as his parcel-gilt beaver to his fool's head.

Rhod. Well, it shall go hard, but he shall be employed. Oh, 'tis a most accomplished ass; the mongrel of a gull, and a villain: the very essence of his soul is pure villany; the substance of his brain, foolery; one that believes nothing from the stars upward; a pagan in belief, an epicure beyond belief; prodigious in lust; prodigal in wasteful expense; in necessary, most penurious. His wit is to admire and imitate; his grace is to censure and detract; he shall to th' court, i' faith he shall thither: I will shape such employment for him, as that he himself shall have no less contentment, in making mirth to the whole court, than the Duke and the whole court shall have pleasure in enjoying his presence. A knave, if he be rich, is fit to make an officer, as a fool, if he be a knave, is fit to make an intelligencer. [*Exeunt.*"

His 'May-day' is not so good. 'All Fools,' the 'Widow's Tears,' and 'Eastward Hoe,' are comedies of great merit, particularly the last. The first is borrowed a good deal from Terence, and the character of Valerio, an accomplished rake, who passes with his father for the person of the greatest economy and rusticity of manners, is an excellent idea, executed with spirit. 'Eastward Hoe' was written in conjunction with Ben Jonson and Marston; and for his share in it, on account of some allusions to the Scotch, just after the accession of James I., our author, with his friends, had nearly lost his ears. Such were the notions of poetical justice in those days! The behaviour of Ben Jonson's mother on this occasion is remarkable. "On his release from prison, he gave an entertainment to his friends, among whom were Camden and Selden. In the midst of the entertainment, his mother, more an antique Roman than a Briton, drank to him, and showed him a paper of poison, which she intended to have given him in his liquor, having first taken a portion of it herself, if the sentence for his punishment had been executed." This play contains the first idea of Hogarth's 'Idle and Industrious Apprentices.'

It remains for me to say something of Webster and Decker. For these two writers I do not know how to show my regard and admiration sufficiently. Noble-minded Webster, gentle-hearted Decker, how may I hope to "express ye unblam'd," and repay to your neglected *manes* some part of the debt of gratitude I owe for proud and soothing recollections? I pass by the 'Appius and Virginia' of the former, which is however a good, sensible, solid tragedy, cast in a frame-work of the most approved models, with little to blame or praise in it, except the affecting speech of Appius to Virginia just before he kills her; as well as Decker's 'Wonder of a Kingdom,' his 'Jacomo Gentili,' that truly ideal character of a magnificent patron, and 'Old Fortunatus and is Wishing-cap,' which last has the idle garrulity of age, with he freshness and gaiety of youth still upon its cheek and in its heart. These go into the common catalogue, and are lost in the crowd; but Webster's 'Vittoria Corombona' I cannot so soon part with; and old honest Decker's Signior Orlando Friscobaldo I shall never forget! I became only of late acquainted with this last-mentioned worthy characte; but the bargain between us is, I trust, for life. We sometimes regret that we had not sooner met with characters like these, that seem to raise, revive, and give a new zest to our being. Vain the complaint! We should never have known their value, if we had not known them always: they are old, very old acquaintance, or we should not recognize them at first sight. We only find in books what is already written within "the red-leaved tables of our hearts." The pregnant materials are there; "the pangs, the internal pangs are ready; and poor humanity's afflicted will struggling in vain with ruthless destiny." But the reading of fine poetry may indeed open the bleeding wounds, or pour balm and consolation into them, or sometimes even close them up for ever! Let any one who has never known cruel disappointment, nor comfortable hopes, read the first scene between Orlando and Hippolito, in Decker's play of the 'Honest Whore,' and he will see nothing in it. But I think few persons will be entirely proof against such passages as some of the following:

"*Enter* ORLANDO FRISCOBALDO.

Omnes. Signior Friscobaldo.

Hippolito. Friscobaldo, oh! pray call him, and leave me; we two have business.

Carolo. Ho, Signior! Signior Friscobaldo, the Lord Hippolito.

[*Exeunt.*

Orlando. My noble Lord! the Lord Hippolito! The Duke's son! his brave daughter's brave husband! How does your honour'd Lordship? Does your nobility remember so poor a gentleman as Signior Orlando Friscobaldo? old mad Orlando?

Hip. Oh, sir, our friends, they ought to be unto us as our jewels; as dearly valued, being locked up and unseen, as when we wear them in our hands. I see, Friscobaldo, age hath not command of your blood; for all Time's sickle hath gone over you, you are Orlando still.

Orl. Why, my Lord, are not the fields mown and cut down, and stript bare, and yet wear they not pied coats again? Though my head be like a leek, white, may not my heart be like the blade, green?

Hip. Scarce can I read the stories on your brow,
Which age hath writ there: you look youthful still.

Orl. I eat snakes, my Lord, I eat snakes. My heart shall never have a wrinkle in it so long as I can cry Hem! with a clear voice. * * *

Hip. You are the happier man, sir.

Orl. May not old Friscobaldo, my Lord, be merry now, ha? I have little, have all things, have nothing. I have no wife, I have no child, have no chick, and why should I not be in my jocundare?

Hip. Is your wife then departed?

Orl. She's an old dweller in those high countries, yet not from me: here, she's here; a good couple are seldom parted.

Hip. You had a daughter, too, sir, had you not?

Orl. Oh, my Lord! this old tree had one branch, and but one branch, growing out of it: it was young, it was fair, it was straight: I pruned it daily, drest it carefully, kept it from the wind, helped it to the sun; yet for all my skill in planting, it grew crooked, it bore crabs: I hew'd it down. What's become of it I neither know nor care.

Hip. Then can I tell you what's become of it: that branch is withered.

Orl. So 'twas long ago.

Hip. Her name, I think, was Bellafront; she's dead.

Orl. Ha! dead?

Hip. Yes, what of her was left, not worth the keeping. Even in my sight, was thrown into a grave.

Orl. Dead! my last and best peace go with her! I see death's a good trencherman; he can eat coarse homely meat as well as the daintiest——Is she dead?

Hip. She's turn'd to earth.

Orl. Would she were turned to heaven. Umh! Is she dead? I am glad the world has lost one of his idols: no whoremonger will at midnight beat at the doors: in her grave sleep all my shame and her own; and all my sorrows and all her sins.

Hip. I'm glad you are wax, not marble; you are made
Of man's best temper; there are now good hopes
That all these heaps of ice about your heart,
By which a father's love was frozen up,
Are thaw'd in those sweet show'rs fetch'd from your eye:
We are ne'er like angels till our passions die.
She is not dead, but lives under worse fate;
I think she's poor; and more to clip her wings
Her husband at this hour lies in the jail,
For killing of a man: to save his blood,
Join all your force with mine; mine shall be shown,
The getting of his life preserves your own.

Orl. In my daughter you will say! Does she live, then? I am sorry I wasted tears upon a harlot! but the best is, I have a handkerchief to drink them up, soap can wash them all out again. Is she poor?

Hip. Trust me, I think she is.

Orl. Then she's a right strumpet. I never knew one of their trade rich two years together; sieves can hold no water, nor harlots hoard up money; taverns, tailors, bawds, panders, fiddlers, swaggerers, fools, and knaves, do all wait upon a common harlot's trencher; she is the gallypot to which these drones fly: not for love to the pot, but for the sweet sucket in it, her money, her money.

Hip. I almost dare pawn my word her bosom gives warmth to no such snakes; when did you see her?

Orl. Not seventeen summers.

Hip. Is your hate so old?

Orl. Older; it has a white head, and shall never die till she be buried; her wrongs shall be my bedfellow.

Hip. Work yet his life, since in it lives her fame.

Orl. No, let him hang, and half her infamy departs out of the world; I hate him for her: he taught her first to taste poison; I hate her for herself, because she refused my physic.

Hip. Nay, but Friscobaldo.

Orl. I detest her, I defy both, she's not mine, she's——

Hip. Hear her, but speak.

Orl. I love no mermaids, I'll not be caught with a quail-pipe.

Hip. You're now beyond all reason. Is't dotage to relieve your child, being poor?

Orl. 'Tis foolery; relieve her! Were her cold limbs stretcht out upon a bier, I would not sell this dirt under my nails to buy her an hour's breath, nor give this hair unless it were to choke her.

Hip. Fare you well, for I'll trouble you no more. [*Exit.*

Orl. And fare you well, sir, go thy ways; we have few lords of thy making, that love wenches for their honesty.—'Las, my girl, art thou poor? Poverty dwells next door to despair, there's but a wall between them: despair is one of hell's catchpoles, and lest that devil arrest her, I'll to her; yet she shall not know me: she shall drink of my wealth as beggars do of running water, freely; yet never know from what fountain's head it flows. Shall a silly bird pick her own breast to nourish her young ones: and can a father see his child starve? That were hard: the pelican does it, and shall not I?"

The rest of the character is answerable to the beginning. The execution is, throughout, as exact as the conception is new and masterly. There is the least colour possible used; the pencil drags; the canvas is almost seen through: but then, what precision of outline, what truth and purity of tone, what firmness of hand, what marking of character! The words and answers all along are so true and pertinent, that we seem to see the gestures, and to hear the tone with which they are accompanied. So when Orlando, disguised, says to his daughter, "You'll forgive me," and she replies, "I am not marble, I forgive you;" or again, when she introduces him to her husband, saying simply, "It is my father," there needs no stage-direction to supply the relenting tones of voice or cordial frankness of manner with which these words are spoken. It is as if there were some fine art to chisel thought, and to embody the inmost movements of the mind in every-day actions and familiar speech. It has been asked,

> "Oh! who can paint a sun-beam to the blind,
> Or make him feel a shadow with his mind?"

But this difficulty is here in a manner overcome. Simplicity and extravagance of style, homeliness and quaintness, tragedy and comedy, interchangeably set their hands and seals to this admirable production. We find the simplicity of prose with the graces of poetry. The stalk grows out of the ground; but the flowers spread their flaunting leaves in the air. The mixture of levity in the chief character bespeaks the bitterness from which it seeks relief; it is the idle echo of fixed despair, jealous of observation or pity. The sarcasm quivers on the lip, while the tear stands congealed on the eye-lid. This "tough senior," this impracticable old gentleman softens into a little child; this choke-pear melts in the mouth like marmalade. In spite of his resolute professions of misanthropy, he watches over his daughter with kindly solicitude; plays the careful housewife; broods over her lifeless hopes; nurses the decay of her husband's fortune, as he had supported her tottering infancy; saves the high-flying Matheo from the gallows more than once, and is twice a father to them The story has all the romance of private life, all the pathos of bearing up against silent grief, all the tenderness of concealed affection:—there is much sorrow patiently borne, and then comes peace. Bellafront, in the two parts of this play taken together, is a most interesting character. It is an extreme, and I am afraid almost an ideal case. She gives the play its title, turns out a true penitent, that is, a practical one, and is the model of an exemplary wife. She seems intended to establish the converse of the position, that *a reformed rake makes the best husband,* the only difficulty in proving which, is, I suppose, to meet with the character. The change of her relative position, with regard to Hippolito, who, in the first part, in the sanguine enthusiasm of youthful generosity, has reclaimed her from vice, and in the second part, his own faith and love of virtue having been impaired with the progress of years, tries in vain to lure her back again to her former follies, has an effect the most striking and beautiful. The pleadings on both sides, for and against female faith and constancy, are managed with great polemical skill, assisted by the grace and vividness of poetical illustration. As an instance of the manner in which Bellafront speaks of the miseries of her former situation, "and she has felt them knowingly," I might give the lines in which she contrasts the different regard shown to the modest or the abandoned of her sex:

"I cannot, seeing she's woven of such bad stuff,
Set colours on a harlot bad enough.
Nothing did make me when I lov'd them best,
To loath them more than this: when in the street
A fair, young, modest damsel, I did meet,
She seem'd to all a dove, when I pass'd by,
And I to all a raven: every eye
That followed her, went with a bashful glance;
At me each bold and jeering countenance
Darted forth scorn: to her, as if she had been
Some tower unvanquished, would they vail;
'Gainst me swoln rumour hoisted every sail.
She crown'd with reverend praises, passed by them;
I, though with face mask'd, could not 'scape the hem;
For, as if heav'n had set strange marks on whores,
Because they should be pointing-stocks to man,
Drest up in civilest shape, a courtesan,
Let her walk saint-like, noteless, and unknown,
Yet she's betray'd by some trick of her own."

Perhaps this sort of appeal to matter of fact and popular opinion, is more convincing than the scholastic subtleties of the Lady in 'Comus.' The manner too, in which Infelice, the wife of Hippolito, is made acquainted with her husband's infidelity, is finely dramatic; and in the scene where she convicts him of his injustice by taxing herself with incontinence first, and then turning his most galling reproaches to her into upbraidings against his own conduct, she acquits herself with infinite spirit and address. The contrivance by which, in the first part, after being supposed dead, she is restored to life, and married to Hippolito, though perhaps a little far-fetched, is affecting and romantic. There is uncommon beauty in the Duke her father's description of her sudden illness. In reply to Infelice's declaration on reviving, "I'm well," he says,

"Thou wert not so e'en now. Sickness' pale hand
Laid hold on thee, ev'n in the midst of feasting:
And when a cup, crown'd with thy lover's health,
Had touch'd thy lips, a sensible cold dew
Stood on thy cheeks, as if that death had wept
To see such beauty altered."

Candido, the good-natured man of this play, is a character of inconceivable quaintness and simplicity. His patience and good-humour cannot be disturbed by anything. The idea (for it is nothing but an idea) is a droll one, and is well supported. He is not only resigned to injuries, but "turns them," as Falstaff says of diseases, "into commodities." He is a patient Grizzel out of petticoats, or a Petruchio reversed. He is as determined upon winking at affronts, and keeping out of scrapes at all events, as the hero of the 'Taming of the Shrew' is bent upon picking quarrels out of straws, and signalizing his manhood without the smallest provocation to do so. The sudden turn of the character of Candido, on his second marriage, is, however, as amusing as it is unexpected.

Matheo, "the high-flying" husband of Bellafront, is a masterly portrait, done with equal ease and effect. He is a person almost without virtue or vice, that is, he is in strictness without any moral principle at all. He has no malice against others, and no concern for himself. He is gay, profligate, and unfeeling, governed entirely by the impulse of the moment, and utterly reckless of consequences. His exclamation, when he gets a new suit of velvet, or a lucky run on the dice, "Do we not fly high," is an answer to all arguments. Punishment or advice has no more effect upon him, than upon the moth that flies into the candle. He is only to be left to his fate. Orlando saves him from it, as we do the moth, by snatching it out of the flame, throwing it out of the window, and shutting down the casement upon it.

Webster would, I think, be a greater dramatic genius than Decker, if he had the same originality; and perhaps is so, even without it. His 'White Devil' and 'Duchess of Malfy,' upon the whole, perhaps, come the nearest to Shakspeare of anything we have upon record; the only drawback to them, the only shade of imputation than can be thrown upon them, "by which they lose some colour," is, that they are too like Shakspeare, and often direct imitations of him, both in general conception and individual expression. So far, there is nobody else whom it would be either so difficult or so desirable to imitate; but it would have been still better, if all his characters had been entirely his own, had stood out as much from others, resting only on their own naked merits, as that of the honest Hidalgo, on whose praises I have dwelt so much above. Decker has, I think, more truth of character, more instinctive depth of sentiment, more of the unconscious simplicity of nature; but he does not, out of his own stores, clothe his subject with the same richness of imagination, or the same glowing colours of language. Decker excels in giving expression to habitual, deeply-rooted feelings, which remain pretty much the same in all circumstances, the simple uncompounded elements of nature and passion:—Webster gives more scope to their various combinations and changeable aspects, brings them into dramatic play by contrast and comparison, flings them into a state of fusion by a kindled fancy, makes them describe a wider arc of oscillation from the impulse of unbridled passion, and carries both terror and pity to a more painful and sometimes unwarrantable excess. Decker is contented with the historic picture of suffering; Webster goes on to suggest horrible imaginings. The pathos of the one tells home and for itself; the other adorns his sentiments with some image of tender or awful beauty. In a word, Decker is more like Chaucer or Boccaccio; as Webster's mind appears to have been cast more in the mould of Shakspeare's, as well naturally as from studious emulation. The Bellafront and Vittoria Corombona of these two excellent writers, show their different powers and turn of mind. The one is all softness; the other "all fire and air." The faithful wife of Matheo sits at home drooping, "like the female dove, the whilst her golden couplets are disclosed;" while the insulted and persecuted Victoria darts killing scorn and pernicious beauty at her enemies. This White Devil (as she is called) is made fair as the leprosy, dazzling as the lightning. She is dressed like a bride in her wrongs and her revenge. In the trial scene in particular, her sudden indignant answers to the questions that are asked her, startle the nearers. Nothing can be imagined finer than the whole conduct and conception of this scene, than her scorn of her accusers and of herself. The sincerity of her sense of guilt triumphs over the hypocrisy of their affected and official contempt for it. In answer to the charge of having received letters from the Duke of Brachiano, she says,

> "Grant I was tempted:—
> Condemn you me, for that the Duke did love me?
> So may you blame some fair and crystal river,
> For that some melancholic distracted man
> Hath drown'd himself in 't."

And again, when charged with being accessary to her husband's death, and showing no concern for it—

> "She comes not like a widow; she comes arm'd
> With scorn and impudence. Is this a mourning habit?"

she coolly replies,

> "Had I foreknown his death, as you suggest,
> I would have bespoke my mourning."

In the closing scene with her cold-blooded assassins, Lodovico and Gasparo, she speaks daggers, and might almost be supposed to exorcise the murdering fiend out of these true devils. Every word probes to the quick. The whole scene is the sublime of contempt and indifference.

> "*Vittoria.* If Florence be i' the Court, he would not kill me.
> *Gasparo.* Fool! Princes give rewards with their own hands,
> But death or punishment by the hands of others.
> *Lodovico* (*to* Flamineo). Sirrah, you once did strike me; I'll strike you
> Unto the centre.
> *Flam.* Thou'lt do it like a hangman, a base hangman,
> Not like a noble fellow, for thou see'st
> I cannot strike again.
> *Lod.* Dost laugh?
> *Flam.* Would'st have me die, as I was born, in whining?
> *Gasp.* Recommend yourself to Heaven.
> *Flam.* No, I will carry mine own commendations thither.
> *Lod.* O! could I kill you forty times a-day,
> And use 't four year together, 'twere too little:
> Nought grieves, but that you are too few to feed
> The famine of our vengeance. What do'st think on?

Flam. Nothing; of nothing: leave thy idle questions—
I am i' th' way to study a long silence.
To prate were idle: I remember nothing;
There's nothing of so infinite vexation
As man's own thoughts.
Lod. O thou glorious strumpet!
Could I divide thy breath from this pure air
When 't leaves thy body, I would suck it up,
And breathe 't upon some dunghill.
Vit. Cor. You my death's-man.
Methinks thou dost not look horrid enough;
Thou hast too good a face to be a hangman:
If thou be, do thy office in right form;
Fall down upon thy knees, and ask forgiveness.
Lod. O! thou hast been a most prodigious comet;
But I'll cut off your train: kill the Moor first.
Vit. Cor. You shall not kill her first; behold my breast;
I will be waited on in death: my servant
Shall never go before me.
Gasp. Are you so brave?
Vit. Cor. Yes, I shall welcome death
As princes do some great embassadours;
I'll meet thy weapon half way.
Lod. Thou dost not tremble!
Methinks, fear should dissolve thee into air.
Vit. Cor. O, thou art deceived, I am too true a woman!
Conceit can never kill me. I'll tell thee what,
I will not in my death shed one base tear
Or if look pale, for want of blood, not fear.
Gasp. (*to* Zanche). Thou art my task, black fury.
Zanche. I have blood
As red as either of theirs! Wilt drink some?
'Tis good for the falling sickness: I am proud
Death cannot alter my complexion,
For I shall ne'er look pale.
Lod. Strike, strike,
With a joint motion.
Vit. Cor. 'Twas a manly blow:
The next thou givest, murther some sucking infant,
And then thou wilt be famous."

Such are some of the *terrible graces* of the obscure, forgotten Webster. There are other parts of this play of a less violent, more subdued, and, if it were possible, even deeper character; such is the declaration of divorce pronounced by Brachiano on his wife:

"Your hand I'll kiss:
This is the latest ceremony of my love;
I'll never more live with you," &c.

which is in the manner of, and equal to, Decker's finest things: —and others, in a quite different style of fanciful poetry and bewildered passion; such as the lamentation of Cornelia, his mother, for the death of Marcello, and the parting scene of Brachiano; which would be as fine as Shakspeare, if they were not in a great measure borrowed from his inexhaustible store. In the former, after Flamineo has stabbed his brother, and Hortensio comes in, Cornelia exclaims,

"Alas! he is not dead; he's in a trance.
Why, here's nobody shall get anything by his death:
Let me call him again, for God's sake.

Hor. I would you were deceived.

Corn. O you abuse me, you abuse me, you abuse me! How many have gone away thus, for lack of 'tendance? Rear up 's head, rear up 's head; his bleeding inward will kill him.

Hor. You see he is departed.

Corn. Let me come to him; give me him as he is. If he be turned to earth, let me but give him one hearty kiss, and you shall put us both into one coffin. Fetch a looking-glass: see if his breath will not stain it; or pull out some feathers from my pillow, and lay them to his lips. Will you lose him for a little pains-taking?

Hor. Your kindest office is to pray for him.

Corn. Alas! I would not pray for him yet. He may live to lay me i' th' ground, and pray for me, if you'll let me come to him.

Enter BRACHIANO, *all armed, save the Bearer, with* FLAMINEO *and Page.*

Brach. Was this your handy-work?

Flam. It was my misfortune.

Corn. He lies, he lies; he did not kill him. These have killed him, that would not let him be better looked to.

Brach. Have comfort, my grieved mother.

Corn. O, yon screech-owl!

Hor. Forbear, good madame.

Corn. Let me go, let me go.

(*She runs to* Flamineo *with her knife drawn, and coming to him, lets it fall.*)

The God of Heaven forgive thee! Dost not wonder
I pray for thee? I'll tell thee what's the reason:
I have scarce breath to number twenty minutes;
I'd not spend that in cursing. Fare thee well!

Half of thyself lies there; and may'st thou live
To fill an hour-glass with his moulder'd ashes,
To tell how thou should'st spend the time to come
In b.est repentance.
Brach. Mother, pray tell me,
How came he by his death? What was the quarrel?
Corn. Indeed, my younger boy presumed too much
Upon his manhood, gave him bitter words,
Drew his sword first; and so, I know not how,
For I was out of my wits, he fell with 's head
Just in my bosom.
Page. This is not true, madam.
Corn. I pr'ythee, peace.
One arrow's graz'd already: it were vain
To lose this; for that will ne'er be found again."

This is a good deal borrowed from Lear; but the inmost folds of the human heart, the sudden turns and windings of the fondest affection, are also laid open with so masterly and original a hand, that it seems to prove the occasional imitations as unnecessary as they are evident. The scene where the Duke discovers that he is poisoned, is as follows, and equally fine:

"*Brach.* Oh! I am gone already. The infection
Flies to the brain and heart. O, thou strong heart,
There's such a covenant 'tween the world and thee,
They're loth to part.
Giovanni. O my most lov'd father!
Brach. Remove the boy away:
Where's this good woman? Had I infinite worlds,
They were too little for thee. Must I leave thee? (*To* Vittoria.)
What say you, screech-owls? (*To the Physicians.*) Is the venom mortal?
Phy. Most deadly.
Brach. Most corrupted politic hangman!
You kill without book; but your art to save
Fails you as oft as great men's needy friends:
I that have given life to offending slaves,
And wretched murderers, have I not power
To lengthen mine own a twelve-month?
Do not kiss me, for I shall poison thee.
This unction is sent from the great Duke of Florence.
Francesco de Medici (in disguise). Sir, be of comfort.
Brach. O thou soft natural death! that art joint-twin
To sweetest slumber!—no rough-bearded comet
Stares on thy mild departure: the dull owl

Beats not against thy casement: the hoarse wolf
Scents not thy carrion. Pity winds thy corse,
Whilst horror waits on princes.
Vit. Cor. I am lost for ever.
Brach. How miserable a thing it is to die
Mongst women howling! What are those?
Flam. Franciscans.
They have brought the extreme unction.
Brach. On pain of death, let no man name death to me:
It is a word most infinitely terrible.
Withdraw into our cabinet."

The deception practised upon him by Lodovico and Gasparo, who offer him the sacrament in the disguise of Monks, and then discover themselves to damn him, is truly diabolical and ghastly. But the genius that suggested it was as profound as it was lofty. When they are at first introduced, Flamineo says,

"See, see how firmly he doth fix his eye
Upon the Crucifix."

To which Vittoria answers,

"Oh, hold it constant:
It settles his wild spirits; and so his eyes
Melt into tears."

The Dutchess of Malfy is not, in my judgment, quite so spirited or effectual a performance as the White Devil. But it is distinguished by the same kind of beauties, clad in the same terrors. I do not know but the occasional strokes of passion are even profounder and more Shakspearian; but the story is more laboured, and the horror is accumulated to an overpowering and insupportable height. However appalling to the imagination and finely done, the scenes of the madhouse to which the Duchess is condemned with a view to unsettle her reason, and the interview between her and her brother, where he gives her the supposed lead hand of her husband, exceed, to my thinking, the just bounds of poetry and of tragedy. At least, the merit is of a kind which, however great, we wish to be rare. A series of such exhibitions obtruded upon the senses or the imagination must tend to stupefy and harden, rather than to exalt the fancy or meliorate the heart. I speak this under correction; but I hope the objection is a venial common-place. In a different style altogether are the directions she gives about her children in her last struggles:

> "I pr'ythee, look thou giv'st my little boy
> Some syrop for his cold, and let the girl
> Say her pray'rs ere she sleep. Now what death you please—"

and her last word, "Mercy," which she recovers just strength enough to pronounce; her proud answer to her tormentors, who taunt her with her degradation and misery—"But I am Duchess of Malfy still"*—as if the heart rose up, like a serpent coiled, to resent the indignities put upon it, and being struck at, struck again; and the staggering reflection her brother makes on her death, "Cover her face: my eyes dazzle: she died young!" Bosola replies:

> "I think not so; her infelicity
> Seem'd to have years too many.
> *Ferdinand.* She and I were twins.
> And should I die this instant, I had liv'd
> Her time to a minute."

This is not the bandying of idle words and rhetorical common-places, but the writhing and conflict, and the sublime colloquy of man's nature with itself!

The 'Revenger's Tragedy,' by Cyril Tourneur, is the only other drama equal to these and to Shakspeare, in "the dazzling fence of impassioned argument," in pregnant illustration, and in those profound reaches of thought which lay open the soul of feeling. The play, on the whole, does not answer to the expectations it excites; but the appeals of Castiza to her mother, who endeavours to corrupt her virtuous resolutions, "Mother, come

* "Am I not the Duchess?

Bosola. Thou art some great woman, sure; for riot begins to sit on thy forehead (clad in grey hairs) twenty years sooner than on a merry milkmaid's. Thou sleep'st worse than if a mouse should be forced to take up his lodging in a cat's ear: a little infant that breeds its teeth, should it lie with thee, would cry out, as if thou wert the more unquiet bed-fellow.

Duch. I am Duchess of Malfy still."

from that poisonous woman there," with others of the like kind, are of as high and abstracted an essence of poetry, as any of those above mentioned.

In short, the great characteristic of the elder dramatic writers is, that there is nothing theatrical about them. In reading them you only think how the persons, into whose mouths certain sentiments are put, would have spoken or looked: in reading Dryden and others of that school, you only think, as the authors themselves seem to have done, how they would be ranted on the stage by some buskined hero or tragedy-queen. In this respect, indeed, some of his more obscure contemporaries have the advantage over Shakspeare himself, inasmuch as we have never seen their works represented on the stage; and there is no stage-trick to remind us of it. The characters of their heroes have not been cut down to fit into the prompt-book, nor have we ever seen their names flaring in the play-bills in small or large capitals.—I do not mean to speak disrespectfully of the stage; but I think higher still of nature, and next to that of books. They are the nearest to our thoughts: they wind into the heart; the poet's verse slides into the current of our blood. We read them when young, we remember them when old. We read there of what has happened to others; we feel that it has happened to ourselves. They are to be had everywhere cheap and good. We breathe but the air of books: we owe everything to their authors, on this side barbarism; and we pay them easily with contempt, while living, and with an epitaph, when dead! Michael Angelo is beyond the Alps; Mrs. Siddons has left the stage and us to mourn her loss. Were it not so, there are neither picture-galleries nor theatres-royal on Salisbury-plain, where I write this; but here, even here, with a few old authors, I can manage to get through the summer or the winter months, without ever knowing what it is to feel *ennui*. They sit with me at breakfast; they walk out with me before dinner. After a long walk through unfrequented tracts, after starting the hare from the fern, or hearing the wing of the raven rustling above my head, or being greeted by the woodman's "stern good-night," as he strikes into his narrow homeward path, I can "take mine ease at mine inn," beside the blazing hearth, and shake hands with Signor Orlando Friscobaldo, as the oldest acquaintance I have. Ben Jonson, learned Chapman, Master Webster, and Master Heywood, are there; and seated round, discourse the silent hours away. Shakspeare is there himself, not in Cibber's manager's coat. Spenser is hardly yet returned from a ramble through the woods, or is concealed behind a group of nymphs, fawns, and satyrs. Milton lies on the table, as on an altar, never taken up or laid down without reverence. Lyly's Endymion sleeps with the Moon, that shines in at the window; and a breath of wind stirring at a distance seems a sigh from the tree under which he grew old. Faustus disputes in one corner of the room with fiendish faces, and reasons of divine astrology. Bellafront soothes Matheo, Vittoria triumphs over her judges, and old Chapman repeats one of the hymns of Homer, in his own fine translation! I should have no objection to pass my life in this manner out of the world, not thinking of it, nor it of me; neither abused by my enemies, nor defended by my friends; careless of the future, but sometimes dreaming of the past, which might as well be forgotten! Mr. Wordsworth has expressed this sentiment well (perhaps I have borrowed it from him)—

"Books, dreams, are both a world; and books, we know,
Are a substantial world, both pure and good,
Round which, with tendrils strong as flesh and blood,
Our pastime and our happiness may grow.
* * * * * *
Two let me mention dearer than the rest,
The gentle lady wedded to the Moor,
And heavenly Una with her milk-white lamb.

Blessings be with them and eternal praise,
The poets, who on earth have made us heirs
Of truth and pure delight in deathless lays.
Oh, might my name be number'd among theirs,
Then gladly would I end my mortal days!"

I have no sort of pretension to join in the concluding wish of the last stanza; but I trust the writer feels that this aspiration of his early and highest ambition is already not unfulfilled!

LECTURE IV.

On Beaumont and Fletcher, Ben Jonson, Ford, and Massinger.

Beaumont and Fletcher, with all their prodigious merits, appear to me the first writers who in some measure departed from the genuine tragic style of the age of Shakspeare. They thought less of their subject, and more of themselves, than some others. They had a great and unquestioned command over the stores both of fancy and passion; but they availed themselves too often of common-place extravagances and theatrical trick. Men at first produce effect by studying nature, and afterwards they look at nature only to produce effect. It is the same in the history of other arts, and of other periods of literature. With respect to most of the writers of this age, their subject was their master. Shakspeare was alone, as I have said before, master of his subject; but Beaumont and Fletcher were the first who made a play-thing of it, or a convenient vehicle for the display of their own powers. The example of preceding or contemporary writers had given them facility; the frequency of dramatic exhibition had advanced the popular taste; and this facility of production, and the necessity for appealing to popular applause, tended to vitiate their own taste, and to make them willing to pamper that of the public for novelty and extraordinary effect. There wants something of the sincerity and modesty of the older writers. They do not wait nature's time, or work out her materials patiently and faithfully, but try to anticipate her, and so far defeat themselves. They would have a catastrophe in every scene; so that you have none at last: they would raise admiration to its height in every line; so that the impression of the whole is comparatively loose and desultory. They pitch the characters at first in too high a key, and exhaust themselves by the eagerness and impatience of their efforts. We find all the prodigality of youth, the confidence inspired by success, an enthusiasm bordering on extravagance, richness running riot, beauty dissolving in its own sweetness. They are like heirs just come to their estates, like lovers in the honey-moon. In the economy of nature's gifts they "misuse the bounteous Pan, and thank the Gods amiss." Their productions shoot up in haste, but bear the marks of precocity and premature decay. Or they are two goodly trees, the stateliest of the forest, crowned with blossoms, and with the verdure springing at their feet; but they do not strike their roots far enough into the ground, and the fruit can hardly ripen for the flowers!

It cannot be denied that they are lyrical and descriptive poets of the highest order; every page of their writings is a *florilegium:* they are dramatic poets of the second class, in point of knowledge, variety, vivacity, and effect; there is hardly a passion, character, or situation, which they have not touched in their devious range, and whatever they touched they adorned with some new grace or striking feature: they are masters of style and versification in almost every variety of melting modulation or sounding pomp, of which they are capable: in comic wit and spirit, they are scarcely surpassed by any writers of any age. There they are in their element, "like eagles newly baited;" but I speak rather of their serious poetry; and this, I apprehend, with all its richness, sweetness, loftiness, and grace, wants something—stimulates more than it gratifies, and leaves the mind in a certain sense exhausted and unsatisfied. Their fault is a too ostentatious and indiscriminate display of power. Everything seems in a state of fermentation and effervescence, and not to have settled and found its centre in their minds. The ornaments, through neglect or abundance, do not always appear sufficiently appropriate: there is evidently a rich wardrobe of words and images, to set off any sentiments that occur, but not equal felicity in the choice of the sentiments to be expressed; the characters in general do not take a substantial form, or excite a growing interest, or leave a permanent impression; the passion does not accumulate by the force of time, of circumstances, and habit, but wastes itself in the first ebullitions of surprise and novelty.

Besides these more critical objections, there is a too frequent mixture of voluptuous softness or effeminacy of character with horror in the subjects, a conscious weakness (I can hardly think it wantonness) of moral constitution struggling with wilful and violent situations, like the tender wings of the moth, attracted to the flame that dazzles and consumes it. In the hey-day of their youthful ardour, and the intoxication of their animal spirits, they take a perverse delight in tearing up some rooted sentiment, to make a mawkish lamentation over it; and fondly and gratuitously cast the seeds of crimes into forbidden grounds, to see how they will shoot up and vegetate into luxuriance, to catch the eye of fancy. They are not safe teachers of morality: they tamper with it, like an experiment tried *in corpore vili;* and seem to regard the decomposition of the common affections, and the dissolution of the strict bonds of society, as an agreeable study and a careless pastime. The tone of Shakspeare's writings is manly and bracing; theirs is at once insipid and meretricious, in the comparison. Shakspeare never disturbs the grounds of moral principle; but leaves his characters (after doing them heaped justice on all sides) to be judged of by our common sense and natural feeling. Beaumont and Fletcher constantly bring in equivocal sentiments and characters, as if to set them up to be debated by sophistical casuistry, or varnished over with the colours of poetical ingenuity. Or Shakspeare may be said to "cast the diseases of the mind, only to restore it to a sound and pristine health:" the dramatic paradoxes of Beaumont and Fletcher are, to all appearance, tinctured with an infusion of personal vanity and laxity of principle. I do not say that this was the character of the men; but it strikes me as the character of their minds. The two things are very distinct. The greatest purits (hypocrisy apart) are often free livers; and some of the most unguarded professors of a gėneral licence of behaviour, have been the last persons to take the benefit of their own doctrine, from which they reap nothing, but the obloquy, and the pleasure of startling their "wonder-wounded" hearers. There is a division of labour, even in vice. Some persons addict themselves to the speculation only, others to the practice. The peccant humours of the body or the mind break out in different ways. One man *sows his wild oats* in his neighbour's field: another on Mount Parnassus; from whence, borne on the breath of fame, they may hope to spread and fructify to distant times and regions. Of the latter class were our poets, who, I believe, led unexceptionable lives, and only indulged their imaginations in occasional unwarrantable liberties with the Muses. What makes them more inexcusable, and confirms this charge against them, is, that they are always abusing "wanton poets," as if willing to shift suspicion from themselves.

Beaumont and Fletcher were the first, also, who laid the foundation of the artificial diction and tinselled pomp of the next generation of poets, by aiming at a profusion of ambitious ornaments, and by translating the commonest circumstances into the language of metaphor and passion. It is this misplaced and inordinate craving after striking effect and continual excitement that had at one time rendered our poetry the most vapid of all things, by not leaving the moulds of poetic diction to be filled up by the overflowings of nature and passion, but by swelling out ordinary and unmeaning topics to certain preconceived and indispensable standards of poetical elevation and grandeur.—I shall endeavour to confirm this praise, mixed with unwilling blame, by remarking on a few of their principal tragedies. If I have done them injustice, the resplendent passages I have to quote will set everything to rights.

The 'Maid's Tragedy' is one of the poorest. The nature of the distress is of the most disagreeable and repulsive kind; and not the less so because it is entirely improbable and uncalled for. There is no sort of reason, or no sufficient reason to the reader's mind, why the king should marry off his mistress to one of his courtiers, why he should pitch upon the worthiest for this purpose, why he should, by such a choice, break off Amintor's match with the sister of another principal support of his throne (whose death is the consequence), why he should insist on the inviolable fidelity of his former mistress to him after she is married, and why her husband should thus inevitably be made acquainted with his dishonour, and roused to madness and revenge, except the mere love of mischief and gratuitous delight in torturing the feelings of others, and tempting one's own fate. The character of Evadne, however, her naked, unblushing impudence, the mixture of folly with vice, her utter insensibility to any motive but her own pride and inclination, her heroic superiority to any signs of shame or scruples of conscience from a recollection of what is due to herself or others, are well described, and the lady is true to herself in her repentance, which is owing to nothing but the accidental impulse and whim of the moment. The deliberate, voluntary disregard of all moral ties and all pretence to virtue, in the structure of the fable, is nearly unaccountable. Amintor (who is meant to be the hero of the piece) is a feeble, irresolute character: his slavish, recanting loyalty to his prince, who has betrayed and dishonoured him, is of a piece with the tyranny and insolence of which he is made the sport; and even his tardy revenge is snatched from his hands, and he kills his former betrothed and beloved mistress, instead of executing vengeance on the man who has destroyed his peace of mind and unsettled her intellects. The king, however, meets his fate from the penitent fury of Evadne; and on this account, the 'Maid's Tragedy' was forbidden to be acted in the reign of Charles II., as countenancing the doctrine of regicide. Aspatia is a beautiful sketch of resigned and heart-broken melancholy, and Calianax, a blunt, satirical courtier, is a character of much humour and novelty. There are striking passages here and there, but fewer than in almost any of their plays. Amintor's speech to Evadne, when she makes confession of her unlooked-for remorse, is, I think, the finest:

> ——— "Do not mock me:
> Though I am tame, and bred up with my wrongs,
> Which are my foster-brothers, I may leap,
> Like a hand-wolf, into my natural wildness,
> And do an outrage. Prithee, do not mock me!"

'King and No King,' which is on a strangely chosen subject as strangely treated, is very superior in power and effect. There is an unexpected reservation in the plot, which, in some measure, relieves the painfulness of the impression. Arbaces is painted in gorgeous, but not alluring colours. His vain-glorious pretensions and impatience of contradiction are admirably displayed, and are so managed as to produce an involuntary comic effect to temper the lofty tone of tragedy, particularly in the scenes in which he affects to treat his vanquished enemy with such condescending kindness; and perhaps this display of upstart pride was meant by the authors as an oblique satire on his low origin, which is afterwards discovered. His pride of self will and fierce impetuosity are the same in war and in love. The haughty voluptuousness and pampered effeminacy of his character admit neither respect for his misfortunes, nor pity for his errors. His ambition is a fever in the blood; and his love is a sudden transport of ungovernable caprice that brooks no restraint, and is intoxicated with the lust of power, even in the lap of pleasure, and the sanctuary of the affections. The passion of Panthea is, as it were, a reflection from, and lighted at the shrine of her lover's flagrant vanity. In the elevation of his rank, and in the consciousness of his personal accomplishments, he seems firmly persuaded (and by sympathy to persuade others) that there is nothing in the world which can be an object of liking or admiration but himself. The first birth and declaration of this perverted sentiment to himself, when he meets with Panthea after his return from conquest, fostered by his presumptuous infatuation and the heat of his inflammable passions, and the fierce and lordly tone in which he repels the suggestion of the natural obstacles to his sudden phrenzy, are in Beaumont and Fletcher's most daring manner; but the rest is not equal. What may be called the love scenes are equally gross and common-place; and instead of any thing like delicacy or a struggle of different feelings, have all the indecency and familiarity of a brothel. Bessus, a comic character in this play, is a swaggering coward, something between Parolles and Falstaff.

The 'False One' is an indirect imitation of Antony and Cleopatra. We have Septimius for Œnobarbus, and Cæsar for Antony. Cleopatra herself is represented in her girlish state, but she is made divine in

> "Youth that opens like perpetual spring,"

and promises the rich harvest of love and pleasure that succeeds it. Her first presenting herself before Cæsar, when she is brought in by Sceva, and the impression she makes upon him, like a vision dropped from the clouds, or

> "Like some celestial sweetness, the treasure of soft love,"

are exquisitely conceived. Photinus is an accomplished villain, well-read in crooked policy and quirks of state; and the description of Pompey has a solemnity and grandeur worthy of his unfortunate end. Septimius says, bringing in his lifeless head,

"'Tis here, 'tis done! Behold, you fearful viewers,
Shake, and behold the model of the world here,
The pride and strength! Look, look again, 'tis finished!
That that whole armies, nay, whole nations,
Many and mighty kings, have been struck blind at,
And fled before, wing'd with their fears and terrors,
That steel War waited on, and fortune courted,
That high-plum'd Honour built up for her own;
Behold that mightiness. behold that fierceness,
Behold that child of war, with all his glories,
By this poor hand made breathless!"

And again Cæsar says of him, who was his mortal enemy (it was not held in the fashion in those days, nor will it be held so in time to come, to lampoon those whom you have vanquished)—

——— "Oh, thou conqueror,
Thou glory of the world once, now the pity,
Thou awe of nations, wherefore didst thou fall thus?
What poor fate followed thee, and plucked thee on
To trust thy sacred life to an Egyptian?
The life and light of Rome to a blind stranger,
That honourable war ne'er taught a nobleness,
Nor worthy circumstance show'd what a man was?
That never heard thy name sung but in banquets,
And loose lascivious pleasures?—to a boy,
That had no faith to comprehend thy greatness,
No study of thy life to know thy goodness?
Egyptians, do you think your highest pyramids,
Built to outdure the sun, as you suppose,
Where your unworthy kings lie raked in ashes,
Are monuments fit for him! No, brood of Nilus,
Nothing can cover his high fame but heaven
No pyramids set off his memories,
But the eternal substance of his greatness,
To which I leave him."

It is something worth living for, to write or even read such poetry as this is, or to know that it has been written, or that there have been subjects on which to write it!—This, of all Beaumont and Fletcher's plays, comes the nearest in style and manner to Shakspeare, not excepting the first act of the 'Two Noble Kinsmen,' which has been sometimes attributed to him.

The 'Faithful Shepherdess,' by Fletcher alone, is "a perpetual feast of nectar'd sweets, where no crude surfeit reigns." The author has in it given a loose to his fancy, and his fancy was his most delightful and genial quality, where, to use his own words,

> "He takes most ease, and grows ambitious
> Thro' his own wanton fire and pride delicious."

The songs and lyrical descriptions throughout are luxuriant and delicate in a high degree. He came near to Spenser in a certain tender and voluptuous sense of natural beauty; he came near to Shakspeare in the playful and fantastic expression of it. The whole composition is an exquisite union of dramatic and pastoral poetry; where the local descriptions receive a tincture from the sentiments and purposes of the speaker, and each character, cradled in the lap of nature, paints "her virgin fancies wild" with romantic grace and classic elegance.

The place and its employments are thus described by Chloe to Thenot:

> ——— "Here be woods as green
> As any, air likewise as fresh and sweet
> As where smooth Zephyrus plays on the fleet
> Face of the curled stream, with flow'rs as many
> As the young spring gives, and as choice as any;
> Here be all new delights, cool streams and wells,
> Arbours o'ergrown with woodbine; caves, and dells
> Chuse where thou wilt, while I sit by and sing,
> Or gather rushes, to make many a ring
> For thy long fingers; tell thee tales of love,
> How the pale Phœbe, hunting in a grove,
> First saw the boy Endymion, from whose eyes
> She took eternal fire that never dies;
> How she conveyed him softly in a sleep,
> His temples bound with poppy, to the steep
> Head of old Latmos, where she stoops each night,
> Gilding the mountain with her brother's light,
> To kiss her sweetest."

There are few things that can surpass in truth and beauty of allegorical description the invocation of Amaryllis to the God of Shepherds, Pan, to save her from the violence of the Sullen Shepherd, for Syrinx's sake:

—— "For her dear sake,
That loves the rivers' brinks, and still doth shake
In cold remembrance of thy quick pursuit!"

Or again, the friendly Satyr promises Clorin—

"Brightest, if there be remaining
Any service, without feigning
I will do it; were I set
To catch the nimble wind, or get
Shadows gliding on the green."

It would be a task no less difficult than this, to follow the flight of the poet's Muse, or catch her fleeting graces, fluttering her golden wings, and singing in notes angelical of youth, of love, and joy!

There is only one affected and ridiculous character in this drama, that of Thenot in love with Clorin. He is attached to her for her inviolable fidelity to her buried husband, and wishes her not to grant his suit, lest it should put an end to his passion. Thus he pleads to her against himself:—

—— "If you yield, I die
To all affection; 'tis that loyalty
You tie unto this grave I so admire;
And yet there's something else I would desire,
If you would hear me, but withal deny.
Oh Pan, what an uncertain destiny
Hangs over all my hopes! I will retire;
For if I longer stay, this double fire
Will lick my life up."

This is paltry quibbling. It is spurious logic, not genuine feeling. A pedant may hang his affections on the point of a dilemma in this manner; but nature does not sophisticate; or when she does, it is to gain her ends, not to defeat them.

The Sullen Shepherd turns out too dark a character in the

end, and gives a shock to the gentle and pleasing sentiments inspired throughout.

The resemblance of Comus to this poem is not so great as has been sometimes contended, nor are the particular allusions important or frequent. Whatever Milton copied, he made his own. In reading the Faithful Shepherdess, we find ourselves breathing the moonlight air under the cope of heaven, and wander by forest side or fountain, among fresh dews and flowers, following our vagrant fancies, or smit with the love of nature's works. In reading Milton's Comus, and most of his other works, we seem to be entering a lofty dome raised over our heads and ascending to the skies, and as if Nature and everything in it were but a temple and an image consecrated by the poet's art to the worship of virtue and true religion. The speech of Clorin, after she has been alarmed by the Satyr, is the only one of which Milton has made a free use:

> " And all my fears go with thee.
> What greatness or what private hidden power
> Is there in me to draw submission
> From this rude man and beast? Sure I am mortal:
> The daughter of a shepherd; he was mortal
> And she that bore me mortal; prick my hand,
> And it will bleed, a fever shakes me, and
> The self-same wind that makes the young lamb shrink,
> Makes me a-cold: my fear says, I am mortal.
> Yet I have heard (my mother told it me,
> And now I do believe it,) if I keep
> My virgin flow'r uncropt, pure, chaste, and fair.
> No goblin, wood-god, fairy, elf, or fiend,
> Satyr, or other power that haunts the groves,
> Shall hurt my body, or by vain illusion
> Draw me to wander after idle fires;
> Or voices calling me in dead of night
> To make me follow, and so tole me on
> Thro' mire and standing pools to find my ruin;
> Else, why should this rough thing, who never knew
> Manners, nor smooth humanity, whose heats
> Are rougher than himself, and more misshapen.
> Thus mildly kneel to me? Sure there's a pow'r
> In that great name of Virgin, that binds fast
> All rude uncivil bloods, all appetites
> That break their confines: then strong Chastity!

> Be thou my strongest guard, for here I'll dwell
> In opposition against fate and hell!"

Ben Jonson's 'Sad Shepherd' comes nearer it in style and spirit, but still with essential differences, like the two men, and without any appearance of obligation. Ben's is more homely and grotesque. Fletcher's is more visionary and fantastical. I hardly know which to prefer. If Fletcher has the advantage in general power and sentiment, Jonson is superior in *naïveté* and truth of local colouring.

The 'Two Noble Kinsmen' is another monument of Fletcher's genius; and it is said also of Shakspeare's. The style of the first act has certainly more weight, more abruptness, and more involution, than the general style of Fletcher, with fewer softenings and fillings-up to sheathe the rough projecting points and piece the disjointed fragments together. For example, the compliment of Theseus to one of the Queens, that Hercules

> "Tumbled him down upon his Nemean hide
> And swore his sinews thaw'd"

at sight of her beauty, is in a bolder and more masculine vein than Fletcher usually aimed at. Again, the supplicating address of the distressed Queen to Hippolita,

> —— "Lend us a knee:
> But touch the ground for us no longer time
> Than a dove's motion, when the head's pluck'd off"—

is certainly in the manner of Shakspeare, with his subtlety and strength of illustration. But, on the other hand, in what immediately follows, relating to their husbands left dead in the field of battle,

> "Tell him if he i' th' blood-siz'd field lay swoln,
> Showing the sun his teeth, grinning at the moon,
> What you would do,"—

I think we perceive the extravagance of Beaumont and Fletcher, not contented with truth or strength of description, but hurried away by the love of violent excitement into an image of disgust and horror, not called for, and not at all proper in the mouth into which it is put. There is a studied exaggeration of the sentiment, and an evident imitation of the parenthetical interruptions and breaks in the line, corresponding to what we sometimes meet in Shakspeare, as in the speeches of Leontes in 'The Winter's Tale;' but the sentiment is overdone, and the style merely mechanical. Thus Hippolita declares, on her lord's going to the wars,

> "We have been soldiers, and we cannot weep,
> When our friends don their helms, or put to sea,
> Or tell of babes broach'd on the lance, or women
> That have seethed their infants in (and after eat them)
> The brine they wept at killing 'em; then if
> You stay to see of us such spinsters, we
> Should hold you here for ever."

One might apply to this sort of poetry what Marvel says of some sort of passions, that it is

> "Tearing our pleasures with rough strife
> Through the iron gates of life."

It is not in the true spirit of Shakspeare, who was "born only heir to all humanity," whose horrors were not gratuitous, and who did not harrow up the feelings for the sake of making mere *bravura* speeches. There are also in this first act several repetitions of Shakspeare's phraseology; a thing that seldom or never occurs in his own works. For instance:

> —— "Past slightly
> *His careless execution*"—
>
> "*The very lees* of such, millions of rates
> Exceed *the wine* of others"—
>
> "Let *the event*,
> That *never-erring arbitrator*, tell us"—
>
> "Like *old importment's bastard*."

There are also words that are never used by Shakspeare in a similar sense:—

> ——"All our surgeons
> *Convent* in their behoof"—
>
> "We *convent* nought else but woes."

in short, it appears to me that the first part of this play was written in imitation of Shakspeare's manner, but I see no reason to suppose that it was his, but the common tradition, which is by no means well established. The subsequent acts are confessedly Fletcher's, and the imitations of Shakspeare which occur there (not of Shakspeare's manner as differing from his, but as it was congenial to his own spirit and feeling of nature) are glorious in themselves, and exalt our idea of the great original which could give birth to such magnificent conceptions in another. The conversation of Palamon and Arcite in prison is of this description—the outline is evidently taken from that of Guiderius, Arviragus, and Bellarius, in 'Cymbelline,' but filled up with a rich profusion of graces that make it his own again.

> "*Pal.* How do you, noble cousin?
> *Arc.* How do you, Sir?
> *Pal.* Why, strong enough to laugh at misery,
> And bear the chance of war yet. We are prisoners,
> I fear for ever, cousin.
> *Arc.* I believe it;
> And to that destiny have patiently
> Laid up my hour to come.
> *Pal.* Oh, cousin Arcite,
> Where is Thebes now? Where is our noble country?
> Where are our friends and kindreds? Never more
> Must we behold those comforts; never see
> The hardy youths strive for the games of honour,
> Hung with the painted favours of their ladies,
> Like tall ships under sail: then start amongst 'em,
> And, as an east wind, leave 'em all behind us
> Like lazy clouds, whilst Palamon and Arcite
> Even in the wagging of a wanton leg,
> Outstript the people's praises, won the garland,
> Ere they have time to wish 'em ours. Oh, never
> Shall we two exercise, like twins of honour,
> Our arms again, and feel our fiery horses,
> Like proud seas, under us! Our good swords now
> (Better the red-eyed god of war ne'er wore)
> Ravish'd our sides, like age, must run to rust,
> And deck the temples of those gods that hate us:
> These hands shall never draw 'em out like lightning,
> To blast whole armies more.
> *Arc.* No, Palamon,
> Those hopes are prisoners with us: here we are,
> And here the graces of our youth must wither.

Like a too timely spring: here age must find us,
And, which is heaviest, Palamon, unmarried;
The sweet embraces of a loving wife,
Loaden with kisses, arm'd with thousand Cupids,
Shall never clasp our necks! No issue know us,
No figures of ourselves shall we e'er see,
To glad our age, and like young eaglets teach 'em
Boldly to gaze against bright arms, and say,
Remember what your fathers were, and conquer!
The fair-eyed maids shall weep our banishments,
And in their songs curse ever-blinded fortune,
Till she for shame see what a wrong she has done
To youth and nature. This is all our world:
We shall know nothing here, but one another;
Hear nothing but the clock that tells our woes;
The vine shall grow, but we shall never see it:
Summer shall come, and with her all delights,
But dead-cold winter must inhabit here still.

Pal. 'Tis too true, Arcite! To our Theban hounds,
That shook the aged forest with their echoes,
No more now must we hallow; no more shake
Our pointed javelins, while the angry swine
Flies, like a Parthian quiver, from our rages,
Struck with our well-steel'd darts! All valiant uses
(The food and nourishment of noble minds)
In us two here shall perish; we shall die
(Which is the curse of honour) lazily,
Children of grief and ignorance.

Arc. Yet, cousin,
Even from the bottom of these miseries,
From all that fortune can inflict upon us,
I see two comforts rising, two mere blessings,
If the gods please to hold here; a brave patience,
And the enjoying of our griefs together.
Whilst Palamon is with me, let me perish
If I think this our prison!

Pal. Certainly,
'Tis a main goodness, cousin, that our fortunes
Were twinn'd together; 'tis most true, two souls
Put in two noble bodies, let 'em suffer
The gall of hazard, so they grow together,
Will never sink; they must not, say they could;
A willing man dies sleeping, and all's done.

Arc. Shall we make worthy uses of this place
That all men hate so much?

Pal. How, gentle cousin?

Arc. Let's think this prison a holy sanctuary

To keep us from corruption of worse men
We 're young, and yet desire the ways of honour;
That, liberty and common conversation,
The poison of pure spirits, might, like women,
Woo us to wander from. What worthy blessing
Can be, but our imaginations
May make it ours? And here, being thus together
We are an endless mine to one another,
We 're father, friends, acquaintance;
We are, in one another, families;
I am your heir, and you are mine; this place
Is our inheritance; no hard oppressor
Dare take this from us; here, with a little patience,
We shall live long, and loving; no surfeits seek us:
The hand of war hurts none here, nor the seas
Swallow their youth; were we at liberty,
A wife might part us lawfully, or business;
Quarrels consume us; envy of ill men
Crave our acquaintance; I might sicken, cousin
Where you should never know it, and so perish
Without your noble hand to close mine eyes,
Or prayers to the gods: a thousand chances,
Were we from hence, would sever us.
Pal. You have made me
(I thank you, cousin Arcite) almost wanton
With my captivity; what a misery
It is to live abroad, and everywhere!
'Tis like a beast, methinks! I find the court here,
I'm sure a more content; and all those pleasures,
That woo the wills of men to vanity,
I see through now; and am sufficient
To tell the world 'tis but a gaudy shadow
That old Time, as he passes by, takes with him.
What had we been, old in the court of Creon,
Where sin is justice, lust and ignorance
The virtues of the great ones? Cousin Arcite,
Had not the loving gods found this place for us,
We had died as they now, ill old men unwept,
And had their epitaphs,—the people's curses!
Shall I say more?
Arc. I would hear you still.
Pal. You shall.
Is there the record of any two that lov'd
Better than we do, Arcite?
Arc. Sure there cannot.
Pal. I do not think it possible our friendship
Should ever leave us.
Arc. Till our deaths it cannot."

Thus they "sing their bondage freely;" but just then enters Æmilia, who parts all this friendship between them, and turns them to deadliest foes.

The jailor's daughter, who falls in love with Palamon, and goes mad, is a wretched interpolation in the story, and a fantastic copy of Ophelia. But they readily availed themselves of all the dramatic common-places to be found in Shakspeare,—love, madness, processions, sports, imprisonment, &c., and copied him too often in earnest, to have a right to parody him, as they sometimes did, in jest. The story of 'The Two Noble Kinsmen' is taken from Chaucer's 'Palamon and Arcite;' but the latter part, which in Chaucer is full of dramatic power and interest, degenerates in the play into a mere narrative of the principal events, and possesses little value or effect. It is not improbable that Beaumont and Fletcher's having dramatized this story, put Dryden upon modernizing it.

I cannot go through all Beaumont and Fletcher's dramas (52 in number), but I have mentioned some of the principal, and the excellences and defects of the rest may be judged of from these. 'The Bloody Brother', 'A Wife for a Month,' 'Bonduca,' 'Thierry and Theodoret,' are among the best of their tragedies: among the comedies, 'The Night Walker,' 'The Little French Lawyer,' and 'Monsieur Thomas,' come perhaps next to 'The Chances,' 'The Wild Goose Chase,' and 'Rule a Wife and Have a Wife.'—'Philaster, or, Love Lies a-Bleeding,' is one of the most admirable productions of these authors (the last I shall mention); and the patience of Euphrasia, disguised as Bellario, the tenderness of Arethusa, and the jealousy of Philaster, are beyond all praise. The passages of extreme romantic beauty and high-wrought passion that I might quote are out of number. One only must suffice, the account of the commencement of Euphrasia's love to Philaster:

——" Sitting in my window,
Printing my thought in lawn, I saw a God
I thought (but it was you) enter our gates;
My blood flew out, and back again as fast
As I had puffed it forth and suck'd it in
Like breath; then was I called away in haste
To entertain you. Never was a man

Heav'd from a sheep-cote to a sceptre, rais'd
So high in thoughts as I: you left a kiss
Upon these lips then, which I mean to keep
From you for ever. I did hear you talk
Far above singing!"

And so it is our poets themselves write, "far above singing."* I am loth to part with them, and wander down, as we now must,

"Into a lower world, to theirs obscure
And wild—to breathe in other air
Less pure, accustomed to immortal fruits."

Ben Jonson's serious productions are, in my opinion, superior to his comic ones. What he does, is the result of strong sense and painful industry; but sense and industry agree better with the grave and severe, than with the light and gay productions of the muse. "His plays were works," as some one said of them, "while others' works were plays." The observation had less of compliment than of truth in it. He may be said to mine his way into a subject, like a mole, and throws up a prodigious quantity of matter on the surface, so that the richer the soil in which he labours, the less dross and rubbish we have. His fault is, that he sets himself too much to his subject, and cannot let go his hold of an idea, after the insisting on it becomes tiresome or painful to others. But his tenaciousness of what is grand and lofty, is more praiseworthy than his delight in what is low and disagreeable. His pedantry accords better with didactic pomp than with illiterate and vulgar gabble; his learning, engrafted on romantic tradition or classical history, looks like genius.

"Miraturque novas frondes et non sua poma."

He was equal, by an effort, to the highest things, and took the same, and even more successful pains to grovel to the lowest. He raised himself up or let himself down to the level of his sub-

* Euphrasia as the Page, just before speaking of her life, which Philaster threatens to take from her, says,

——"'Tis not a life;
'Tis but a piece of childhood thrown away."

What exquisite beauty and delicacy!

ject, by ponderous machinery. By dint of application, and a certain strength of nerve, he could do justice to Tacitus and Sallust no less than to mine host of the New Inn. His tragedy of 'The Fall of Sejanus,' in particular, is an admirable piece of ancient mosaic. The principal character gives one the idea of a lofty column of solid granite, nodding to its base from its pernicious height, and dashed in pieces by a breath of air, a word of its creator—feared, not pitied, scorned, unwept, and forgotten. The depth of knowledge and gravity of expression sustain one another throughout: the poet has worked out the historian's outline, so that the vices and passions, the ambition and servility of public men, in the heated and poisoned atmosphere of a luxurious and despotic court, were never described in fuller or more glowing colours. I am half afraid to give any extracts, les. they should be tortured into an application to other times and characters than those referred to by the poet, Some of the sounds, indeed, may bear (for what I know) an awkward construction: some of the objects may look double to squint-eyed suspicion. But that is not my fault. It only proves that the characters of prophet and poet are implied in each other; that he who describes human nature well once, describes it for good and all, as it was, is, and, I begin to fear, will ever be. Truth always was, and must always remain, a libel to the tyrant and the slave. Thus Satrius Secundus and Pinnarius Natta, two public informers in those days, are described as

> "Two of Sejanus' blood-hounds, whom he breeds
> With human flesh, to bay at citizens."

But Rufus, another of the same well-bred gang, debating the point of his own character with two senators whom he has entrapped, boldly asserts, in a more courtly strain,

> —— "To be a spy on traitors
> Is honourable vigilance."

This sentiment of the respectability of the employment of a government spy, which had slept in Tacitus for near two thousand years, has not been without its modern patrons. The effects of such "honourable vigilance" are very finely exposed in the following high-spirited dialogue between Lepidus and Arruntius, two noble Romans, who loved their country, but were not unfashionable enough to confound their country with its oppressors, and the extinguishers of its liberty.

"*Arr.* What are thy arts (good patriot, teach them me)
That have preserv'd thy hairs to this white dye,
And kept so reverend and so dear a head
Safe on his comely shoulders?
Lep. Arts, Arruntius!
None but the plain and passive fortitude
To suffer and be silent; never stretch
These arms against the torrent; live at home
With my own thoughts and innocence about me,
Not tempting the wolves' jaws: these are my arts.
Arr. I would begin to study 'em, if I thought
They would secure me. May I pray to Jove
In secret, and be safe? ay, or aloud?
With open wishes? so I do not mention
Tiberius or Sejanus! Yes, I must,
If I speak out. 'Tis hard, that. May I think,
And not be rack'd? What danger is't to dream?
Talk in one's sleep, or cough? Who knows the law?
May I shake my head without a comment? Say
It rains, or it holds up, and not be thrown
Upon the Gemonies? These now are things
Whereon men's fortunes, yea, their fate depends;
Nothing hath privilege 'gainst the violent ear.
No place, no day, no hour (we see) is free
(Not our religious and most sacred times)
From some one kind of cruelty; all matter,
Nay, all occasion pleaseth. Madman's rage,
The idleness of drunkards, women's nothing,
Jesters' simplicity, all, all is good
That can be catch'd at."

'Tis a pretty picture; and the duplicates of it, though multiplied without end, are seldom out of request.

The following portrait of a prince besieged by flatterers (taken from 'Tiberius') has unrivalled force and beauty, with historic truth

—— "If this man
Had but a mind allied unto his words,

How blest a fate were it to us, and Rome?
Men are deceived, who think there can be thrall
Under a virtuous prince. Wish'd liberty
Ne'er lovelier looks than under such a crown.
But when his grace is merely but lip-good,
And that, no longer than he airs himself
Abroad in public, there to seem to shun
The strokes and stripes of flatterers, which within
Are lechery unto him, and so feed
His brutish sense with their afflicting sound,
As (dead to virtue) he permits himself
Be carried like a pitcher by the ears
To every act of vice; this is a case
Deserves our fear, and doth presage the nigh
And close approach of bloody tyranny.
Flattery is midwife unto princes' rage:
And nothing sooner doth help forth a tyrant
Than that, and whisperers' grace, that have the time,
The place, the power, to make all men offenders!"

The only part of this play in which Ben Jonson has completely forgotten himself (or rather seems not to have done so) is in the conversations between Livia and Eudemus, about a wash for her face, here called a *fucus*, to appear before Sejanus. 'Catiline's Conspiracy' does not furnish by any means an equal number of striking passages, and is spun out to an excessive length with Cicero's artificial and affected orations against Catiline, and in praise of himself. His apologies for his own eloquence, and declarations that in all his art he uses no art at all, put one in mind of Polonius's circuitous way of coming to the point. Both these tragedies, it might be observed, are constructed on the exact principles of a French historical picture, where every head and figure is borrowed from the antique; but, somehow, the precious materials of old Roman history and character are better preserved in Jonson's page than on David's canvas.

Two of the most poetical passages in Ben Jonson are the description of Echo in 'Cynthia's Revels,' and the fine comparison of the mind to a temple, in the 'New Inn;' a play which, on the whole, however, I can read with no patience.

I must hasten to conclude this Lecture with some account of Massinger and Ford, who wrote in the time of Charles I. I am sorry I cannot do it *con amore*. The writers of whom I have chiefly had to speak were true poets, impassioned, fanciful, "musical as is Apollo's lute;" but Massinger is harsh and crabbed, Ford finical and fastidious. I find little in the works of these two dramatists, but a display of great strength or subtlety of understanding, inveteracy of purpose, and perversity of will. This is not exactly what we look for in poetry, which, according to the most approved recipes, should combine pleasure with profit, and not owe all its fascination over the mind to its power of shocking or perplexing us. The muses should attract by grace or dignity of mien. Massinger makes an impression by hardness and repulsiveness of manner. In the intellectual processes which he delights to describe, "reason panders will:" he fixes arbitrarily on some object which there is no motive to pursue, or every motive combined against it, and then, by screwing up his heroes or heroines to the deliberate and blind accomplishment of this, thinks to arrive at "the true pathos and sublime of human life." That is not the way. He seldom touches the heart, or kindles the fancy. It is in vain to hope to excite much sympathy with convulsive efforts of the will, or intricate contrivances of the understanding, to obtain that which is better left alone, and where the interest arises principally from the conflict between the absurdity of the passion and the obstinacy with which it is persisted in. For the most part, his villains are a sort of *lusus naturæ;* his impassioned characters are like drunkards or madmen. Their conduct is extreme and outrageous, their motives unaccountable and weak; their misfortunes are without necessity, and their crimes without temptation, to ordinary apprehensions. I do not say that this is invariably the case in all Massinger's scenes, but I think it will be found that a principle of playing at cross-purposes is the ruling passion throughout most of them. This is the case in the tragedy of 'The Unnatural Combat,' in 'The Picture,' 'The Duke of Milan,' 'A New Way to Pay Old Debts,' and even in 'The Bondman,' and 'The Virgin Martyr,' &c. In 'The Picture,' Matthias nearly loses his wife's affections, by resorting to the far-fetched and unnecessary device of procuring a magical portrait to read the slightest variation in her thoughts. In the same play, Honoria risks her reputation and her life to gain a clandestine interview with Matthias, merely to shake his fidelity to his wife, and when she has gained her object, tells the king her husband in pure caprice and fickleness of purpose. 'The Virgin Martyr' is nothing but a tissue of instantaneous conversions to and from Paganism and Christianity. The only scenes of any real beauty and tenderness in this play, are those between Dorothea and Angelo, her supposed friendless beggar-boy, but her guardian angel in disguise, which are understood to be by Decker. The interest of 'The Bondman' turns upon two different acts of penance and self-denial, in the persons of the hero and heroine, Pisander and Cleora. In the Duke of Milan (the most poetical of Massinger's productions), Sforza's resolution to destroy his wife, rather than bear the thought of her surviving him, is as much out of the verge of nature and probability, as it is unexpected and revolting, from the want of any circumstances of palliation leading to it. It stands out alone, a pure piece of voluntary atrocity, which seems not the dictate of passion, but a start of phrensy ; as cold-blooded in the execution as it is extravagant in the conception.

Again, Francesco, in this play, is a person whose actions we are at a loss to explain till the conclusion of the piece, when the attempt to account for them from motives originally amiable and generous, only produces a double sense of incongruity, and instead of satisfying the mind, renders it totally incredulous. He endeavours to seduce the wife of his benefactor, he then (failing) attempts her death, slanders her foully, and wantonly causes her to be slain by the hand of her husband, and has him poisoned by a nefarious stratagem, and all this to appease a high sense of injured honour, that "felt a stain like a wound," and from the tender overflowing of fraternal affection, his sister having, it appears, been formerly betrothed to, and afterwards deserted by, the Duke of Milan. Sir Giles Overreach is the most successful and striking effort of Massinger's pen, and the best known to the reader, but it will hardly be thought to form an exception to the tenor of the above remarks.* The same spirit of caprice and

* The following criticism on this play has appeared in another publication, but may be not improperly inserted here:

"'A New Way to Pay Old Debts' is certainly a very admirable play, and highly characteristic of the genius of its author, which was hard and forcible,

sullenness survives in Rowe's 'Fair Penitent,' taken from this author's 'Fatal Dowry.'

Ford is not so great a favourite with me as with some others, from whose judgment I dissent with diffidence. It has been la-

and calculated rather to produce a strong impression than a pleasing one. There is considerable unity of design and a progressive interest in the fable, though the artifice by which the catastrophe is brought about (the double assumption of the character of favoured lovers by Wellborn and Lovell) is some what improbable, and out of date; and the moral is peculiarly striking, because its whole weight falls upon one who all along prides himself in setting every principle of justice and all fear of consequences at defiance.

"The character of Sir Giles Overreach (the most prominent feature of the play, whether in the perusal, or as it is acted) interests us less by exciting our sympathy than our indignation. We hate him very heartily, and yet not enough; for he has strong, robust points about him that repel the impertinence of censure, and he sometimes succeeds in making us stagger in our opinion of his conduct, by throwing off any idle doubts or scruples that might hang upon it in his own mind, 'like dew-drops from the lion's mane.' His steadiness of purpose scarcely stands in need of support from the common sanctions of morality, which he intrepidly breaks through, and he almost conquers our prejudices by the consistent and determined manner in which he braves them. Self-interest is his idol, and he makes no secret of his idolatry: he is only a more devoted and unblushing worshipper at this shrine than other men. Self-will is the only rule of his conduct, to which he makes every other feeling bend: or rather, from the nature of his constitution, he has no sickly, sentimental obstacles to interrupt him in his headstrong career. He is a char acter of obdurate self-will, without fanciful notions or natural affections; one who has no regard to the feelings of others, and who professes an equal disregard to their opinions. He minds nothing but his own ends, and takes the shortest and surest way to them. His understanding is clear-sighted, and his passions strong-nerved. Sir Giles is no flincher, and no hypocrite; and he gains almost as much by the hardihood with which he avows his impudent and sordid designs as others do by their caution in concealing them. He is the demon of selfishness personified; and carves out his way to the objects of his unprincipled avarice and ambition with an arm of steel, that strikes but does not feel the blow it inflicts. The character of calculating, systematic self-love, as the master-key to all his actions, is preserved with great truth of keeping and in the most trifling circumstances. Thus ruminating to himself, he says, "I'll walk, to get me an appetite: 'tis but a mile; and exercise will keep me from being pursy!'—Yet, to show the absurdity and impossibility of a man's being governed by any such pretended exclusive regard to his own interest, this very Sir Giles, who laughs at conscience, and scorns opinion, who ridicules every thing as fantastical but wealth, solid, substantial wealth, and boasts of himself as having been the founder of his own fortune, by his contempt for every other consideration, is ready to sacrifice the whole of his

mented that the play of his which has been most admired ('’Tis Pity She's a Whore') had not a less exceptionable subject. I do not know, but I suspect that the exceptionableness of the subject is that which constitutes the chief merit of the play. The re-

enormous possessions—to what?—to a title, a sound, to make his daughter 'right honourable,' the wife of a lord whose name he cannot repeat without loathing, and in the end he becomes the dupe of, and falls a victim to, that very opinion of the world which he despises!

"The character of Sir Giles Overreach has been found fault with as unnatural; and it may, perhaps, in the present refinement of our manners, have become in a great measure obsolete. But we doubt whether even still, in remote and insulated parts of the country, sufficient traces of the same character of wilful selfishness, mistaking the inveteracy of its purposes for their rectitude, and boldly appealing to power, as justifying the abuses of power, may not be found to warrant this an undoubted original—probably a facsimile of some individual of the poet's actual acquaintance. In less advanced periods of society than that in which we live, if we except rank, which can neither be an object of common pursuit nor immediate attainment, money is the only acknowledged passport to respect. It is not merely valuable as a security from want, but it is the only defence against the insolence of power. Avarice is sharpened by pride and necessity. There are then few of the arts, the amusements, and accomplishments, that soften and sweeten life, that raise or refine it: the only way in which any one can be of service to himself or another, is by his command over the gross commodities of life; and a man is worth just so much as he has. Where he who is not 'lord of acres' is looked upon as a slave and a beggar, the soul becomes wedded to the soil by which its worth is measured, and takes root in it in proportion to its own strength and stubbornness of character. The example of Wellborn may be cited in illustration of these remarks. The loss of his land makes all the difference between 'young master Wellborn' and 'rogue Wellborn;' and the treatment he meets with in this latter capacity is the best apology for the character of Sir Giles. Of the two, it is better to be the oppressor than the oppressed.

"Massinger, it is true, dealt generally in extreme characters, as well as in very repulsive ones. The passion is with him wound up to its height at first, and he never lets it down afterwards. It does not gradually arise out of previous circumstances, nor is it modified by other passions. This gives an appearance of abruptness, violence, and extravagance to all his plays. Shakspeare's characters act from mixed motives, and are made what they are by various circumstances. Massinger's characters act from single motives, and become what they are, and remain so, by a pure effort of the will, in spite of circumstances. This last author endeavoured to embody an abstract principle; labours hard to bring out the same individual trait in its most exaggerated state; and the force of his impassioned characters arises for the most part from the obstinacy with which they exclude every other feeling. Their vices look of a gigantic stature from their standing alone. Their actions seem extrava-

pulsiveness of the story is what gives it its critical interest; for it is a studiously prosaic statement of facts, and naked declaration of passions. It was not the least of Shakspeare's praise, that he never tampered with unfair subjects. His genius was above it; his taste kept aloof from it. I do not deny the power of simple painting and polished style in this tragedy in general, and of a great deal more in some few of the scenes, particularly in the quarrel between Annabella and her husband, which is wrought up to a pitch of demoniac scorn and phrensy with consummate art and knowledge; but I do not find much other power in the author (generally speaking) than that of playing with edged tools, and knowing the use of poisoned weapons. And what confirms me in this opinion is the comparative inefficiency of his other plays. Except the last scene of 'The Broken Heart' (which I think extravagant—others may think it sublime, and be right), they are merely exercises of style and effusions of wire-drawn sentiment. Where they have not the sting of illicit passion, they are quite pointless, and seem painted on gauze, or spun of cobwebs. The affected brevity and division of some of the lines into hemisticks, &c. so as to make in one case a

gant from their having always the same fixed aim—the same incorrigible purpose. The fault of Sir Giles Overreach, in this respect, is less in the excess to which he pushes a favourite propensity, than in the circumstance of its being unmixed with any other virtue or vice.

"We may find the same simplicity of dramatic conception in the comic as in the tragic characters of the author. Justice Greedy has but one idea or subject in his head throughout. He is always eating, or talking of eating. His belly is always in his mouth, and we know nothing of him but his appetite; he is as sharpset as travellers from off a journey. His land of promise touches on the borders of the wilderness: his thoughts are constantly in apprehension of feasting or famishing. A fat turkey floats before his imagination in royal state, and his hunger sees visions of chines of beef, venison pasties, and Norfolk dumplings, as if it were seized with a calenture. He is a very amusing personage; and in what relates to eating and drinking, as peremptory as Sir Giles himself.—Marrall is another instance of confined comic humour, whose ideas never wander beyond the ambition of being the implicit drudge of another's knavery or good fortune. He sticks to his stewardship, and resists the favour of a salute from a fine lady, as not entered in his accounts. The humour of this character is less striking in the play than in Munden's personification of it. The other characters do not require any particular analysis. They are very insipid, good sort of people."

mathematical stair-case of the words and answers given to different speakers,* is an instance of frigid and ridiculous pedantry. An artificial elaborateness is the general characteristic of Ford's style. In this respect his plays resemble Miss Baillie's more than any others I am acquainted with, and are quite distinct from the exuberance and unstudied force which characterized his immediate predecessors. There is too much of scholastic subtlety, an innate perversity of understanding or predominance of will, which either seeks the irritation of inadmissible subjects, or to stimulate its own faculties by taking the most barren, and making something out of nothing, in a spirit of contradiction. He does not *draw along with* the reader: he does not work upon our sympathy, but on our antipathy or our indifference, and there is as little of the social or gregarious principle in his productions as there appears to have been in his personal habits, if we are to believe Sir John Suckling, who says of him, in the Sessions of the Poets—

"In the dumps John Ford alone by himself sat
With folded arms and melancholy hat."

I do not remember without considerable effort the plot or persons of most of his plays—'Perkin Warbeck,' 'The Lover's Melancholy,' 'Love's Sacrifice,' and the rest. There is little character, except of the most evanescent or extravagant kind (to which last class we may refer that of the sister of Calantha in 'The Broken Heart')—little imagery or fancy, and no action. It is but fair, however, to give a scene or two, in illustration of these remarks (or in confutation of them, if they are wrong), and I shall take the concluding one of 'The Broken Heart,' which is held up as the author's master-piece.

* "*Ithocles.* Soft peace enrich this room.
Orgilus. How fares the lady?
Philema. Dead!
Christalla. Dead!
Philema. Starv'd!
Christalla. Starv'd!
Ithocles. Me miserable!"

" SCENE—*A Room in the Palace.*

A Flourish.—Enter EUPHRANEA, *led by* GRONEAS *and* HEMOPHIL: PROPHILUS *led by* CHRISTALLA *and* PHILEMA: NEARCHUS *supporting* CALANTHA, CROTOLON, *and* AMELUS.

Cal. We miss our servants, Ithocles and Orgilus. On whom attend they?
Crot. My son, gracious princess,
Whisper'd some new device, to which these revels
Should be but usher: wherein I conceive
Lord Ithocles and he himself are actors.
Cal. A fair excuse for absence. As for Bassanes,
Delights to him are troublesome. Armostes
Is with the king?
Crot. He is.
Cal. On to the dance!
Cousin, hand you the bride: the bridegroom must be
Entrusted to my courtship. Be not jealous,
Euphranea; I shall scarcely prove a temptress.
Fall to our dance!

(*They dance the first change, during which enter* ARMOSTES.)

Arm. (*In a whisper to* Calantha.) The king your father's dead.
Cal. To the other change.
Arm. Is't possible?

They dance the second change.—Enter BASSANES

Bass. (*Whispers* Calantha). Oh! Madam,
Penthea, poor Penthea's starv'd.
Cal. Beshrew thee!
Lead to the next!
Bass. Amazement dulls my senses.

They dance the third change.—Enter ORGILUS.

Org. Brave Ithocles is murder'd, murder'd cruelly.
Cal. How dull this music sounds! Strike up more sprightly
Our footings are not active like our heart,*
Which treads the nimbler measure,
Org. I am thunderstruck.

The last change.

Cal. So; let us breathe awhile. (*Music ceases.*) Hath not this motion
Rais'd fresher colours on our cheek?
Near. Sweet princess,
A perfect purity of blood enamels
The beauty of your white.
Cal. We all look cheerfully:
And, cousin, 'tis, methinks, a rare presumption

* " High as our heart."—See passage from the 'Malcontent.'

In any who prefers our lawful pleasures
Before their own sour censure, to interrupt
The custom of this ceremony bluntly.
Near. None dares, lady.
Cal. Yes, yes; some hollow voice deliver'd to me
How that the king was dead.
Arm. The king is dead," &c. &c.

This, I confess, appears to me to be tragedy in masquerade. Nor is it, I think, accounted for, though it may be in part redeemed by her solemn address at the altar to the dead body of her husband.

" *Cal.* Forgive me. Now I turn to thee, thou shadow
Of my contracted lord! Bear witness all,
I put my mother's wedding-ring upon
His finger; 'twas my father's last bequest:
(*Places a ring on the finger of* ITHOCLES.)
Thus I new marry him, whose wife I am:
Death shall not separate us. Oh, my lords,
I but deceived your eyes with antic gesture,
When one news strait came huddling on another
Of death, and death, and death: still I danced forward;
But it struck home and here, and in an instant.
Be such mere women, who with shrieks and outcries
Can vow a present end to all their sorrows,
Yet live to court new pleasures, and outlive them:
They are the silent griefs which cut the heartstrings:
Let me die smiling.
Near. 'Tis a truth too ominous.
Cal. One kiss on these cold lips—my last: crack, crack
Argos, now Sparta's king, command the voices
Which wait at th' altar, now to sing the song
I fitted for my end."

And then, after the song, she dies.

This is the true false gallop of sentiment: anything more artificial and mechanical I cannot conceive. The boldness of the attempt, however, the very extravagance, might argue the reliance of the author on the truth of feeling prompting him to hazard it; but the whole scene is a forced transposition of that already alluded to in Marston's 'Malcontent.' Even the form of the stage directions is the same.

Enter MENDOZO, *supporting the* DUCHESS; GUERRINO; *the Ladies that are on the stage rise.* FERRARDO *ushers in the* DUCHESS; *then takes a Lady to tread a measure.*

Aurelia. We will dance. Music! we will dance. * *

Enter PREPASSO.

Who saw the Duke? the Duke?

Aurelia. Music!

Prepussa. The Duke? is the Duke returned?

Aurelia. Music!

Enter CELSO.

The Duke is quite invisible, or else is not.

Aurelia. We are not pleased with your intrusion upon our private retirement; we are not pleased: you have forgot yourselves.

Enter a PAGE.

Celso. Boy, thy master? where's the Duke?

Page. Alas, I left him burying the earth with his spread joyless limbs; he told me he was heavy, would sleep: bid me walk off, for the strength of fantasy oft made him talk in his dreams: I strait obeyed, nor ever saw him since; but wheresoe'er he is, he's sad.

Aurelia. Music, sound high, as is our heart; sound high.

Enter MALEVOLE *and her Husband, disguised like a Hermit.*

Malevole. The Duke? Peace, the Duke is dead.

Aurelia. Music!" *Act IV. Scene* 3.

The passage in Ford appears to me an ill-judged copy from this. That a woman should call for music, and dance on in spite of the death of her husband whom she hates, without regard to common decency, is but too possible: that she should dance on with the same heroic perseverance in spite of the death of her husband, of her father, and of every one else whom she loves, from regard to common courtesy or appearance, is not surely natural. The passions may silence the voice of humanity, but it is, I think, equally against probability and decorum to make both the passions and the voice of humanity give way (as in the example of Calantha) to a mere form of outward behaviour. Such a suppression of the strongest and most uncontroulable feelings can only be justified from necessity, for some great purpose, which is not the case in Ford's play; or it must be done for the effect and *eclat* of the thing, which is not fortitude but affectation. Mr. Lamb, in his impressive eulogy on this passage in 'The

Broken Heart,' has failed (as far as I can judge) in establishing the parallel between this uncalled-for exhibition of stoicism, and the story of the Spartan boy.

It may be proper to remark here, that most of the great men of the period I have treated of (except the greatest of all, and one other,) were men of classical education. They were learned men in an unlettered age; not self-taught men in a literary and critical age. This circumstance should be taken into the account in a theory of the dramatic genius of that age. Except Shakspeare, nearly all of them, indeed, came up from Oxford or Cambridge, and immediately began to write for the stage. No wonder. The first coming up to London in those days must have had a singular effect upon a young man of genius, almost like visiting Babylon or Susa, or a journey to the other world. The stage (even as it then was,) after the recluseness and austerity of a college life, must have appeared like Armida's enchanted palace, and its gay votaries like

> "Fairy elves beyond the Indian mount,
> Whose midnight revels, by a forest side
> Or fountain, some belated peasant sees,
> Or dreams he sees; while overhead the moon
> Sits arbitress, and nearer to the earth
> Wheels her pale course: they on their mirth and dance
> Intent, with jocund music charm his ear:
> At once with joy and fear his heart rebounds."

So our young novices must have felt when they first saw the magic of the scene, and heard its syren sounds with rustic wonder and the scholar's pride: and the joy that streamed from their eyes at that fantastic vision, at that gaudy shadow of life, of all its business and all its pleasures, and kindled their enthusiasm to join the mimic throng, still has left a long lingering glory behind it; and though now "deaf the praised ear, and mute the tuneful tongue," lives in their eloquent page, "informed with music, sentiment, and thought, never to die!"

LECTURE V.

On Single Plays, Poems, &c.—The Four P's, The Return from Parnassus, Gammer Gurton's Needle, and other Works.

I SHALL, in this lecture, turn back to give some account of single plays, poems, &c.; the authors of which are either not known or not very eminent, and the productions themselves, in general, more remarkable for their singularity, or as specimens of the style and manners of the age, than for their intrinsic merit or poetical excellence. There are many more works of this kind, however, remaining, than I can pretend to give an account of; and what I shall chiefly aim at, will be to excite the curiosity of the reader, rather than to satisfy it.

'The Four P's' is an interlude, or comic dialogue, in verse, between a Palmer, a Pardoner, a Poticary, and a Pedlar, in which each exposes the tricks of his own and his neighbours' profession, with much humour and shrewdness. It was written by John Heywood, the Epigrammatist, who flourished chiefly in the reign of Henry VIII., was the intimate friend of Sir Thomas More, with whom he seems to have had a congenial spirit, and died abroad, in consequence of his devotion to the Roman Catholic cause, about the year 1565. His zeal, however, on this head, does not seem to have blinded his judgment, or to have prevented him from using the utmost freedom and severity in lashing the abuses of Popery, at which he seems to have looked "with the malice of a friend." 'The Four P's' bears the date of 1547. It is very curious, as an evidence both of the wit, the manners, and opinions of the time. Each of the parties in the dialogue gives an account of the boasted advantages of his own particular calling, that is, of the frauds which he practises on credulity and ignorance, and is laughed at by the others in turn. In fact, they all of them strive to outbrave each other, till the contest becomes a jest, and it ends in a wager who shall tell the greatest lie, when the prize is adjudged to him who says that he had found a patient woman.* The common superstitions (here recorded) in civil and religious matters are almost incredible; and the chopped logic, which was the fashion of the time, and which comes in aid of the author's shrewd and pleasant sallies to expose them, is highly entertaining. Thus the Pardoner, scorning the Palmer's long pilgrimages and circuitous road to heaven, flouts him to his face, and vaunts his own superior pretensions:

"*Pard.* By the first part of this last tale,
It seemeth you came of late from the ale:
For reason on your side so far doth fail,
That you leave reasoning, and begin to rail.
Wherein you forget your own part clearly,
For you be as untrue as I:
But in one part you are beyond me,
For you may lie by authority,
And all that have wandered so far,
That no man can be their controller,
And where you esteem your labour so much
I say yet again, my pardons are such,
That if there were a thousand souls on a heap,
I would bring them all to heaven as good sheep,
As you have brought yourself on pilgrimage,
In the last quarter of your voyage,
Which is far a-this side heaven, by God:
There your labour and pardon is odd.
With small cost without any pain,
These pardons bring them to heaven plain:
Give me but a penny or two-pence,
And as soon as the soul departeth hence,
In half an hour, or three quarters at the most,
The soul is in heaven with the Holy Ghost."

The Poticary does not approve of this arrogance of the Friar, and undertakes, in mood and figure, to prove them both "false knaves." It is he, he says, who sends most souls to heaven, and who ought, therefore, to have the credit of it.

"No soul, ye know, entereth heaven-gate,
Till from the body he be separate:
And whom have ye known die honestly,

* Or, never known one otherwise than patient.

Without help of the Poticary ?
Nay, all that cometh to our handling,
Except ye hap to come to hanging.
Since of our souls the multitude
I send to heaven, when all is view'd
Who should but I then altogether
Have thank of all their coming thither ?"

The Pardoner here interrupts him captiously—

"If ye kill'd a thousand in an hour's space,
When come they to heaven, dying out of grace ?"

But the Poticary, not so baffled, retorts—

"If a thousand pardons about your necks were tied;
When come they to heaven, if they never died
* * * * * * *
But when ye feel your conscience ready,
I can send you to heaven very quickly."

The Pedlar finds out the weak side of his new companions, and tells them very bluntly, on their referring their dispute to him, a piece of his mind.

"Now have I found one mastery,
That ye can do indifferently;
And it is neither selling nor buying,
But even only very lying."

At this game of imposture, the cunning dealer in pins and laces undertakes to judge their merits ; and they accordingly set to work like regular graduates. The Pardoner takes the lead, with an account of the virtues of his relics ; and here we may find a plentiful mixture of popish superstition and indecency. The bigotry of any age is by no means a test of its piety, or even sincerity. Men seemed to make themselves amends for the enormity of their faith by levity of feeling, as well as by laxity of principle ; and in the indifference or ridicule with which they treated the wilful absurdities and extravagances to which they hood-winked their understandings, almost resembled children playing at blindman's-buff, who grope their way in the dark, and make blunders on purpose to laugh at their own idleness and folly. The sort of mummery at which popish bigotry used to play at the time when this old comedy was written, was not quite so harmless as blindman's-buff: what was sport to her, was death to others. She laughed at her own mockeries of common sense and true religion, and murdered while she laughed. The tragic farce was no longer to be borne, and it was partly put an end to. At present, though her eyes are blind-folded, her hands are tied fast behind her, like the false Duessa's. The sturdy genius of modern philosophy has got her in much the same situation that Count Fathom has the old woman that he lashes before him from the robbers' cave in the forest. In the following dialogue of this lively satire, the most sacred mysteries of the Catholic faith are mixed up with its idlest legends by old Heywood, who was a martyr to his religious zeal, without the slightest sense of impropriety. The Pardoner cries out in one place (like a lusty Friar John, or a trusty Friar Onion)—

"Lo, here be pardons, half a dozen,
For ghostly riches they have no cousin
And, moreover, to me they bring
Sufficient succour for my living.
And here be relics of such a kind
As in this world no man can find.
Kneel down all three, and when ye leave kissing,
Who list to offer shall have my blessing.
Friends, here shall ye see, even anon,
Of All-Hallows the blessed jaw-bone.
Mark well this, this relic here is a whipper;
My friends unfeigned, here's a slipper
Of one of the seven sleepers, be sure.—
Here is an eye-tooth of the great Turk:
Whose eyes be once set on this piece of work,
May happily lose part of his eye-sight,
But not all till he be blind outright.
Kiss it hardly, with good devotion.
Pot. This kiss shall bring us much promotion:
Fogh! by St. Saviour, I never kiss'd a worse.
* * * * * * * *
For, by All-Hallows, yet methinketh
That All-Hallows' breath stinketh.
Palm. Ye judge All-Hallows' breath unknown:
If any breath stink, it is your own.

Pot. I know mine own breath from All-Hallows,
Or else it were time to kiss the gallows.
Pard. Nay, sirs, here may ye see
The great toe of the Trinity:
Who to this toe any money voweth,
And once may roll it in his mouth,
All his life after I undertake
He shall never be vex'd with the tooth-ache.
Pot. I pray you turn that relic about;
Either the Trinity had the gout,
Or else, because it is three toes in one,
God made it as much as three toes alone.
Pard. Well, let that pass, and look upon this:
Here is a relic that doth not miss
To help the least as well as the most:
This is a buttock-bone of Pentecost.
* * * * * * *
Here is a box full of humble-bees,
That stung Eve as she sat on her knees
Tasting the fruit to her forbidden:
Who kisseth the bees within this hidden,
Shall have as much pardon of right,
As for any relic he kiss'd this night.
Good friends, I have yet here in this glass,
Which on the drink at the wedding was
Of Adam and Eve undoubtedly:
If ye honour this relic devoutly,
Although ye thirst no whit the less,
Yet shall ye drink the more, doubtless.
After which drinking, ye shall be as meet
To stand on your head as on your feet."

The same sort of significant irony runs through the Apothecary's knavish enumeration of miraculous cures in his possession:

" For this medicine helpeth one and other,
And bringeth them in case that they need no other.
Here is a *syrapus de Byzansis*,—
A little thing is enough of this;
For even the weight of one scrippal
Shall make you as strong as a cripple.
These be the things that break all strife
Between man's sickness and his life.
From all pain these shall you deliver,
And set you even at rest for ever.
Here is a medicine no more like the same,

Which commonly is called thus by name.
Not one thing here particularly,
But worketh universally;
For it doth me as much good when I sell it,
As all the buyers that take it or smell it.
If any reward may entreat ye,
I beseech your mastership be good to me,
And ye shall have a box of marmalade,
So fine that you may dig it with a spade."

After these quaint but pointed examples of it, Swift's boast with respect to the invention of irony,

"Which I was born to introduce,
Refin'd it first, and shew'd its use,

can be allowed to be true only in part.

The controversy between them being undecided, the Apothecary, to clench his pretensions "as a liar of the first magnitude," by a *coup de-grace*, says to the Pedlar, "You are an honest man;" but this home-thrust is somehow ingeniously parried. The Apothecary and Pardoner fall to their narrative vein again; and the latter tells a story of fetching a young woman from the lower world, from which I shall only give one specimen more as an instance of ludicrous and fantastic exaggeration. By the help of a passport from Lucifer, "given in the furnace of our palace," he obtains a safe conduct from one of the subordinate imps to his master's presence:

"The devil and I walked arm in arm
So far, till he had brought me thither,
Where all the devils of hell together
Stood in array in such apparel,
As for that day there meetly fell.
Their horns well gilt, their claws full clean,
Their tails well kempt, and, as I ween,
With sothery butter their bodies anointed;
I never saw devils so well appointed.
The master-devil sat in his jacket,
And all the souls were playing at racket.
None other rackets they had in hand,
Save every soul a good fire-brand;
Wherewith they play'd so prettily,
That Lucifer laughed merrily.

And all the residue of the fiends
Did laugh thereat full well, like friends.
But of my friend I saw no whit,
Nor durst not ask for her as yet.
Anon all this rout was brought in silence,
And I by an usher brought to presence
Of Lucifer; then low, as well I could,
I kneeled, which he so well allow'd
That thus he beck'd, and by St. Antony
He smiled on me well-favour'dly,
Bending his brows as broad as barn-doors;
Shaking his ears as rugged as burrs;
Rolling his eyes as round as two bushels;
Flashing the fire out of his nostrils;
Gnashing his teeth so vain-gloriously,
That methought time to fall to flattery,
Wherewith I told, as I shall tell;
Oh pleasant picture! O prince of hell!" &c.

The piece concludes with some good wholesome advice from the Pedlar, who here, as well as in the poem of the 'Excursion,' performs the part of Old Morality; but he does not seem, as in the latter case, to be acquainted with the "mighty stream of Tendency." He is more full of "wise saws" than "modern instances;" as prosing, but less paradoxical!

"But where ye doubt, the truth not knowing,
Believing the best, good may be growing.
In judging the best, no harm at the least;
In judging the worst, no good at the best.
But best in these things, it seemeth to me,
To make no judgment upon ye;
But as the church does judge or take them,
So do ye receive or forsake them.
And so be you sure you cannot err,
But may be a fruitful follower."

Nothing can be clearer than this.

The 'Return from Parnassus' was "first publicly acted," as the title-page imports, "by the students in St. John's College, Cambridge." It is a very singular, a very ingenious, and, as I think, a very interesting performance. It contains criticisms on contemporary authors, strictures on living manners, and the earliest denunciation (I know of) of the miseries and unprofitableness of a scholar's life. The only part I object to in our author's criticism is his abuse of Marston; and that, not because he says what is severe, but because he says what is not true of him. Anger may sharpen our insight into men's defects; but nothing should make us blind to their excellences. The whole passage is, however, so curious in itself (like the 'Edinburgh Review' lately published for the year 1755) that I cannot forbear quoting a great part of it. We find in the list of candidates for praise many a name—

"That like a trumpet makes the spirits dance;"

there are others that have long since sunk to the bottom of the stream of time, and no Humane Society of Antiquarians and Critics is ever likely to fish them up again.

"*Judicio.* Read the names.

Ingenioso. So I will, if thou wilt help me to censure them.

Edmund Spenser,	John Davis,
Henry Constable,	John Marston,
Thomas Lodge,	Kit Marlowe,
Samuel Daniel,	William Shakspeare;
Thomas Watson,	and one Churchyard,
Michael Drayton,	[who is consigned to an untimely grave.]

Good men and true, stand together, hear your censure: what's thy judgment of Spenser?

Jud. A sweeter swan than ever sung in Po;
A shriller nightingale than ever blest
The prouder groves of self-admiring Rome,
Blithe was each valley, and each shepherd proud,
While he did chaunt his rural minstrelsy.
Attentive was full many a dainty ear:
Nay, hearers hung upon his melting tongue,
While sweetly of his Faery Queen he sung,
While to the water's fall he tun'd her fame,
And in each bark engrav'd Eliza's name.
And yet for all, this unregarding soil
Unlaced the line of his desired life,
Denying maintenance for his dear relief;
Careless even to prevent his exequy,
Scarce deigning to shut up his dying eye.

Ing. Pity it is that gentler wits should breed,
Where thick-skinned chuffs laugh at a scholar's need.
But softly may our honour'd ashes rest,
That lie by merry Chaucer's noble chest.

But I pray thee proceed briefly in thy censure, that I may be proud of myself, as in the first, so in the last, my censure may jump with thine. Henry Constable, Samuel Daniel, Thomas Lodge, Thomas Watson.

Jud. Sweet Constable doth take the wondering ear,
And lays it up in willing prisonment:
Sweet honey-dropping Daniel doth wage
War with the proudest big Italian,
That melts his heart in sugar'd sonnetting.
Only let him more sparingly make use
Of others' wit, and use his own the more,
That well may scorn base imitation.
For Lodge and Watson, men of some desert,
Yet subject to a critic's marginal:
Lodge for his oar in every paper boat,
He that turns over Galen every day,
To sit and simper Euphues' legacy.

Ing. Michael Drayton.

Jud. Drayton's sweet Muse is like a sanguine dye,
Able to ravish the rash gazer's eye.

Ing. However, he wants one true note of a poet of our times; and that is this, he cannot swagger in a tavern, nor domineer in a pot-house. John Davis—

Jud. Acute John Davis, I affect thy rhymes,
That jerk in hidden charms these looser times:
Thy plainer verse, thy unaffected vein,
Is graced with a fair and sweeping train.

Ing. John Marston—

Jud. What, Monsieur Kinsayder, put up, man, put up for shame.
Methinks he is a ruffian in his style,
Withouten bands or garters' ornament.
He quaffs a cup of Frenchman's helicon,
Then royster doyster in his oily terms
Cuts, thrusts, and foins at whomsoe'er he meets,
And strews about Ram-alley meditations.
Tut, what cares he for modest close-couch'd terms
Cleanly to gird our looser libertines?
Give him plain naked words stript from their shirts
That might beseem plain-dealing Aretine.

Ing. Christopher Marlowe—

Jud. Marlowe was happy in his buskin'd Muse:
Alas! unhappy in his life and end.
Pity it is that wit so ill should dwell,
Wit lent from heaven, but vices sent from hell.

Ing. Our theatre hath lost, Pluto hath got
A tragic penman for a dreary plot.
Benjamin Jonson—

Jud. The wittiest fellow of a bricklayer in England.

Ing. A mere empiric, one that gets what he hath by observation, and makes only nature privy to what he endites: so slow an inventor, that he were better betake himself to his old trade of bricklaying; a blood whoreson, as confident now in making of a book, as he was in times past in laying of a brick.

William Shakspeare.

Jud. Who loves Adonis' love, or Lucrece' rape,
His sweeter verse contains heart-robbing life.
Could but a graver subject him content,
Without love's lazy foolish languishment."

This passage might seem to ascertain the date of the piece, as it must be supposed to have been written before Shakspeare had become known as a dramatic poet. Yet he afterwards introduces Kempe the actor talking with Burbage, and saying, "Few (of the University) pens play well: they smell too much of that writer Ovid, and of that writer Metamorphosis, and talk too much of Proserpina and Jupiter. Why, here's our fellow Shakspeare puts them all down; ay, and Ben Jonson too."—There is a good deal of discontent in all this; but the author complains of want of success in a former attempt, and appears not to have been on good terms with fortune. The miseries of a poet's life forms one of the favourite topics of 'The Return from Parnassus,' and are treated as if by some one who had "felt them knowingly." Thus Philomusus and Studioso chaunt their griefs in concert.

"*Phil.* Bann'd be those hours, when 'mongst the learned throng,
By Granta's muddy bank we whilom sung.
Stud. Bann'd be that hill which learned wits adore,
Where erst we spent our stock and little store.
Phil. Bann'd be those musty mews, where we have spent
Our youthful days in paled languishment.
Stud. Bann'd be those cozening arts that wrought our woe,
Making us wandering pilgrims to and fro.
Phil. Curst be our thoughts whene'er they dream of hope;
Bann'd be those haps that henceforth flatter us,
When mischief dogs us still, and still for aye,
From our first birth until our burying day.
In our first gamesome age, our doting sires
Carked and car'd to have us lettered:
Sent us to Cambridge where our oil is spent:
Us our kind college from the teat did tent,
And forced us walk before we weaned were.

From that time since wandered have we still
In the wide world, urg'd by our forced will;
Nor ever have we happy fortune tried;
Then why should hope with our rent state abide?"

"Out of our proof we speak."—This sorry matter-of-fact retrospect of the evils of a college life is very different from the hypothetical aspirations after its incommunicable blessings expressed by a living writer of true genius and a lover of true learning, who does not seem to have been cured of the old-fashioned prejudice in favour of classic lore, two hundred years after its vanity and vexation of spirit had been denounced in 'The Return from Parnassus:'—

"I was not trained in academic bowers;
And to those learned streams I nothing owe,
Which copious from those fair twin founts do flow:
Mine have been anything but studious hours.
Yet can I fancy wandering 'mid thy towers,
Myself a nursling, Granta, of thy lap.
My brow seems tightening with the Doctor's cap;
And I walk gowned; feel unusual powers.
Strange forms of logic clothe my admiring speech;
Old Ramus' ghost is busy at my brain,
And my skull teems with notions infinite:
Be still, ye reeds of Camus, while I teach
Truths which transcend the searching schoolmen's vein;
And half had stagger'd that stout Stagyrite."*

Thus it is that our treasure always lies where our knowledge does not, and fortunately enough perhaps; for the empire of imagination is wider and more prolific than that of experience.

The author of the old play, whoever he was, appears to have belonged to that class of mortals, who, as Fielding has it, feed upon their own hearts; who are egotists the wrong way, made desperate by too quick a sense of constant infelicity; and have the same intense uneasy consciousness of their own defects that most men have self-complacency in their supposed advantages. Thus venting the driblets of his spleen still upon himself, he prompts the Page to say, "A mere scholar is a creature that can strike fire in the morning at his tinder-box, put on a pair of lined

* 'Sonnet to Cambridge,' by Charles Lamb.

slippers, sit rheuming till dinner, and then go to his meat when the bell rings; one that hath a peculiar gift in a cough, and a license to spit: or if you will have him defined by negatives, he is one that cannot make a good leg, one that cannot eat a mess of broth cleanly, one that cannot ride a horse without spur-galling, one that cannot salute a woman and look on her directly, one that cannot ——"

If I was not afraid of being tedious, I might here give the examination of Signor Immerito, a raw ignorant clown (whose father has purchased him a living,) by Sir Roderick and the Recorder, which throws a considerable light on the state of wit and humour, as well as of ecclesiastical patronage in the reign of Elizabeth. It is to be recollected that one of the titles of this play is "A Scourge for Simony.'

Rec. For as much as nature has done her part in making you a handsome likely man—in the next place some art is requisite for the perfection of nature: for the trial whereof, at the request of my worshipful friend, I will in some sort propound questions fit to be resolved by one of your profession. Say what is a person that was never at the university?

Im. A person that was never in the university, is a living creature that can eat a tythe pig.

Rec. Very well answered: but you should have added—and must be officious to his patron. Write down that answer, to shew his learning in logic.

Sir Rod. Yea, boy, write that down: very learnedly, in good faith. I pray now let me ask you one question that I remember, whether is the masculine gender or the feminine more worthy?

Im. The feminine, sir.

Sir Rod. The right answer, the right answer. In good faith, I have been of that mind always: write, boy, that, to shew he is a grammarian.

Rec. What university are you of?

Im. Of none.

Sir Rod. He tells truth: to tell truth is an excellent virtue: boy, make two heads, one for his learning, another for his virtues, and refer this to the head of his virtues, not of his learning. Now, Master Recorder, if it please you, I will examine him in an author, that will sound him to the depth; a book of astronomy, otherwise called an almanack.

Rec. Very good, Sir Roderick; it were to be wished there were no other book of humanity; then there would not be such busy state-prying fellows as are now a-days. Proceed, good sir.

Sir Rod. What is the dominical letter?

Im. C, sir, and please your worship.

Sir Rod. A very good answer, a very good answer, the very answer of the book. Write down that, and refer it to his skill in philosophy. How many days hath September?

Im. Thirty days hath September, April, June, and November, February hath twenty-eight alone, and all the rest hath thirty and one.

Sir Rod. Very learnedly, in good faith: he hath also a smack in poetry. Write down that, boy, to show his learning in poetry. How many miles from Waltham to London?

Im. Twelve, sir.

Sir Rod. How many from Newmarket to Grantham?

Im. Ten, sir.

Sir Rod. Write down that answer of his, to show his learning in arithmetic.

Page. He must needs be a good arithmetician that counted [out] money so lately.

Sir Rod. When is the new moon?

Im. The last quarter, the fifth day, at two of the clock, and thirty-eight minutes, in the morning.

Sir Rod. How call you him that is weather-wise?

Rec. A good astronomer.

Sir Rod. Sirrah, boy, write him down for a good astronomer. What day of the month lights the queen's day on?

Im. The 17th of November.

Sir Rod. Boy, refer this to his virtues, and write him down a good subject.

Page. Faith, he were an excellent subject for two or three good wits; he would make a fine ass for an ape to ride upon.

Sir Rod. And these shall suffice for the parts of his learning. Now it remains to try, whether you be a man of a good utterance, that is, whether you can ask for the strayed heifer with the white face, as also chide the boys in the belfry, and bid the sexton whip out the dogs: let me hear your voice.

Im. If any man or woman—

Sir Rod. That's too high.

Im. If any man or woman.

Sir Rod. That's too low.

Im. If any man or woman can tell any tidings of a horse with four feet, two ears, that did stray about the seventh hour, three minutes in the forenoon, the fifth day—

Sir Rod. Boy, write him down for a good utterance. Master Recorder, I think he hath been examined sufficiently.

Rec. Ay, Sir Roderick, 'tis so: we have tried him very thoroughly.

Page. Ay, we have taken an inventory of his good parts, and prized them accordingly.

Sir Rod. Signior Immerito, forasmuch as we have made a double trial of thee, the one of your learning, the other of your erudition; it is expedient, also, in the next place, to give you a few exhortations, considering the greatest clerks are not the wisest men: this is therefore first to exhort you to abstain from controversies; secondly, not to gird at men of worship, such as myself, but to use yourself discreetly; thirdly, not to speak when any man or woman coughs: do so, and in so doing, I will persevere to be your worshipful friend and loving patron. Lead Immerito in to my son, and let him despatch him, and remember my tythes to be reserved, paying twelve-pence a-year.

'Gammer Gurton's Needle'* is a still older and more curious relic; and is a regular comedy in five acts, built on the circumstance of an old woman having lost her needle, which throws the whole village into confusion, till it is at last providentially found sticking in an unlucky part of Hodge's dress. This must evidently have happened at a time when the manufacturers of Sheffield and Birmingham had not reached the height of perfection which they have at present done. Suppose that there is only one sewing-needle in a parish, that the owner, a diligent, notable old dame, loses it, that a mischief-making wag sets it about that another old woman has stolen this valuable instrument of household industry, that strict search is made everywhere in-doors for it in vain, and that then the incensed parties sally forth to scold it out in the open air, till words end in blows, and the affair is referred over to the higher authorities, and we shall have an exact idea (though perhaps not so lively a one) of what passes in this authentic document between Gammer Gurton and her Gossip Dame Chat, Diccon the Bedlam (the causer of these harms), Hodge, Gammer Gurton's servant, Tyb, her maid, Cocke, her 'prentice boy, Doll, Scapethrift, Master Baillie, his master, Doctor Rat, the curate, and Gib the Cat, who may be fairly reckoned one of the *dramatis personæ*, and performs no mean part.

"Gog's crosse, Gammer" (says Cocke, the boy), "if ye will laugh, look in
but at the door.
And see how Hodge lieth tumbling and tossing amidst the floor.
Raking there some fire to find among the ashes dead†
Where there is not a spark so big as a pin's head:
At last in a dark corner two sparks he thought he sees,
Which were indeed nought else but Gib our cat's two eyes.

* The name of Still has been assigned as the author of this singular production, with the date of 1566.

† That is, to light a candle to look for the lost needle.

Puff, quoth Hodge; thinking thereby to have fire without doubt;
With that Gib shut her two eyes, and so the fire was out;
And by and by them opened, even as they were before,
With that the sparks appeared, even as they had done of yore;
And even as Hodge blew the fire, as he did think,
Gib, as he felt the blast, straightway began to wink;
Till Hodge fell of swearing, as came best to his turn;
The fire was sure bewitch'd, and therefore would not burn.
At last Gib up the stairs, among old posts and pins,
And Hodge he hied him after, till broke were both his shins;
Cursing and swearing oaths, were never of his making.
That Gib would fire the house, if that she were not taken."

Diccon, the strolling beggar (or Bedlam, as he is called,) steals a piece of bacon from behind Gammer Gurton's door, and in answer to Hodge's complaint of being dreadfully pinched for hunger, asks—

"Why, Hodge, was there none at home thy dinner for to set?
Hodge. Gog's bread, Diccon, I came too late, was nothing there to get:
Gib (a foul fiend might on her light) lik'd the milk-pan so clean:
See, Diccon, 'twas not so well washed this seven year I ween.
A pestilence light on all ill luck, I had thought yet for all this,
Of a morsel of bacon behind the door, at worst I should not miss:
But when I sought a slip to cut, as I was wont to do,
Gog's souls, Diccon, Gib our cat had eat the bacon too."

Hodge's difficulty in making Diccon understand what the nee dle is which his dame has lost, shows his superior acquaintance with the conveniences and modes of abridging labour in more civilized life, of which the other had no idea.

"*Hodge.* Has she not gone, trowest now thou, and lost her neele?" [So it is called here.]
"*Dic.* (*says staring.*) Her eel, Hodge? Who fished of late? That was a dainty dish.
Hodge. Tush, tush, her neele, her neele, her neele, man, 'tis neither flesh nor fish:
A little thing with a hole in the end, as bright as any siller [silver],
Small, long, sharp at the point, and strait as any pillar.
Dic. I know not what a devil thou mean'st, thou bring'st me more in doubt.
Hodge, (*answers with disdain*). Know'st not with what Tom tailor's man sits broching through a clout?
A neele, a neele, my Gammer's neele is gone."

The rogue Diccon threateus to show Hodge a spirit; but though Hodge runs away through pure fear before it has time to appear, he does not fail, in the true spirit of credulity, to give a faithful and alarming account of what he did not see to his mistress, concluding with a hit at the Popish clergy.

"By the mass, I saw him of late call up a great black devil.
Oh, the knave cried, ho, ho, he roared and thunder'd;
And ye had been there, I am sure, you'd murrainly ha' wonder'd.
Gam. Wast not thou afraid, Hodge, to see him in his plaee?
Hodge, (*lies and says*). No and he had come to me, should have laid him on his face,
Should have promised him.
Gam. But, Hodge, had he no horns to push?
Hodge. As long as your two arms. Saw ye never Friar Rush,
Painted on a cloth, with a fine long cow's tail,
And crooked cloven feet, and many a hooked nail?
For all the world (if I should judge) should reckon him his brother:
Look even what face Friar Rush had, the devil had such another."

He then adds (quite apocryphally) while he is in for it, that "the devil said plainly that Dame Chat had got the needle," which makes all the disturbance. The same play contains the well-known good old song, beginning and ending—

"Back and side go bare, go bare,
Both foot and hand go cold:
But belly, God send thee good ale enough,
Whether it be new or old,
I cannot eat but little meat,
My stomach is not good;
But sure I think, that I can drink
With him that wears a hood:
Though I go bare, take ye no care,
I nothing am a-cold:
I stuff my skin so full within
Of jolly good ale and old.
Back and side go bare, &c.

I love no roast, but a nut-brown toast,
And a crab laid in the fire:
A little bread, shall do me stead,
Much bread I do not desire.
No frost or snow, no wind I trow,
Can hurt me if I wolde,
I am so wrapt, and thoroughly lapt

In jolly good ale and old.
  Back and side go bare, &c

And Tib, my wife, that as her life
Loveth well good ale to seek;
Full oft drinks she, till ye may see
The tears run down her cheek
Then doth she troll to me the bowl,
Even as a malt-worm sholde:
And saith, sweetheart, I took my part
Of this jolly good ale and old.
  Back and side go bare, go bare,
  Both foot and hand go cold:
  But belly, God send thee good ale enough,
  Whether it be new or old.

Such was the wit, such was the mirth of our ancestors:—homely, but hearty; coarse perhaps, but kindly. Let no man despise it, for "Evil to him that evil thinks." To think it poor and beneath notice because it is not just like ours, is the same sort of hypercriticism that was exercised by the person who refused to read some old books, because they were "such very poor spelling." The meagreness of their literary or their bodily fare was at least relished by themselves; and this is better than a surfeit or an indigestion. It is refreshing to look out of ourselves sometimes, not to be always holding the glass to our own peerless perfections; and as there is a dead wall which always intercepts the prospect of the future from our view, (all that we can see beyond it is the heavens,) it is as well to direct our eyes now and then without scorn to the page of history, and repulsed in our attempts to penetrate the secrets of the next six thousand years, not to turn our backs on auld lang syne!

The other detached plays of nearly the same period of which I proposed to give a cursory account, are 'Green's Tu Quoque,' 'Microcosmus,' 'Lingua,' 'The Merry Devil of Edmonton,' 'The Pinner of Wakefield,' and 'The Spanish Tragedy.' Of the spurious plays attributed to Shakspeare, and to be found in some of the editions of his works, such as 'The Yorkshire Tragedy,' 'Sir John Oldcastle,' 'The Widow of Watling Street,' &c., I shall say nothing here, because I suppose the reader to be already acquainted with them, and because I have given a general account of them in another work.

'Green's Tu Quoque,' by George Cook, a contemporary of Shakspeare's, is so called from Green the actor, who played the part of Bubble in this very lively and elegant comedy, with the cant phrase of *Tu quoque* perpetually in his mouth. The double change of situation between this fellow and his master, Staines, each passing from poverty to wealth, and from wealth to poverty again, is equally well imagined and executed. A gay and gallant spirit pervades the whole of it; wit, poetry, and morality, each take their turn in it. The characters of the two sisters, Joyce and Gertrude, are very skilfully contrasted, and the manner in which they mutually betray one another into the hands of their lovers, first in the spirit of mischief, and afterwards of retaliation, is quite dramatic. "If you cannot find in your heart to tell him you love him, I'll sigh it out for you. Come, we little creatures must help one another," says the Madcap to the Madonna. As to style and matter, this play has a number of pigeon-holes full of wit and epigrams which are flying out in almost every sentence. I could give twenty pointed conceits, wrapped up in good set terms. Let one or two at the utmost suffice. A bad hand at cards is thus described. Will Rash says to Scattergood, "Thou hast a wild hand indeed; thy small cards show like a troop of rebels, and the knave of clubs is their chief leader." Bubble expresses a truism very gaily on finding himself equipped like a gallant—"How apparel makes a man respected! The very children in the street do adore me." We find here the first mention of Sir John Suckling's "melancholy hat," as a common article of wear—the same which he chose to clap on Ford's head, and the first instance of the theatrical *double entendre* which has been repeated ever since of an actor's ironically abusing himself in his feigned character.

"*Gervase.* They say Green's a good clown.
Bubble, (*played by Green, says*) Green! Green's an ass,
Scattergood. Wherefore do you say so?
Bub. Indeed, I ha' no reason; for they say he's as like me as ever he can look."

The following description of the dissipation of a fortune in the hands of a spendthrift is ingenious and beautiful:

> "Know that which made him gracious in your eyes,
> And gilded o'er his imperfections,
> Is wasted and consumed even like ice,
> Which by the vehemence of heat dissolves,
> And glides to many rivers: so his wealth,
> That felt a prodigal hand, hot in expense,
> Melted within his gripe, and from his coffers
> Ran like a violent stream to other men's."

'Microcosmus,' by Thomas Nabbes, is a dramatic mask or allegory, in which the Senses, the Soul, a Good and a Bad Genius, Conscience, &c., contend for the dominion of a man; and notwithstanding the awkwardness of the machinery, is not without poetry, elegance, and originality. Take the description of morning as a proof:

> "What do I see? Blush, grey-eyed morn, and spread
> Thy purple shame upon the mountain tops;
> Or pale thyself with envy, since here comes
> A brighter Venus than the dull-eyed star
> That lights thee up."

But what are we to think of a play, of which the following is a literal list of the *dramatis personæ?*

"NATURE, a fair woman, in a white robe, wrought with birds, beasts, fruits, flowers, clouds, stars, &c.; on her head a wreath of flowers interwoven with stars.

JANUS, a man with two faces, signifying Providence, in a yellow robe, wrought with snakes, as he is deus anni; on his head a crown. He is Nature's husband.

FIRE, a fierce-countenanced young man, in a flame-coloured robe, wrought with gleams of fire; his hair red, and on his head a crown of flames. His creature a Vulcan.

AIR, a young man of a variable countenance, in a blue robe, wrought with divers coloured clouds; his hair blue; and on his head a wreath of clouds. His creature a giant or silvan.

WATER, a young woman in a sea-greeen robe, wrought with waves; her hair a sea-green, and on her head a wreath of sedge bound about with waves. Her creature a syren.

EARTH, a young woman of a sad countenance. in a grass-green robe, wrought with sundry fruits and flowers; her hair black, and on her head a chaplet of flowers. Her creature a pigmy.

LOVE, a Cupid in a flame-coloured habit; bow and quiver, a crown of flaming hearts, &c.

PHYSANDER, a perfect grown man, in a long white robe, and on his head a garland of white lilies and roses mixed. His name ἀπο τῆς φύσεος καὶ τῦ ἀνδρος.

CHOLER, a fencer; his clothes red.

BLOOD, a dancer, in a watchet-coloured suit.

PHLEGM, a physician, an old man; his doublet white and black; trunk hose.

MELANCHOLY, a musician; his complexion, hair, and clothes black; a lute in his hand. He is likewise an amorist.

BELLANIMA, a lovely woman, in a long white robe; on her head a wreath of white flowers. She signifies the soul.

BONUS GENIUS, an angel, in a like white robe; wings and wreath white.

MALUS GENIUS, a devil, in a black robe; hair, wreath, and wings black.

THE FIVE SENSES—Seeing, a chambermaid; Hearing, the usher of the hall; Smelling, a huntsman or gardener; Tasting, a cook; Touching, a gentleman usher.

SENSUALITY, a wanton woman, richly habited, but lasciviously dressed, &c.

TEMPERANCE, a lovely woman, of a modest countenance; her garments plain, but decent, &c.

A Philosopher,
An Eremite,
A Ploughman,
A Shepherd, } all properly habited.

Three Furies as they are commonly fancied.

Fear, the crier of the court, with a tipstaff.

Conscience, the Judge of the court.

Hope and Despair, an advocate and a lawyer.

The other three Virtues, as they are frequently expressed by painters.

The Heroes, in bright antique habits, &c.

The front of a workmanship proper to the fancy of the rest, adorned with brass figures of angels and devils, with several inscriptions; the title is an escutcheon, supported by an angel and a devil. Within the arch a continuing perspective of ruins, which is drawn still before the other scenes, whilst they are varied.

THE INSCRIPTIONS.

Hinc gloria.	Hinc pœna.
Appetitus boni.	Appetitus mali."

Antony Brewer's 'Lingua' (1607) is of the same cast. It is much longer as well as older than 'Microcosmus.' It is also an allegory celebrating the contention of the Five Senses for the crown of superiority, and the pretensions of Lingua, or the Tongue, to be admitted as a sixth sense. It is full of child's play, and old wives' tales; but is not unadorned with passages displaying strong good sense, and powers of fantastic description.

Mr. Lamb has quoted two passages from it—the admirable enumeration of the characteristics of different languages, 'The Chaldee wise, the Arabian physical,' &c.; and the striking description of the ornaments and uses of tragedy and comedy. The dialogue between Memory, Common Sense, and Phantastes, is curious and worth considering:

"*Common Sense.* Why, good father, why are you so late now-a-days?

Memory. Thus 'tis; the most customers I remember myself to have, are, as your lordship knows, scholars, and now-a-days the most of them are become critics, bringing me home such paltry things to lay up for them, that I can hardly find them again.

Phantastes. Jupiter, Jupiter, I had thought these flies had bit none but myself; do critics tickle you, i' faith?

Mem. Very familiarly; for they must know of me, forsooth, how every idle word is written in all the musty moth-eaten manuscripts, kept in all the old libraries in every city, betwixt England and Peru.

Common Sense. Indeed I have noted these times to affect antiquities more than is requisite.

Mem. I remember in the age of Assaracus and Ninus, and about the wars of Thebes, and the siege of Troy, there were few things committed to my charge, but those that were well worthy the preserving; but now every trifle must be wrapp'd up in the volume of eternity. A rich pudding-wife, or a cobbler, cannot die but I must immortalize his name with an epitaph; a dog cannot water in a nobleman's shoe, but it must be sprinkled into the chronicles; so that I never could remember my treasure more full, and never emptier of honourable and true heroical actions."

And again, Mendacio put in his claim with great success to many works of uncommon merit:

"*Appe.* Thou boy! how is this possible? Thou art but a child, and there were sects of philosophy before thou wert born.

Men. Appetitus, thou mistakest me; I tell thee, three thousand years ago was Mendacio born in Greece, nursed in Crete, and ever since honoured every where: I'll be sworn I held old Homer's pen when he writ his Iliads and his Odysseys.

Appe. Thou hadst need, for I hear say he was blind.

Men. I helped Herodotus to pen some part of his Muses; lent Pliny ink to write his history; rounded Rabelais in the ear when he historified Pantagruel; as for Lucian, I was his genius. O, those two books, 'De Vera Historia,' however they go under his name, I'll be sworn I writ them every tittle.

Appe. Sure as I am hungry, thou'lt have it for lying. But hast thou rusted this latter time for want of exercise?

Men. Nothing less. I must confess I would fain have jogged Stow and great Hollingshed on their elbows, when they were about their Chronicles; and, as I remember, Sir John Mandevill's Travels, and a great part of the 'Decades," were of my doing; but for the 'Mirror of Knighthood,' 'Bevis of Southampton,' 'Palmerin of England,' 'Amadis of Gaul,' 'Huon de Bordeaux,' 'Sir Guy of Warwick,' 'Martin Marprelate,' 'Robin Hood,' 'Garagantua,' 'Gerilion,' and a thousand such exquisite monuments as these, no doubt but they breathe in my breath up and down."

'The Merry Devil of Edmonton,' which has been sometimes attributed to Shakspeare, is assuredly not unworthy of him. It is more likely, however, both from the style and subject matter, to have been Heywood's than any other person's. It is perhaps the first example of sentimental comedy we have—romantic, sweet, tender, it expresses the feelings of honour, love, and friendship in their utmost delicacy, enthusiasm, and purity. The names alone, Raymond Mounchersey, Frank Jerningham, Clare, Millisent, "sound silver sweet, like lovers' tongues by night." It sets out with a sort of story of Doctor Faustus, but this is dropt as jarring on the tender chords of the rest of the piece. The wit of 'The Merry Devil of Edmonton' is as genuine as the poetry. Mine Host of the George is as good a fellow as Boniface, and the deer-stealing scenes in the forest between him, Sir John the curate, Smug the smith, and Banks the miller, are "very honest knaveries," as Sir Hugh Evans has it. The air is delicate, and the deer, shot by their cross-bows, fall without a groan! Frank Jerningham says to Clare,

"The way lies right: hark, the clock strikes at Enfield: what's the hour?

Young Clare. Ten, the bell says.

Jern. It was but eight when we set out from Cheston: Sir John and his sexton are at their ale to-night, the clock runs at random.

Y. Clare. Nay, as sure as thou livest, the villanous vicar is abroad in the chase. The priest steals more venison than half the country.

Jern. Millisent, how dost thou?

Mil. Sir, very well.
I would to God we were at Brian's lodge."

A volume might be written to prove this last answer Shakspeare's, in which the tongue says one thing in one line, and the heart contradicts it in the next; but there were other writers living in the time of Shakspeare, who knew these subtle windings of the passions besides him,—though none so well as he!

'The Pinner of Wakefield, or George a Green,' is a pleasant interlude, of an early date, and the author unknown, in which kings and cobblers, outlaws and Maid Marians, are "hail-fellow well met," and in which the features of the antique world are made smiling and amiable enough. Jenkin, George a Green's servant, is a notorious wag. Here is one of his pretended pranks:

"*Jenkin.* This fellow comes to me,
And takes me by the bosom: you slave,
Said he, hold my horse, and look
He takes no cold in his feet.
No, marry shall he, sir, quoth I.
I'll lay my cloak underneath him.
I took my cloak, spread it all along,
And his horse on the midst of it.
George. Thou clown, did'st thou set his horse upon thy cloak?
Jenk. Aye, but mark how I served him.
Madge and he was no sooner gone down into the ditch
But I plucked out my knife, cut four holes in my cloak, and made his horse stand on the bare ground."

The first part of 'Jeronymo' is an indifferent piece of work, and the second, or 'The Spanish Tragedy,' by Kyd, is like unto it, except the interpolations idly said to have been added by Ben Jonson, relating to Jeronymo's phrensy, "which have all the melancholy madness of poetry, if not the inspiration."

LECTURE VI.

On Miscellaneous Poems; F. Beaumont, P. Fletcher, Drayton, Daniel, etc.; Sir P. Sidney's 'Arcadia,' and other works.

I SHALL, in the present Lecture, attempt to give some idea of the lighter productions of the Muse in the period before us, in order to show that grace and elegance are not confined entirely to later times, and shall conclude with some remarks on Sir Philip Sidney's 'Arcadia.'

I have already made mention of the lyrical pieces of Beaumont and Fletcher. It appears from his poems, that many of these were composed by Francis Beaumont, particularly the very beautiful ones in the tragedy of 'The False One,' the 'Praise of Love' in that of 'Valentinian,' and another in 'The Nice Valour, or Passionate Madman,' an "Address to Melancholy," which is the perfection of this kind of writing.

"Hence, all you vain delights,
As short as are the nights
Wherein you spend your folly
There's nought in this life sweet,
If man were wise to see't,
But only melancholy,
Oh, sweetest melancholy,
Welcome folded arms and fixed eyes,
A sight that piercing mortifies;
A look that's fasten'd to the ground,
A tongue chain'd up without a sound;
Fountain heads, and pathless groves,
Places which pale passion loves:
Moon-light walks, where all the fowls
Are warmly hous'd, save bats and owls;
A midnight bell, a passing groan,
These are the sounds we feed upon:
Then stretch our bones in a still, gloomy valley;
Nothing so dainty sweet as lovely melancholy."

It has been supposed (and not without every appearance of good reason) that this pensive strain, "most musical, most melancholy," gave the first suggestion of the spirited introduction to Milton's 'Il Penseroso.'

> "Hence, vain deluding joys,
> The brood of folly without father bred!
> But hail, thou Goddess, sage and holy,
> Hail, divinest melancholy,
> Whose saintly visage is too bright
> To hit the sense of human sight," &c.

The same writer thus moralises on the life of man, in a set of similes, as apposite as they are light and elegant:

> "Like to the falling of a star,
> Or as the flights of eagles are,
> Or like the fresh spring's gaudy hue,
> Or silver drops of morning dew,
> Or like a wind that chafes the flood,
> Or bubbles which on water stood:
> E'en such is man, whose borrow'd light
> Is straight call'd in and paid to-night:—
> The wind blows out, the bubble dies:
> The spring entomb'd in autumn lies;
> The dew's dried up, the star is shot,
> The flight is past, and man forgot."

"The silver foam which the wind severs from the parted wave" is not more light or sparkling than this: the dove's downy pinion is not softer and smoother than the verse. We are too ready to conceive of the poetry of that day, as altogether old-fashioned, meagre, squalid, deformed, withered and wild in its attire, or as a sort of uncouth monster, like "grim-visaged, comfortless despair," mounted on a lumbering, unmanageable Pegasus, dragon-winged and leaden-hoofed; but it as often wore a sylph-like form with Attic vest, with fairy feet, and the butterfly's gaudy wings. The bees were said to have come, and built their hive in the mouth of Plato when a child; and the fable might be transferred to the sweeter accents of Beaumont and Fletcher! Beaumont died at the age of five-and-twenty. One of these writers makes Bellario the Page say to Philaster, who threatens to take his life—

"'Tis not a life;
'Tis but a piece of childhood thrown away."

But here was youth, genius, aspiring hope, growing reputation, cut off like a flower in its summer-pride, or like "the lily on its stalk green," which makes us repine at fortune and almost at nature, that seems to set so little store by their greatest favourites. The life of poets is, or ought to be (judging of it from the light it lends to ours,) a golden dream, full of brightness and sweetness, "lapt in Elysium;" and it gives one a reluctant pang to see the splendid vision, by which they are attended in their path of glory, fade like a vapour, and their sacred heads laid low in ashes, before the sand of common mortals has run out. Fletcher too was prematurely cut off by the plague. Raphael died at four-and-thirty, and Correggio at forty. Who can help wishing that they had lived to the age of Michael Angelo and Titian? Shakspeare might have lived another half century, enjoying fame and repose, "now that his task was smoothly done," listening to the music of his name, and better still, of his own thoughts, without minding Rymer's abuse of "the tragedies of the last age." His native stream of Avon would then have flowed with softer murmurs to the ear, and his pleasant birthplace, Stratford, would in that case have worn even a more gladsome smile than it does, to the eye of fancy!—Poets, however, have a sort of privileged after-life, which does not fall to the common lot; the rich and mighty are nothing but while they are living; their power ceases with them: but "the sons of memory, the great heirs of fame," leave the best part of what was theirs, their thoughts, their verse, what they most delighted and prided themselves in, behind them—imperishable, incorruptible, immortal!—Sir John Beaumont (the brother of our dramatist), whose loyal and religious effusions are not worth much, very feelingly laments his brother's untimely death in an epitaph upon him:

"Thou shouldst have followed me, but Death (to blame)
Miscounted years, and measured age by fame;
So dearly hast thou bought thy precious lines,
Their praise grew swiftly; so thy life declines,

Thy Muse, the hearer's Queen, the readers Love,
All ears, all hearts (but Death's) could please and move."

Beaumont's verses addressed to Ben Jonson at the Mermaid are a pleasing record of their friendship, and of the way in which they "fleeted the time carelessly" as well as studiously "in the golden age" of our poetry:

Lines sent from the country with two unfinished Comedies, which deferred their merry meetings at the Mermaid.]

"The sun which doth the greatest comfort bring
To absent friends, because the self-same thing
They know they see, however absent, is
Here our best hay-maker, (forgive me this,
It is our country style) in this warm shine
I lie and dream of your full Mermaid wine:
Oh, we have water mixt with claret lees,
Drink apt to bring in drier heresies
Than here, good only for the sonnet's strain,
With fustian metaphors to stuff the brain:
Think with one draught a man's invention fades,
Two cups had quite spoil'd Homer's Iliads.
'Tis liquor that will find out Sutcliffe's wit,
Like where he will, and make him write worse yet:
Fill'd with such moisture, in most grievous qualms*
Did Robert Wisdom write his singing psalms:
And so must I do this: and yet I think
It is a potion sent us down to drink
By special providence, keep us from fights,
Make us not laugh when we make legs to knights;
'Tis this that keeps our minds fit for our states,
A medicine to obey our magistrates.
* * * * * * * *
Methinks the little wit I had is lost
Since I saw you, for wit is like a rest
Held up at tennis, which men do the best
With the best gamesters. What things have we seen
Done at the Mermaid! Hard words that have been
So nimble, and so full of subtile flame,
As if that every one from whence they came
Had meant to put his whole wit in a jest,
And had resolved to live a fool the rest

* So in Rochester's epigram:

"Sternhold and Hopkins had great qualms,
When they translated David's Psalms."

Of his dull life; then when there hath been thrown
Wit able enough to justify the town
For three days past, wit that might warrant be
For the whole city to talk foolishly,
Till that were cancell'd; and when that was gone,
We left an air behind us, which alone
Was able to make the two next companies
Right witty, though but downright fools more wise."

I shall not in this place repeat Marlowe's celebrated song 'Come live with me and be my love,' nor Sir Walter Raleigh's no less celebrated answer to it (they may both be found in Walton's 'Complete Angler,' accompanied with scenery and remarks worthy of them); but I may quote, as a specimen of the high and romantic tone in which the poets of this age thought and spoke of each other, the 'Vision upon the Conceipt of the Faëry Queen,' understood to be by Sir Walter Releigh:

"Methought I saw the grave where Laura lay,
Within that temple, where the vestal flame
Was wont to burn, and passing by that way
To see that buried dust of living fame,
Whose tomb fair Love, and fairer Virtue kept.
All suddenly I saw the Faery Queen:
At whose approach the soul of Petrarch wept;
And from thenceforth those Graces were not seen,
For they this Queen attended, in whose stead
Oblivion laid him down on Laura's hearse.
Hereat the hardest stones were seen to bleed,
And groans of buried ghosts the heavens did pierce,
Where Homer's spright did tremble all for grief,
And curst th' access of that celestial thief."

A higher strain of compliment cannot well be conceived than this, which raises your idea even of that which it disparages in the comparison, and makes you feel that nothing could have torn the writer from his idolatrous enthusiasm for Petrarch and his Laura's tomb, but Spenser's magic verses and diviner 'Faëry Queen'—the one lifted above mortality, the other brought from the skies!

The name of Drummond of Hawthornden is in a manner entwined in cypher with that of Ben Jonson. He has not done himself or Jonson any credit by his account of their conversaion; but his sonnets are in the highest degree elegant, harmonious, and striking. It appears to me that they are more in the manner of Petrarch than any others that we have, with a certain intenseness in the sentiment, an occasional glitter of thought, and uniform terseness of expression. The reader may judge for himself from a few examples.

"I know that all beneath the moon decays,
And what by mortals in this world is wrought
In time's great periods shall return to nought;
That fairest states have fatal nights and days.
I know that all the Muse's heavenly lays,
With toil of spright which are so dearly bought,
As idle sounds, of few or none are sought;
That there is nothing lighter than vain praise.
I know frail beauty's like the purple flow'r,
To which one morn oft birth and death affords;
That love a jarring is of mind's accords,
Where sense and will bring under reason's pow'r.
Know what I list, this all cannot me move,
But that, alas! I both must write and love."

Another—

"Fair moon, who with thy cold and silver shine
Mak'st sweet the horror of the dreadful night,
Delighting the weak eye with smiles divine,
Which Phœbus dazzles with his too much light;
Bright queen of the first Heav'n, if in thy shrine
By turning oft, and Heav'n's eternal might,
Thou hast not yet that once sweet fire of thine,
Endymion, forgot, and lovers' plight:
If cause like thine may pity breed in thee,
And pity somewhat else to it obtain,
Since thou hast power of dreams as well as he
That holds the golden rod and mortal chain;
Now while she sleeps,* in doleful guise her show
These tears, and the black map of all my woe."

This is the eleventh sonnet: the twelfth is full of [illegible] and forced conceits, without any sentiment at all; such as calling the sun "the goldsmith of the stars," "the enameller of the moon," and "the Apelles of the flowers." This is as bad as

* His mistress.

Cowley or Sir Philip Sidney. Here is one that is worth a million of such quaint devices:

" *To the Nightingale.*

Dear chorister, who from these shadows sends*,
Ere that the blushing morn dare show her light,
Such sad lamenting strains, that night attends
(Become all ear†) stars stay to hear thy plight.
If one whose grief even reach of thought transcends,
Who ne'er (not in a dream) did taste delight,
May thee importune who like case pretends,
And seem'st to joy in woe, in woe's despite:
Tell me (so may thou milder fortune try,
And long, long sing!) for what thou thus complains,*
Since winter's gone, and sun in dappled sky
Enamour'd smiles on woods and flow'ry plains?
The bird, as if my questions did her move,
With trembling wings sigh'd forth, 'I love, I love.' "

Or if a mixture of the Della Cruscan style be allowed to en shrine the true spirit of love and poetry, we have it in the following address to the river Forth, on which his mistress had embarked:

" Slide soft, fair Forth, and make a crystal plain,
Cut your white locks, and on your foamy face
Let not a wrinkle be, when you embrace
The boat that earth's perfection doth contain.
Winds wonder, and through wondering hold your peace,
Or if that you your hearts cannot restrain
From sending sighs, feeling a lover's case,
Sigh, and in her fair hair yourselves enchain.
Or take these sighs, which absence makes arise
From my oppressed breast, and fill the sails.
Or some sweet breath new brought from Paradise.
The floods do smile, love o'er the winds prevails,
And yet huge waves arise; the cause is this,
The ocean strives with Forth the boat to kiss."

This to the English reader will express the very soul of Petrarch, the molten breath of sentiment converted into the glassy essence of a set of glittering but still graceful conceits.

"The fly that sips treacle is lost in the sweets," and the critic

* Scotch for send'st; for complain'st, &c.
† "I was all ear;" see Milton's 'Comus.'

that tastes poetry "ruin meets." His feet are clogged with its honey, and his eyes blinded with its beauties; and he forgets his proper vocation, which is to buzz and sting. I am afraid of losing my way in Drummond's "sugar'd sonnetting:" and have determined more than once to break off abruptly; but another and another tempts the rash hand and curious eye, which I am loth not to give, and I give it accordingly: for if I did not write these Lectures to please myself, I am at least sure I should please nobody else. In fact, I conceive that what I have undertaken to do in this and former cases, is merely to read over a set of authors with the audience, as I would do with a friend, to point out a favourite passage, to explain an objection; or if a remark or a theory occurs, to state it in illustration of the subject, but neither to tire him nor puzzle myself with pedantic rules and pragmatical formulas of criticism that can do no good to anybody. I do not come to the task with a pair of compasses or a ruler in my pocket, to see whether a poem is round or square, or to measure its mechanical dimensions, like a metre and alnager of poetry: it is not in my bond to look after exciseable articles or contraband wares, or to exact severe penalties and forfeitures for trifling oversights, or to give formal notice of violent breaches of the three unities, of geography and chronology; or to distribute printed stamps and poetical licences (with blanks to be filled up) on Mount Parnassus. I do not come armed from top to toe with colons and semi-colons, with glossaries and indexes, to adjust the spelling or reform the metre, or to prove by everlasting contradiction and querulous impatience, that former commentators did not know the meaning of their author, any more than I do, who am angry at them, only because I am out of humour with myself—as if the genius of poetry lay buried under the rubbish of the press; and the critic was the dwarf-enchanter who was to release its airy form from being stuck through with blundering points and misplaced commas; or to prevent its vital powers from being worm-eaten and consumed, letter by letter, in musty manuscripts and black-letter print. I do not think that is the way to learn "the gentle craft" of poesy, or to teach it to others:—to imbibe or to communicate its spirit; which, if it does not disentangle itself and soar above the obscure and trivial re searches of antiquarianism, is no longer itself, "a phœnix gazed by all." At least, so it appeared to me; it is for others to judge whether I was right or wrong. In a word, I have endeavoured to feel what was good, and to "give a reason for the faith that was in me," when necessary, and when in my power. This is what I have done, and what I must continue to do.

To return to Drummond.—I cannot but think that his sonnets come as near as almost any others to the perfection of this kind of writing, which should embody a sentiment, and every shade of a sentiment, as it varies with time and place and humour, with the extravagance or lightness of a momentary impression, and should, when lengthened out into a series, form a history of the wayward moods of the poet's mind, the turns of his fate; and imprint the smile or frown of his mistress in indelible characters on the scattered leaves. I will give the two following, and have done with this author:

"In vain I haunt the cold and silver springs,
To quench the fever burning in my veins:
In vain (love's pilgrim) mountains, dales, and plains
I over-run; vain help long absence brings.
In vain, my friends, your counsel me constrains
To fly, and place my thoughts on other things.
Ah, like the bird that fired hath her wings,
The more I move the greater are my pains.
Desire, alas! desire a Zeuxis new,
From th' orient borrowing gold, from western skies
Heavenly cinnabar, sets before my eyes
In every place her hair, sweet look and hue;
That fly, run, rest I, all doth prove but vain;
My life lies in those eyes which have me slain."

The other is a direct imitation of Petrarch's description of the bower where he first saw Laura:

"Alexis, here she stay'd among these pines,
Sweet hermitress, she did alone repair:
Here did she spread the treasure of her hair,
More rich than that brought from the Colchian mines;
Here sat she by these musked eglantines;
The happy flowers seem yet the print to bear:
Her voice did sweeten here thy sugar'd lines,
To which winds, trees, beasts, birds, did lend an ear.
She here me first perceiv'd, and here a morn
Of bright carnations did o'erspread her face:

> Here did she sigh, here first my hopes were born,
> Here first I got a pledge of promised grace;
> But ah! what serves to have been made happy so,
> Sith past pleasures double but new woe!"

I should, on the whole, prefer Drummond's sonnets to Spenser's; and they leave Sydney's, picking their way through verbal intricacies and "thorny queaches,"* at an immeasurable distance behind. Drummond's other poems have great though not equal merit; and he may be fairly set down as one of our old English classics.

Ben Jonson's detached poetry I like much, as indeed I do all about him, except when he degraded himself by "the laborious foolery" of some of his farcical characters, which he could not deal with sportively, and only made stupid and pedantic. I have been blamed for what I have said, more than once, in disparagement of Ben Jonson's comic humour; but I think he was himself aware of his infirmity, and has (not improbably) alluded to it in the following speech of Crites in 'Cynthia's Revels:'

> "Oh, how despised and base a thing is man,
> If he not strive to erect his groveling thoughts
> Above the strain of flesh! But how more cheap,
> When even his best and understanding part
> (The crown and strength of all his faculties)
> Floats like a dead-drown'd body, on the stream
> Of vulgar humour, mix'd with common'st dregs:
> I suffer for their guilt now; and my soul
> (Like one that looks on ill-affected eyes)
> Is hurt with mere intention on their follies.
> Why will I view them then? my sense might ask me:
> Or is't a rarity or some new object
> That strains my strict observance to this point:
> But such is the perverseness of our nature,
> That if we once but fancy levity,
> (How antic and ridiculous soever
> It suit with us) yet will our muffled thought
> Chuse rather not to see it than avoid it," &c.

Ben Jonson had self-knowledge and self-reflection enough to apply this to himself. His tenaciousness on the score of critical

* Chapman's Hymn to Pan.

objections does not prove that he was not conscious of them himself, but the contrary. The greatest egotists are those whom it is impossible to offend, because they are wholly and incurably blind to their own defects; or if they could be made to see them, would instantly convert them into so many beauty-spots and ornamental graces. Ben Jonson's fugitive and lighter pieces are not devoid of the characteristic merits of that class of composition; but still often in the happiest of them, there is a specific gravity in the author's pen, that sinks him to the bottom of his subject, though buoyed up for a time with art and painted plumes, and produces a strange mixture of the mechanical and fanciful, of poetry and prose, in his songs and odes. For instance, one of his most airy effusions is the 'Triumph of his Mistress:' yet there are some lines in it that seem inserted almost by way of burlesque. It is, however, well worth repeating.

"See the chariot at hand here of love
Wherin my lady rideth!
Each that draws it is a swan or a dove;
And well the car love guideth!
As she goes all hearts do duty
 Unto her beauty:
And enamour'd, do wish so they might
 But enjoy such a sight,
That they still were to run by her side,
Through swords, through seas, whither she would ride.
Do but look on her eyes, they do light
 All that love's world compriseth!
Do but look on her hair, it is bright
 As love's star when it riseth!
Do but mark, her forehead's smoother
 Than words that soothe her:
And from her arch'd brows, such a grace
 Sheds itself through the face,
As alone their triumphs to the life
All the gain, all the good of the elements' strife.

Have you seen but a bright lily glow,
Before rude hands have touch'd it?
Ha' you mark'd but the fall of the snow
Before the soil hath smutch'd it?
Ha' you felt *the wool of beaver?*
Or swan's down ever?

Or have smelt o' the bud o' the briar?
Or *the nard in the fire?*
Or have tasted the bag of the bee?
Oh, so white! Oh, so soft! Oh, so sweet is she!"

His 'Discourse with Cupid,' which follows, is infinitely delicate and *piquant*, and without one single blemish. It is a perfect "nest of spicery."

"Noblest Charis, you that are
Both my fortune and my star!
And do govern more my blood,
Than the various moon the flood!
Hear, what late discourse of you,
Love and I have had; and true.
'Mongst my Muses finding me,
Where he chanc'd your name to see
Set, and to this softer strain;
'Sure,' said he, 'If I have brain,
This here sung can be no other,
By description, but my mother!
So hath Homer prais'd her hair;
So Anacreon drawn the air
Of her face, and made to rise,
Just about her sparkling eyes,
Both her brows bent like my bow.
By her looks I do her know,
Which you call my shafts. And see!
Such my mother's blushes be,
As the bath your verse discloses
In her cheeks, of milk and roses;
Such as oft I wanton in.
And, above her even chin,
Have you plac'd the bank of kisses,
Where you say, men gather blisses,
Ripen'd with a breath more sweet,
Than when flowers and west-winds meet,
Nay, her white and polish'd neck,
With the lace that doth it deck,
Is my mother's! hearts of slain
Lovers, made into a chain!
And between each rising breast
Lies the valley, call'd my nest,
Where I sit and proyne my wings
After flight; and put new stings
To my shafts! Her very name

With my mother's is the same.'—
'I confess all,' I replied,
'And the glass hangs by her side,
And the girdle 'bout her waist,
All is Venus: save unchaste.
But, alas! thou seest the least
Of her good, who is the best
Of her sex; but could'st thou, Love,
Call to mind the forms that strove
For the apple, and those three
Make in one, the same were she.
For this beauty yet doth hide
Something more than thou hast spied.
Outward grace weak love beguiles:
She is Venus when she smiles,
But she's Juno when she walks,
And Minerva when she talks.'"

In one of the songs in 'Cynthia's Revels,' we find, amidst some very pleasing imagery, the origin of a celebrated line in modern poetry—

"Drip, drip, drip, drip, drip," &c.

This has not even the merit of originality, which is hard upon it. Ben Jonson had said two hundred years before,

"Oh, I could still
(Like melting snow upon some craggy hill)
Drop, drop, drop, drop,
Since nature's pride is now a wither'd daffodil."

His 'Ode to the Memory of Sir Lucius Cary and Sir H. Morrison' has been much admired, but I cannot but think it one of his most fantastical and perverse performances.

I cannot, for instance, reconcile myself to such stanzas as these:

"Of which we priests and poets say
Such truths as we expect for happy men,
And there he lives with memory; and Ben

The Stand.

Jonson, who sung this of him, ere he went
Himself to rest,

Or taste a part of that full joy he meant
To have exprest,
In this bright asterism;
Where it were friendship's schism
(Were not his Lucius long with us to tarry)
To separate these twi-
Lights, the Dioscori;
And keep the one half from his Harry.
But fate doth so alternate the design,
While that in Heaven, this light on earth doth shine."

This seems as if because he cannot without difficulty write smoothly, he becomes rough and crabbed in a spirit of defiance, like those persons who cannot behave well in company, and affect rudeness to show their contempt for the opinions of others.

His 'Epistles' are particularly good, equally full of strong sense and sound feeling. They show that he was not without friends, whom he esteemed, and by whom he was deservedly esteemed in return. The controversy started about his character is an idle one, carried on in the mere spirit of contradiction, as if he were either made up entirely of gall, or dipped in "the milk of human kindness." There is no necessity or ground to suppose either. He was no doubt a sturdy, plain-spoken, honest, well-disposed man, inclining more to the severe than the amiable side of things; but his good qualities, learning, talents, and convivial habits preponderated over his defects of temper or manners; and in a course of friendship some difference of character, even a little roughness or acidity, may relish to the palate; and olives may be served up with effect as well as sweetmeats. Ben Jonson, even by his quarrels and jealousies, does not seem to have been curst with the last and damning disqualification for friendship,—heartless indifference. He was also what is understood by a *good fellow*, fond of good cheer and good company: and the first step for others to enjoy your society, is for you to enjoy theirs. If any one can do without the world, it is certain that the world can do quite as well without him. His 'Verses Inviting a Friend to Supper' give us as familiar an idea of his private habits and character, as his 'Epistle to Michael Drayton,' that to Selden, &c.; his 'Lines to the Memory of Shakspeare,' and his noble prose 'Eulogy on Lord Bacon,' in his disgrace. do a favourable one.

Among the best of these (perhaps the very best) is the 'Address to Sir Robert Wroth,' which, besides its manly moral sentiments, conveys a strikingly picturesque description of rural sports and manners at this interesting period:

"How blest art thou, canst love the country, Wroth,
Whether by choice, or fate, or both!
And though so near the city and the court,
Art ta'en with neither's vice nor sport:
That at great times, art no ambitious guest
Of sheriff's dinner, or of mayor's feast;
Nor com'st to view the better cloth of state,
The richer hangings, or the crown-plate;
Nor throng'st (when masquing is) to have a sight
Of the short bravery of the night;
To view the jewels, stuffs, the pains, the wit
There wasted, some not paid for yet!
But canst at home, in thy securer rest,
Live with unbought provision blest;
Free from proud porches or their gilded roofs,
'Mongst lowing heards and solid hoofs:
Along the curled woods and painted meads,
Through which a serpent river leads
To some cool courteous shade, which he calls his,
And makes sleep softer than it is!
Or if thou list the night in watch to break,
A-bed canst hear the loud stag speak,
In spring oft roused for their master's sport,
Who for it makes thy house his court;
Or with thy friends, the heart of all the year,
Divid'st upon the lesser deer;
In autumn, at the partrich mak'st a flight,
And giv'st thy gladder guests the sight;
And in the winter hunt'st the flying hare,
More for thy exercise than fare;
While all that follows, their glad ears appty
To the full greatness of the cry:
Or hawking at the river or the bush,
Or shooting at the greedy thrush,
Thou dost with some delight the day out-wear,
Although the coldest of the year!
The whilst the several seasons thou hast seen
Of flow'ry fields, of copses green,

The mowed meadows, with the fleeced sheep,
And feasts that either shearers keep;
The ripened ears yet humble in their height,
And furrows laden with their weight;
The apple-harvest that doth longer last;
The hogs return'd home fat from mast;
The trees cut out in log; and those boughs made
A fire now, that lent a shade!
Thus Pan and Sylvan having had their rites,
Comus puts in for new delights;
And fills thy open hall with mirth and cheer,
As if in Saturn's reign it were;
Apollo's harp and Hermes' lyre resound,
Nor are the Muses strangers found:
The rout of rural folk come thronging in
(Their rudeness then is thought no sin),
Thy noblest spouse affords them welcome grace:
And the great heroes of her race
Sit mixt with loss of state or reverence.
Freedom doth with degree dispense.
The jolly wassall walks the often round,
And in their cups their cares are drown'd:
They think not then which side the cause shall leese,
Nor how to get the lawyer fees.
Such, and no other, was that age of old,
Which boasts t' have had the head of gold.
And such since thou canst make thine own content,
Strive, Wroth, to live long innocent.
Let others watch in guilty arms, and stand
The fury of a rash command,
Go enter breaches, meet the cannon's rage,
That they may sleep with scars in age,
And show their feathers shot and colours torn,
And brag that they were therefore born.
Let this man sweat, and wrangle at the bar
For every price in every jar,
And change possessions oftener with his breath,
Than either money, war, or death:
Let him, than hardest sires, more disinherit,
And eachwhere boast it as his merit,
To blow up orphans, widows, and their states,
And think his power doth equal Fate's.
Let that go heap a mass of wretched wealth,
Purchas'd by rapine, worse than stealth;
And brooding o'er it sit, with broadest eyes,
Not doing good, scarce when he dies.

Let thousands more go flatter vice, and win,
By being organs to great sin;
Get place and honour, and be glad to keep
The secrets that shall break their sleep:
And, so they ride in purple, eat in plate,
Though poison, think it a great fate.
But thou, my Wroth, if I can truth apply,
Shalt neither that nor this envy:
Thy peace is made; and, when man's state is well,
'Tis better, if he there can dwell.
God wisheth none should wrack on a strange shelf;
To him man's dearer than t' himself.
And howsoever, we may think things sweet,
He always gives what he knows meet;
Which who can use is happy: such be thou.
Thy morning's and thy evening's vow
Be thanks to him, and earnest prayer, to find
A body sound, with sounder mind;
To do thy country service, thyself right;
That neither want do thee affright,
Nor death; but when thy latest sand is spent,
Thou mayst think life a thing but lent."

Of all the poetical Epistles of this period, however, that of Daniel to the Countess of Cumberland, for weight of thought and depth of feeling, bears the palm. The reader will not peruse this effusion with less interest or pleasure, from knowing that it is a favourite with Mr. Wordsworth:

"He that of such a height hath built his mind,
And rear'd the dwelling of his thoughts so strong,
As neither fear nor hope can shake the frame
Of his resolved powers; nor all the wind
Of vanity or malice pierce to wrong
His settled peace, or to disturb the same:
What a fair seat hath he, from whence he may
The boundless wastes and wilds of man survey!
And with how free an eye doth he look down
Upon these lower regions of turmoil,
Where all the storms of passions mainly beat
On flesh and blood; where honour, pow'r, renown,
Are only gay afflictions, golden toil;
Where greatness stands upon as feeble feet
As frailty doth; and only great doth seem
To little minds, who do it so esteem.

He looks upon the mightiest monarch's wars
But only as on stately robberies;
Where evermore the fortune that prevails
Must be the right: the ill-succeeding mars
The fairest and the best fac'd enterprize.
Great pirate Pompey lesser pirates quails:
Justice, he sees (as if seduced) still
Conspires with pow'r, whose cause must not be ill.
He sees the face of right t' appear as manifold
As are the passions of uncertain man;
Who puts it in all colours, all attires,
To serve his ends, and make his courses hold.
He sees, that let deceit work what it can,
Plot and contrive base ways to high desires;
That the all-guiding Providence doth yet
All disappoint, and mocks this smoke of wit.
Nor is he mov'd with all the thunder-cracks
Of tyrants' threats, or with the surly brow
Of pow'r, that proudly sits on others' crimes,
Charg'd with more crying sins than those he checks.
The storms of sad confusion, that may grow
Up in the present for the coming times,
Appal not him; that hath no side at all,
But of himself, and knows the worst can fall.
Although his heart (so near allied to earth)
Cannot but pity the perplexed state
Of troublous and distress'd mortality,
That thus make way unto the ugly hirth
Of their own sorrows, and do still beget
Affliction upon imbecility:
Yet seeing thus the course of things must run,
He looks thereon not strange, but as fore-done.
And whilst distraught ambition compasses,
And is encompass'd; whilst as craft deceives,
And is deceiv'd; whilst man doth ransack man,
And builds on blood, and rises by distress;
And th' inheritance of desolation leaves
To great expecting hopes; he looks thereon,
As from the shore of peace, with unwet eye,
And bears no venture in impiety."

Michael Drayton's 'Poly-Olbion' is a work of great length and of unabated freshness and vigour in itself, though the monotony of the subject tires the reader. He describes each place with the accuracy of a topographer, and the enthusiasm of a poet, as if his muse were the very *genius loci.* His 'Heroical Epistles' are also excellent. He has a few lighter pieces, but none of exquisite beauty or grace. His mind is a rich marly soil that produces an abundant harvest, and repays the husbandman's toil; but few flaunting flowers, the garden's pride, grow in it, nor any poisonous weeds.

P. Fletcher's 'Purple Island' is nothing but a long enigma, describing the body of a man, with the heart and veins, and the blood circulating in them, under the fantastic designation of 'The Purple Island.'

The other poets whom I shall mention, and who properly be long to the age immediately following, were William Browne, Carew, Crashaw, Herrick, and Marvell. Browne was a pastoral poet, with much natural tenderness and sweetness, and a good deal of allegorical quaintness and prolixity. Carew was an elegant court-trifler. Herrick was an amorist, with perhaps more fancy than feeling, though he has been called by some the English Anacreon. Crashaw was a hectic enthusiast in religion and in poetry, and erroneous in both. Marvell deserves to be remembered as a true poet as well as patriot, not in the best of times. I will, however, give short specimens from each of these writers, that the reader may judge for himself, and be led by his own curiosity, rather than my recommendation, to consult the originals. Here is one by T. Carew:

"Ask me no more where Jove bestows,
When June is past, the fading rose:
For in your beauties, orient deep
These flow'rs, as in their causes, sleep.

Ask me no more, whither do stray
The golden atoms of the day;
For in pure love, Heaven did prepare
Those powders to enrich your hair.

Ask me no more, whither doth haste
The nightingale, when May is past;
For in your sweet dividing throat
She winters, and keeps warm her note.

Ask me no more, where those stars light,
That downwards fall in dead of night;

For in your eyes they sit, and there
Fixed become, as in their sphere.

Ask me no more, if east or west
The phœnix builds her spicy nest;
For unto you at last she flies,
And in your fragrant bosom dies."

'The Hue and Cry of Love,' 'The Epitaphs on Lady Mary Villiers,' and 'The Friendly Reproof to Ben Jonson for his Angry Farewell to the Stage,' are in the author's best manner. We may perceive, however, a frequent mixture of the superficial and common-place, with far-fetched and improbable conceits.

Herrick is a writer who does not answer the expectations I had formed of him. He is in a manner a modern discovery, and so far has the freshness of antiquity about him. He is not trite and thread-bare. But neither is he likely to become so. He is a writer of epigrams, not of lyrics. He has point and ingenuity, but I think little of the spirit of love or wine. From his frequent allusion to pearls and rubies, one might take him for a lapidary instead of a poet. One of his pieces is entitled

" *The Rock of Rubies and the Quarry of Pearls.*

Some ask'd me where the rubies grew;
And nothing I did say;
But with my finger pointed to
The lips of Julia.

Some ask'd how pearls did grow, and where;
Then spoke I to my girl
To part her lips, and show them there
The quarrelets of pearl."

Now this is making a petrifaction both of love and poetry.

His poems, from their number and size, are "like the moats that play in the sun's beams;" that glitter to the eye of fancy, but leave no distinct impression on the memory. The two best are a translation of Anacreon, and a successful and spirited imitation of him.

" *The Wounded Cupid.*

Cupid, as he lay among
Roses, by a bee was stung.
Whereupon, in anger flying
To his mother, said thus, crying,
Help, oh help, your boy's a-dying!
And why, my pretty lad? said she.
Then, blubbering, replied he,
A winged snake has bitten me,
Which country-people call a bee.
At which she smiled; then with her hairs
And kisses drying up his tears,
Alas, said she, my wag! if this
Such a pernicious torment is;
Come, tell me then, how great 's the smart
Of those thou woundest with thy dart?"

'The Captive Bee, or the Little Filcher,' is his own:

" As Julia once a slumbering lay,
It chanced a bee did fly that way,
After a dew, or dew-like show'r,
To tipple freely in a flow'r.
For some rich flow'r he took the lip
Of Julia, and began to sip:
But when he felt he suck'd from thence
Honey, and in the quintessence,
He drank so much he scarce could stir;
So Julia took the pilferer.
And thus surpris'd, as filchers use,
He thus began himself to excuse:
Sweet lady-flow'r! I never brought
Hither the least one thieving thought;
But taking those rare lips of your's
For some fresh, fragrant, luscious flow'rs,
I thought I might there take a taste,
Where so much syrup run at waste;
Besides, know this, I never sting
The flow'r that gives me nourishing;
But with a kiss of thanks do pay
For honey that I bear away.
This said, he laid his little scrip
Of honey 'fore her ladyship;
And told her, as some tears did fall,
That that he took, and that was all.
At which she smil'd, and bid him go,

And take his bag, but thus much know,
When next he came a pilfering so,
He should from her full lips derive
Honey enough to fill his hive."

Of Marvell I have spoken with such praise as appears to me his due, on another occasion; but the public are deaf, except to proof or to their own prejudices, and I will therefore give an example of the sweetness and power of his verse.

" *To his Coy Mistress.*

Had we but world enough, and time,
This coyness, lady, were no crime.
We would sit down and think which way
To walk, and pass our long love's day.
Thou by the Indian Ganges' side
Should'st rubies find: I by the tide
Of Humber would complain. I would
Love you ten years before the flood;
And you should, if you please, refuse
Till the conversion of the Jews.
My vegetable love should grow
Vaster than empires, and more slow.
An hundred years should go to praise
Thine eyes, and on thy forehead gaze;
Two hundred to adore each breast;
But thirty thousand to the rest.
An age at least to every part,
And the last age should show your heart.
For, lady, you deserve this state;
Nor would I love at lower rate.
  But at my back I always hear
Time's winged chariot hurrying near:
And yonder all before us lie
Deserts of vast eternity.
Thy beauty shall no more be found;
Nor in thy marble vault shall sound
My echoing song; then worms shall try
That long preserved virginity;
And your quaint honour turn to dust;
And into ashes all my lust.
The grave's a fine and private place,
But none, I think, do there embrace.
  Now, therefore, while the youthful hue
Sits on thy skin, like morning dew,

And while thy willing soul transpires
At every pore with instant fires,
Now let us sport us while we may;
And now, like amorous birds of prey,
Rather at once our time devour,
Than languish in his slow-chapp'd pow'r.
Let us roll all our strength, and all
Our sweetness up into one ball;
And tear our pleasures with rough strife,
Through the iron gates of life.
Thus, though we cannot make our sun
Stand still, yet we will make him run."

In Browne's 'Pastorals,' notwithstanding the weakness and prolixity of his general plan, there are repeated examples of single lines and passages of extreme beauty and delicacy, both of sentiment and description, such as the following Picture of Night:

"Clamour grew dumb, unheard was shepherd's song,
And silence girt the woods: no warbling tongue
Talk'd to the echo; satyrs broke their dance,
And all the upper world lay in a trance,
Only the curled streams soft chidings kept;
And little gales that from the green leaf swept
Dry summer's dust, in fearful whisperings stirr'd,
As loth to waken any singing bird."

Poetical beauties of this sort are scattered, not sparingly, over the green lap of nature through almost every page of our author's writings. His description of the squirrel hunted by mischievous boys, of the flowers stuck in the windows like the hues of the rainbow, and innumerable others, might be quoted.

His 'Philarete' (the fourth song of the 'Shepherd's Pipe') has been said to be the origin of 'Lycidas;' but there is no resemblance, except that both are pastoral elegies for the loss of a friend. 'The Inner Temple Mask' has also been made the foundation of 'Comus,' with as little reason. But so it is: if an author is once detected in borrowing, he will be suspected of plagiarism ever after; and every writer that finds an ingenious or partial editor, will be made to set up his claim to originality against him. A more serious charge of this kind has been urged against the principal character in 'Paradise Lost' (that of Satan), which is said to have been taken from Marino, an Italian poet. Of this we may be able to form some judgment, by a comparison with Crashaw's translation of Marino's 'Sospetto d'Herode.' The description of Satan alluded to is given in the following stanzas :—

"Below the bottom of the great abyss,
There where one centre reconciles all things,
The world's profound heart pants; there placed is
Mischief's old master; close about him clings
A curl'd knot of embracing snakes, that kiss
His correspondent cheeks; these loathsome strings
Hold the perverse prince in eternal ties
Fast bound, since first he forfeited the skies.

The judge of torments, and the king of tears,
He fills a burnish'd throne of quenchless fire;
And for his own fair robes of light, he wears
A gloomy mantle of dark flames; the tire
That crowns his hated head, on high appears;
Where seven tall horns (his empire's pride) aspire;
And, to make up hell's majesty, each horn
Seven crested hydras horribly adorn.

His eyes, the sullen dens of death and night,
Startle the dull air with a dismal red;
Such his fell glances as the fatal light
Of staring comets, that look kingdoms dead.
From his black nostrils and blue lips, in spite
Of hell's own stink, a worser stench is spread.
His breath hell's lightning is; and each deep groan
Disdains to think that heaven thunders alone.

His flaming eyes' dire exhalation
Unto a dreadful pile gives fiery breath;
Whose unconsum'd consumption preys upon
The never-dying life of a long death.
In this sad house of slow destruction
(His shop of flames) he fries himself beneath
A mass of woes; his teeth for torment gnash,
While his steel sides sound with his tail's strong lash."

This portrait of monkish superstition does not equal the grandeur of Milton's description:

—— "His form had not yet lost
All her original brightness, nor appear'd
Less than archangel ruin'd and the excess
Of glory obscured."

Milton has got rid of the horns and tail, the vulgar and physical insignia of the devil, and clothed him with other greater and intellectual terrors, reconciling beauty and sublimity, and converting the grotesque and deformed into the ideal and classical. Certainty, Milton's mind rose superior to all others in this respect, on the outstretched wings of philosophic contemplation, in not confounding the depravity of the will with physical distortion, or supposing that the distinctions of good and evil were only to be subjected to the gross ordeal of the senses. In the subsequent stanzas, we however find the traces of some of Milton's boldest imagery, though its effect be injured by the incongruous mixture above stated.

"Struck with these great concurrences of things,*
Symptoms so deadly unto death and him:
Fain would he have forgot what fatal strings
Eternally bind each rebellious limb,
He shook himself, and spread his spacious wings,
Which like two bosom'd sails† embrace the dim
Air, with a dismal shade, but all in vain:
Of sturdy adamant is his strong chain.

While thus heav'n's counsels, by the low
Footsteps of their effects, he traced too well,
He tost his troubled eyes, embers that glow
Now with new rage, and wax too hot for hell.
With his foul claws he fenced his furrow'd brow,
And gave a ghastly shriek, whose horrid yell
Ran trembling through the hollow vaults of night."

The poet adds–

"The while his twisted tail he gnaw'd for spite."

There is no keeping in this. This action of meanness and mere vulgar spite, common to the most contemptible creatures.

* Alluding to the fulfilment of the prophecies and the birth of the Messiah

† "He spreads his sail-broad vans."—'Par. Lost,' b. ii., l. 927.

takes away from the terror and power just ascribed to the prince of Hell, and implied in the nature of the consequences attributed to his every movement of mind or body. Satan's soliloquy to himself is more beautiful and more in character at the same time:

"Art thou not Lucifer? he to whom the droves
Of stars that gild the morn in charge were given?
The nimblest of the lightning-winged loves?
The fairest and the first-born smile of heav'n?
Look in what pomp the mistress planet moves,
Reverently circled by the lesser seven:
Such and so rich the flames that from thine eyes
Opprest the common people of the skies?
Ah! wretch! what boots it to cast back thine eyes
Where dawning hope no beam of comfort shows?" &c.

This is true beauty and true sublimity: it is also true pathos and morality: for it interests the mind, and affects it powerfully with the idea of glory tarnished, and happiness forfeited with the loss of virtue; but from the horns and tail of the brute-demon, imagination cannot re-ascend to the Son of the morning, nor be dejected by the transition from weal to woe, which it cannot without a violent effort picture to itself.

In our author's account of Cruelty, the chief minister of Satan, there is also a considerable approach to Milton's description of Death and Sin, the portress of hell-gates:

"Thrice howl'd the caves of night, and thrice the sound,
Thundering upon the banks of those black lakes,
Rung through the hollow vaults of hell profound:
At last her listening ears the noise o'ertakes,
She lifts her sooty lamps and looking round,
A general hiss,* from the whole tire of snakes
Rebounding through hell's inmost caverns came,
In answer to her formidable name.

'Mongst all the palaces in hell's command,
No one so merciless as this of hers,
The adamantine doors for ever stand
Impenetrable, both to prayers and tears.

* See Satan's reception on his return to Pandemonium, in book x. of 'Paradise Lost.'

> The walls' inexorable steel, no hand
> Of time, or teeth of hungry ruin fears."

On the whole, this poem, though Milton has undoubtedly availed himself of many ideas and passages in it, raises instead of lowering our conception of him, by showing how much more he added to it than he has taken from it.

Crashaw's translation of Strada's description of the contention between a nightingale and a musician, is elaborate and spirited, but not equal to Ford's version of the same story in his 'Lover's Melancholy.' One line may serve as a specimen of delicate quaintness, and of Crashaw's style in general:

> "And with a quavering coyness tastes the strings."

Sir Philip Sidney is a writer for whom I cannot acquire a taste. As Mr. Burke said, "he could not love the French Republic"—so I may say, that I cannot love 'The Countess of Pembroke's Arcadia,' with all my good-will to it. It will not do for me, however, to imitate the summary petulance of the epigrammatist:

> "The reason why I cannot tell,
> But I don't like thee, Dr. Fell."

I must give my reasons, "on compulsion," for not speaking well of a person like Sir Philip Sidney—

> "The soldier's, scholar's, courtier's eye, tongue, sword,
> The glass of fashion, and the mould of form;"

the splendour of whose personal accomplishments, and of whose wide-spread fame, was, in his life-time,

> ——— "Like a gate of steel,
> Fronting the sun, that renders back
> His figure and his heat"

a writer, too, who was universally read and enthusiastically admired for a century after his death, and who has been admired with scarce less enthusiastic, but with a more distant homage, for another century, after ceasing to be read.

We have lost the art of reading, or the privilege of writing, voluminously, since the days of Addison. Learning no longer weaves the interminable page with patient drudgery, nor ignorance pores over it with implicit faith. As authors multiply in number, books diminish in size; we cannot now, as formerly, swallow libraries whole in a single folio: solid quarto has given place to slender duodecimo, and the dingy letter-press contracts its dimensions, and retreats before the white, unsullied, faultless margin. Modern authorship is become a species of stenography: we contrive even to read by proxy. We skim the cream of prose without any trouble; we get at the quintessence of poetry without loss of time. The staple commodity, the coarse, heavy, dirty, unwieldy bullion of books, is driven out of the market of learning, and the intercourse of the literary world is carried on, and the credit of the great capitalists sustained by the flimsy circulating medium of magazines and reviews. Those who are chiefly concerned in catering for the taste of others, and serving up critical opinions in a compendious, elegant, and portable form, are not forgetful of themselves: they are not scrupulously solicitous, idly inquisitive, about the real merits, the *bona fide* contents of the works they are deputed to appraise and value, any more than the reading public who employ them. They look no farther for the contents of the work than the title-page, and pronounce a peremptory decision on its merits or defects by a glance at the name and party of the writer. This state of polite letters seems to admit of improvement in only one respect, which is to go a step farther, and write for the amusement and edification of the world, accounts of works that were never either written or read at all, and to cry up or abuse the authors by name, though they have no existence but in the critic's invention. This would save a great deal of labour in vain; anonymous critics might pounce upon the defenceless heads of fictitious candidates for fame and bread; reviews, from being novels founded upon facts, would aspire to be pure romances; and we should arrive at the *beau ideal* of a commonwealth of letters, at the euthanasia of thought, and millennium of criticism!

At the time that Sir Philip Sidney's 'Arcadia' was written, those middle-men, the critics, were not known. The author and reader came into immediate contact, and seemed never tired of each other's company. We are more fastidious and dissipated the effeminacy of modern taste would, I am afraid, shrink back affrighted at the formidable sight of this once popular work, which is about as long (*horresco referens!*) as all Walter Scott's novels put together; but besides its size and appearance, it has, I think, other defects of a more intrinsic and insuperable nature. It is to me one of the greatest monuments of the abuse of intellectual power upon record. It puts one in mind of the court dresses and preposterous fashions of the time, which are grown obsolete and disgusting. It is not romantic, but scholastic; not poetry, but casuistry; not nature, but art, and the worst sort of art, which thinks it can do better than nature. Of the number of fine things that are constantly passing through the author's mind, there is hardly one that he has not contrived to spoil, and to spoil purposely and maliciously, in order to aggrandize our idea of himself. Out of five hundred folio pages, there are hardly, I conceive, half a dozen sentences expressed simply and directly, with the sincere desire to convey the image implied, and without a systematic interpolation of the wit, learning, ingenuity, wisdom, and everlasting impertinence of the writer, so as to disguise the object, instead of displaying it in its true colours and real proportions. Every page is with "centric and eccentric scribbled o'er;" his muse is tattooed and tricked out like an Indian goddess. He writes a court-hand, with flourishes like a schoolmaster; his figures are wrought in chain-stitch. All his thoughts are forced and painful births, and may be said to be delivered by the Cæsarean operation. At last, they become distorted and rickety in themselves; and before they have been cramped and twisted and swaddled into lifelessness and deformity. Imagine a writer to have great natural talents, great powers of memory and invention, an eye for nature, a knowledge of the passions, much learning, and equal industry: but that he is so full of a consciousness of all this, and so determined to make the reader conscious of it at every step, that he becomes a complete intellectual coxcomb, or nearly so;—that he never lets a casual observation pass without perplexing it with an endless, running commentary, that he never states a feeling without so many *circumambages*, without so many interlineations and parenthetical remarks on all that can be said for it, and anticipations of all that can be said against it, and that he never mentions a fact without giving so many circumstances, and conjuring up so many things that it is like or not like, that you lose the main clue of the story in its infinite ramifications and intersections; and we may form some faint idea of 'The Countess of Pembroke's Arcadia,' which is spun with great labour out of the author's brains, and hangs like a huge cobweb over the face of nature! This is not, as far as I can judge, an exaggerated description; but as near the truth as I can make it. The proofs are not far to seek. Take the first sentence, or open the volume anywhere and read. I will, however, take one of the most beautiful passages, near the beginning, to show how the subject matter, of which the noblest use might have been made, is disfigured by the affectation of the style, and the importunate and vain activity of the writer's mind. The passage I allude to is the celebrated description of Arcadia.

"So that the third day after, in the time that the morning did strew roses and violets in the heavenly floor against the coming of the sun, the nightingales (striving one with the other which could in most dainty variety recount their wrong-caused sorrow) made them put off their sleep, and rising from under a tree (which that night had been their pavilion) they went on their journey, which by-and-by welcomed Musidorus' eyes (wearied with the wasted soil of Laconia) with welcome prospects. There were hills which garnished their proud heights with stately trees: humble valleys whose base estate seemed comforted with the refreshing of silver rivers; meadows enamelled with all sorts of eye-pleasing flowers; thickets, which being lined with most pleasant shade were witnessed so to, by the cheerful disposition of many well-tuned birds; each pasture stored with sheep feeding with sober security, while the pretty lambs, with bleating oratory craved the dam's comfort; here a shepherd's boy piping, as though he should never be old: there a young shepherdess knitting, and withal singing, and it seemed that her voice comforted her hands to work, and her hands kept time to her voice-music. As for the houses of the country (for many houses came under their eye) they were scattered, no two being one by the other, and yet not so far off, as that it barred mutual succour; a show, as it were, of an accompaniable solitariness, and of a civil wildness. I pray you, said Musidorus (then first unsealing his long-silent lips), what countries be these we pass through, which are so divers in show, the one wanting no store, the other having no store but of want? The country, answered Claius, where you were cast ashore, and now are passed through, is Laconia; but this country (where you now set your foot) is Arcadia."

One would think the very name might have lulled his senses to delightful repose in some still, lonely valley, and have laid the restless spirit of Gothic quaintness, witticism, and conceit in the lap of classic elegance and pastoral simplicity. Here are images, too, of touching beauty and everlasting truth that needed nothing but to be simply and nakedly expressed to have made a picture equal (nay superior) to the allegorical representation of 'The Four Seasons of Life,' by Giorgione. But no! He cannot let his imagination, or that of the reader, dwell for a moment on the beauty or power of the real object. He thinks nothing is done, unless it is his doing. He must officiously and gratuitously interpose between you and the subject, as the Cicerone of Nature, distracting the eye and the mind by continual uncalled-for interruptions, analyzing, dissecting, disjointing, murdering everything, and reading a pragmatical, self-sufficient lecture over the dead body of nature. The moving-spring of his mind is not sensibility or imagination, but dry, literal, unceasing craving after intellectual excitement, which is indifferent to pleasure or pain, to beauty or deformity, and likes to owe everything to its own perverse efforts, rather than the sense of power in other things. It constantly interferes to perplex and neutralize. It never leaves the mind in a wise passiveness. In the infancy of taste, the froward pupils of art took nature to pieces, as spoiled children do a watch, to see what was in it. After taking it to pieces they could not, with all their cunning, put it together again, so as to restore circulation to the heart, or its living hue to the face! The quaint and pedantic style here objected to was not, however, the natural growth of untutored fancy, but an artificial excrescence transferred from logic and rhetoric to poetry. It was not owing to the excess of imagination, but of the want of it, that is, to the predominance of the mere understanding or dialectic faculty over the imaginative and the sensitive. It is, in fact, poetry degenerating at every step into prose, sentiment entangling itself into a controversy, from the habitual leaven of polemics and casuistry in the writer's mind. The poet insists upon matters of fact from the beauty or grandeur that accompanies them; our prose-poet insists upon them because they are matters of fact, and buries the beauty and grandeur in a heap of common rubbish, "like two grains of wheat in a bushel of chaff." The true poet illustrates for ornament or use: the fantastic pretender only because he is not easy till he can translate everything out of itself into something else. Imagination consists in enriching one idea by another, which has the same feeling or set of associations belonging to it in a higher or more striking degree; the quaint or scholastic style consists in comparing one thing to another by the mere process of abstraction, and the more forced and naked the comparison, the less of harmony or congruity there is in it, the more wire-drawn and ambiguous the link of generalization by which objects are brought together, the greater is the triumph of the false and fanciful style. There was a marked instance of the difference in some lines from Ben Jonson, which I have above quoted, and which, as they are alternate examples of the extremes of both in the same author, and in the same short poem, there can be nothing invidious in giving. In conveying an idea of female softness and sweetness, he asks—

"Have you felt the wool of the beaver,
Or swan's down ever?
Or smelt of the bud of the briar,
Or the nard in the fire?"

Now "the swan's down" is a striking and beautiful image of the most delicate and yielding softness; but we have no associations of a pleasing sort with the wool of the beaver. The comparison is dry, hard, and barren of effect. It may establish the matter of fact, but detracts from and impairs the sentiment. The smell of the "bud of the briar" is a double-distilled essence of sweetness: besides, there are all the other concomitant ideas of youth, beauty, and blushing modesty, which blend with and heighten the immediate feeling: but the poetical reader was not bound to know even what *nard* is (it is merely a learned substance, a nonentity to the imagination), nor whether it has a fragrant or disagreeable scent when thrown into the fire, till Ben Jonson went out of his way to give him this pedantic piece of information. It is a mere matter of fact or of experiment; and while the experiment is making in reality or fancy, the sentiment stands still; or even taking it for granted in the literal and scientific sense, we are where we were; it does not enhance the passion to be expressed: we have no love for the smell of nard in the fire, but we have an old, a long cherished one from infancy, for the bud of the briar. Sentiment, as Mr. Burke said of nobility, is a thing of inveterate prejudice; and cannot be created, as some people (learned and unlearned) are inclined to suppose, out of fancy or out of anything by the wit of man. The artificial and natural style do not alternate in this way in the 'Arcadia:' the one is but the Helot, the eyeless drudge of the other. Thus even in the above passage, which is comparatively beautiful and simple in its general structure, we have "the bleating oratory" of lambs, as if anything could be more unlike oratory than the bleating of lambs. We have a young shepherdess knitting, whose hands keep time not to her voice, but to her "voice-music," which introduces a foreign and questionable distinction, merely to perplex the subject; we have meadows enamelled with all the sorts of "eye-pleasing flowers," as if it were necessary to inform the reader that flowers pleased the eye, or as if they did not please any other sense: we have valleys refreshed "with *silver* streams," an epithet that has nothing to do with the refreshment here spoken of: we have "an accompaniable solitariness and a civil wildness," which are a pair of very laboured antitheses; in fine, we have "want of store, and store of want."

Again, the passage describing the shipwreck of Pyrochles has been much and deservedly admired: yet it is not free from the same inherent faults.

"But a little way off they saw the mast (of the vessel) whose proud height now lay along, like a widow having lost her mate, of whom she held her honour." [This needed explanation.] "But upon the mast they saw a young man (at least if it were a man) bearing show of about eighteen years of age, who sat (as on horseback) having nothing upon him but his shirt, which being wrought with blue silk and gold, had a kind of resemblance to the sea," [this is a sort of alliteration in natural history,] "on which the sun [then near his western home] did shoot some of his beams. His hair [which the young men of Greece used to wear very long] was stirred up and down with the wind, which seemed to have a sport to play with it, as the sea had to kiss his feet; himself full of admirable beauty, set forth by the strangeness both of his seat and gesture; for, holding his head up full of unmoved majesty, he held a sword aloft with his fair arm, which often he waved about his crown, as though he would threaten the world in that extremity."

If the original sin of alliteration, antithesis, and metaphysical conceit could be weeded out of this passage, there is hardly a more heroic one to be found in prose or poetry.

Here is one more passage marred in the making. A shepherd is supposed to say of his mistress,

"Certainly, as her eyelids are more pleasant to behold than two white kids climbing up a fair tree and browsing on its tenderest branches, and yet are nothing compared to the day-shining stars contained in them; and as her breath is more sweet than a gentle south-west wind, which comes creeping over flowery fields and shadowed waters in the extreme heat of summer; and yet is nothing compared to the honey-flowing speech that breath doth carry; no more all that our eyes can see of her [though when they have seen her, what else they shall ever see is but dry stubble after clover grass], is to be matched with the flock of unspeakable virtues laid up delightfully in that best builded fold."

Now here are images of singular beauty and of Eastern originality and daring, followed up with enigmatical or unmeaning common-places, because he never knows when to leave off, and thinks he can never be too wise or too dull for his reader. He loads his prose Pegasus like a pack-horse, with all that comes, and with a number of little trifling circumstances, that fall off, and you are obliged to stop to pick them up by the way. He cannot give his imagination a moment's pause, thinks nothing done while any thing remains to do, and exhausts nearly all that can be said upon the subject, whether good, bad, or indifferent. The above passages are taken from the beginning of the 'Arcadia,' when the author's style was hardly yet formed. The following is a less favourable, but fairer specimen of the work. It is the model of a love-letter, and is only longer than that of Adriano de Armada, in 'Love's Labour's Lost.'

"Most blessed paper, which shall kiss that hand, whereto all blessedness is in nature a servant, do not yet disdain to carry with thee the woful words of a miser now despairing: neither be afraid to appear before her, bearing the base title of the sender. For no sooner shall that divine hand touch thee, bu that thy baseness shall be turned to most high preferment. Therefore mourn boldly my ink: for while she looks upon you your blackness will shine: cry put boldly my lamentation, for while she reads you your cries will be music. Say then (O happy messenger of a most unhappy message) that the too soon born and too late dying creature, which dares not speak, no, not look, no not scarcely think (as from his miserable self unto her heavenly highness) only presumes to desire thee (in the time that her eyes and voice do exalt thee) to say, and in this manner to say, not from him, oh, no, that were not fit, but of him, thus much unto her sacred judgment. O you, the only honour to women, to men the admiration, you that being armed by love, defy him that armed you in this high estate wherein you have placed me" [*i. e.* the letter], "yet let me remember him to whom I am bound for bringing me to your presence: and let me remember him, who (since he is yours, how mean soever he be) it is reason you have an account of him. The wretch (yet your wretch) though with languishing steps runs fast to his grave; and will you suffer a temple (how poorly built soever, but yet a temple of your deity) to be rased? But he dieth: it is most true, he dieth: and he in whom you live, to obey you, dieth. Whereof though he plain, he doth not complain: for it is a harm, but no wrong, which he hath received. He dies, because in woeful language all his senses tell him, that such is your pleasure: for if you will not that he live, alas, alas, what followeth, what followeth of the most ruined Dorus, but his end? End, then, evil destined Dorus, end; and end, thou woeful letter, end; for it sufficeth her wisdom to know, that her heavenly will shall be accomplished."—Lib. ii., p. 117.

This style relishes neither of the lover nor the poet. Nine-tenths of the work are written in this manner. It is in the very manner of those books of gallantry and chivalry, which, with the labyrinths of their style, and "the reason of their unreasonableness," turned the fine intellects of the Knight of La Mancha. In a word (and not to speak it profanely), the Arcadia is a riddle, a rebus, an acrostic in folio: it contains about 4,000 far-fetched similes, and 6,000 impracticable dilemmas; about 10,000 reasons for doing nothing at all, and as many more against it; numberless alliterations, puns, questions and commands, and other figures of rhetoric; about a score good passages that one may turn to with pleasure, and the most involved, irksome, improgressive, and heteroclite subject that ever was chosen to exercise the pen or patience of man. It no longer adorns the toilette or lies upon the pillow of Maids of Honour and Peeresses in their own right (the Pamelas and Philocleas of a later age), but remains upon the shelves of the libraries of the curious in long works and great names, a monument to show that the author was one of the ablest men and worst writers of the age of Elizabeth.

His Sonnets, inlaid in the Arcadia, are jejune, far-fetched and frigid. I shall select only one that has been much commended. It is 'To the Highway, where his Mistress had passed,' a strange subject, but not unsuitable to the author's genius.

> " Highway, since you my chief Parnassus be,
> And that my Muse (to some ears not unsweet)
> Tempers her words to trampling horses' feet
> More oft than to a chamber melody;
> Now blessed you bear onward blessed me
> To her, where I my heart safe left shall meet;
> My Muse, and I must you of duty greet
> With thanks and wishes, wishing thankfully.
> Be you still fair, honoured by public heed,
> By no encroachment wrong'd, nor time forgot:
> Nor blamed for blood, nor shamed for sinful deed;
> And that you know, I envy you no lot
> Of highest wish, I wish you so much bliss,
> Hundreds of years you Stella's feet may kiss."

The answer of the Highway has not been preserved, but the sincerity of this appeal must no doubt have moved the stocks and stones to rise and sympathize. His 'Defence of Poesy' is his most readable performance; there he is quite at home, in a sort of special pleader's office, where his ingenuity, scholastic subtlety, and tenaciousness in argument stand him in good stead; and he brings off poetry with flying colours; for he was a man of wit, of sense, and learning, though not a poet of true taste or unsophisticated genius.

LECTURE VII.

Character of Lord Bacon's Works—compared as to style with Sir Thomas Brown and Jeremy Taylor.

Lord Bacon has been called (and justly) one of the wisest of mankind. The word *wisdom* characterizes him more than any other. It was not that he did so much himself to advance the knowledge of man or nature, as that he saw what others had done to advance it, and what was still wanting to its full accomplishment. He stood upon the high 'vantage ground of genius and learning; and traced, "as in a map the voyager his course," the long devious march of human intellect, its elevations and depressions, its windings and its errors. He had a "large discourse of reason, looking before and after." He had made an exact and extensive survey of human acquirements: he took the gauge and metre, the depths and soundings of human capacity. He was master of the comparative anatomy of the mind of man, of the balance of power among the different faculties. He had thoroughly investigated and carefully registered the steps and processes of his own thoughts, with their irregularities and failures, their liabilities to wrong conclusions, either from the difficulties of the subject, or from moral causes, from prejudice, indolence, vanity, from conscious strength or weakness; and he applied this self-knowledge on a mighty scale to the general advances or retrograde movements of the aggregate intellect of the world. He knew well what the goal and crown of moral and intellectual power was, how far men had fallen short of it, and how they came to miss it. He had an instantaneous perception of the quantity of truth or good in any given system; and of the analogy of any given result or principle to others of the same kind scattered through nature or history. His observations take in a larger range, have more profundity from the fineness of his tact, and more comprehension from the extent of his knowledge, along the line of which his imagination ran with equal celerity and certainty, than any other person's whose writings I know. He however seized upon these results, rather by intuition than by inference: he knew them in their mixed modes and combined effects, rather than by abstraction or analysis, as he explains them to others, not by resolving them into their component parts and elementary principles, so much as by illustrations drawn from other things operating in like manner, and producing similar results; or, as he himself has finely expressed it, "by the same footsteps of nature treading or printing upon several subjects or matters." He had great sagacity of observation, solidity of judgment and scope of fancy; in this resembling Plato and Burke, that he was a popular philosopher and philosophical declaimer. His writings have the gravity of prose with the fervour and vividness of poetry. His sayings have the effect of axioms, and are at once striking and self-evident. He views objects from the greatest height, and his reflections acquire a sublimity in proportion to their profundity, as in deep wells of water we see the sparkling of the highest fixed stars. The chain of thought reaches to the centre, and ascends the brightest heaven of invention. Reason in him works like an instinct; and his slightest suggestions carry the force of conviction. His opinions are judicial. His induction of particulars is alike wonderful for learning and vivacity, for curiosity and dignity, and an all-prevading intellect binds the whole together in a graceful and pleasing form. His style is equally sharp and sweet, flowing and pithy, condensed and expansive, expressing volumes in a sentence, or amplifying a single thought into pages of rich, glowing, and delightful eloquence. He had great liberality from seeing the various aspects of things (there was nothing bigotted, or intolerant, or exclusive about him), and yet he had firmness and decision from feeling their weight and consequences. His character was then an amazing insight into the limits of human knowledge and acquaintance with the landmarks of human intellect, so as to trace its past history or point out the path to future inquirers, but when he quits the ground of contemplation of what others have done or left undone to project himself into future discoveries, he becomes quaint and fantastic, instead of original. His strength was in reflection, not in production; he was the surveyor, not the builder of the fabric of science. He had not strictly the constructive faculty. He was the principal pioneer in the march of modern philosophy, and has completed the education and discipline of the mind for the acquisition of truth, by explaining all the impediments or furtherances that can be applied to it or cleared out of its way. In a word, he was one of the greatest men this country has to boast, and his name deserves to stand, where it is generally placed, by the side of those of our greatest writers, whether we consider the variety, the strength, or the splendour of his faculties, for ornament or use.

His 'Advancement of Learning' is his greatest work; and next to that I like the 'Essays;' for the 'Novum Organum' is more laboured and less effectual than it might be. I shall give a few instances from the first of these chiefly, to explain the scope of the above remarks.

'The Advancement of Learning' is dedicated to James I., and he there observes, with a mixture of truth and flattery, which looks very much like a bold irony—

"I am well assured that this which I shall say is no amplification at all, but a positive and measured truth: which is, that there hath not been, since Christ's time, any king or temporal monarch which hath been so learned in all literature and erudition, divine and human (as your majesty). For let a man seriously and diligently revolve and peruse the succession of the Emperors of Rome, of which Cæsar the Dictator, who lived some years before Christ, and Marcus Antoninus, were the best-learned; and so descend to the Emperors of Grecia, or of the West, and then to the lines of France, Spain, England, Scotland, and the rest, and he shall find this judgment is truly made. For it seemeth much in a king, if by the compendious extractions of other men's wits and labour, he can take hold of any superficial ornaments and shows of learning, or if he countenance and prefer learning and learned men; but to drink indeed of the true fountain of learning, nay, to have such a fountain of learning in himself, in a king, and in a king born, is almost a miracle."

To any one less wrapped up in self-sufficiency than James, the rule would have been more staggering than the exception could have been gratifying. But Bacon was a sort of prose-laureate to the reigning prince, and his loyalty had never been suspected

In recommending learned men as fit counsellors in a state, he thus points out the deficiencies of the mere empiric or man of business, in not being provided against uncommon emergencies. —" Neither," he says, " can the experience of one man's life furnish examples and precedents for the events of another man's life. For, as it happeneth sometimes, that the grand-child, or other descendant, resembleth the ancestor more than the son; so many times occurrences of present times may sort better with ancient examples, than with those of the latter or immediate times; and lastly, the wit of one man can no more countervail learning, than one man's means can hold way with a common purse."—This is finely put. It might be added, on the other hand, by way of caution, that neither can the wit or opinion of one learned man set itself up, as it sometimes does, in opposition to the common sense or experience of mankind.

When he goes on to vindicate the superiority of the scholar over the mere politician in disinterestedness and inflexibility of principle, by arguing ingeniously enough—" The corrupter sort of mere politiques, that have not their thoughts established by learning in the love and apprehension of duty, nor never look abroad into universality, do refer all things to themselves and thrust themselves into the centre of the world, as if all times should meet in them and their fortunes, never caring, in all tempests, what becomes of the ship of estates, so they may save themselves in the cock-boat of their own fortune; whereas men that feel the weight of duty, and know the limits of self-love, use to make good their places and duties, though with peril."—I can only wish that the practice were as constant as the theory is plausible, or that the time gave evidence of as much stability and sincerity of principle in well-educated minds as it does of versatility and gross egotism in self-taught men. I need not give the instances, " they will receive" (in our author's phrase) " an open allowance:" but I am afraid that neither habits of abstraction nor the want of them will entirely exempt men from a bias to their own interest; that it is neither learning nor ignorance that thrusts us into the centre of our own little world, but that it is nature that has put man there!

His character of the school-men is perhaps the finest philosophical sketch that was ever drawn. After observing that there are "two marks and badges of suspected and falsified science; the one, the novelty and strangeness of terms, the other the strictness of positions, which of necessity doth induce oppositions, and so questions and altercations"—he proceeds—"Surely like as many substances in nature which are solid, do putrefy and corrupt into worms; so it is the property of good and sound knowledge to putrefy and dissolve into a number of subtle, idle, unwholesome, and (as I may term them) *vermiculate* questions; which have, indeed, a kind of quickness and life of spirit, but no soundness of matter or goodness of quality. This kind of degenerate learning did chiefly reign amongst the school-men, who, having sharp and strong wits, and abundance of leisure, and small variety of reading; but their wits being shut up in the cells of a few authors (chiefly Aristotle their dictator) as their persons were shut up in the cells of monasteries and colleges, and knowing little history, either of nature or time, did out of no great quantity of matter, and infinite agitation of wit, spin out unto us those laborious webs of learning which are extant in their books. For the wit and mind of man, if it work upon matter, which is the contemplation of the creatures of God, worketh according to the stuff, and is limited thereby; but if it work upon itself, as the spider worketh his web, then it is endless, and brings forth indeed cobwebs of learning, admirable for the fineness of thread and work, but of no substance or profit."

And a little further on, he adds—"Notwithstanding, certain it is, that if those school-men, to their great thirst of truth and unwearied travel of wit, had joined variety and universality of reading and contemplation, they had proved excellent lights to the great advancement of all learning and knowledge; but, as they are, they are great undertakers indeed, and fierce with dark keeping. But, as in the inquiry of the divine truth, their pride inclined to leave the oracle of God's word, and to varnish in the mixture of their own inventions; so in the inquisition of nature, they ever left the oracle of God's works, and adored the deceiving and deformed images which the unequal mirror of their own minds, or a few received authors or principles did represent unto them."

One of his acutest (I might have said profoundest) remarks relates to the near connection between deceiving and being deceived. Volumes might be written in explanation of it. "This vice, therefore," he says, "brancheth itself into two sorts; delight in deceiving, an aptness to be deceived, imposture and credulity; which, although they appear to be of a diverse nature, the one seeming to proceed of cunning, and the other of simplicity, yet certainly they do for the most part concur. For, as the verse noteth, *Percontatorem fugito, nam garrulus idem est;* an inquisitive man is a prattler: so upon the like reason, a credulous man is a deceiver; as we see it in fame, that he that will easily believe rumours will as easily augment rumours, and add somewhat to them of his own, which Tacitus wisely noteth, when he saith *Fingunt simul creduntque,* so great an affinity hath fiction and belief."

I proceed to his account of the causes of error, and directions for the conduct of the understanding, which are admirable both for their speculative ingenuity and practical use:

"The first of these," says Lord Bacon, "is the extreme affection of two anxieties: the one antiquity, the other novelty, wherein it seemeth the children of time do take after the nature and malice of the father. For as he devoureth his children, so one of them seeketh to devour and suppress the other; while antiquity envieth there should be new additions, and novelty cannot be content to add, but it must deface. Surely, the advice of the prophet is the true direction in this respect, *State super vias antiquas, et videte quænam sit via recta et bona, et ambulate in ea.* Antiquity deserveth that reverence, that men should make a stand thereupon, and discover what is the best way, but when the discovery is well taken, then to take progression. And to speak truly," he adds, "*Antiquitas seculi juventus mundi.* These times are the ancient times when the world is ancient; and not those which we count ancient *ordine retrogrado,* by a computation backwards from ourselves.

"Another error, induced by the former, is a distrust that anything should be now to be found out which the world should have missed and passed over so long time, as if the same objection were to be made to time that Lucian makes to Jupiter and other the Heathen Gods, of which he wondereth that they begot so many children in old age, and begot none in his time, and asketh whether they were become septuagenary, or whether the law *Papia* made against old men's marriages had restrained them. So it seemeth men doubt, lest time was become past children and generation; wherein, contrary-wise, we see commonly the levity and unconstancy of men's judgments, which, till a matter be done, wonder that it can be done, and as soon as it is done wonder again that it was done no sooner, as we see in the expedition of Alexander into

Asia, which at first was prejudged as a vast and impossible enterprise, and yet afterwards it pleaseth Livy to make no more of it than this, *nil aliud quam bene ausus vana contemnere.* And the same happened to Columbus in his western navigation. But in intellectual matters it is much more common; as may be seen in most of the propositions in Euclid, which till they be demonstrate, they seem strange to our assent, but being demonstrate, our mind accepteth of them by a kind of relation (as the lawyers speak,) as if we had known them before.

"Another is an impatience of doubt and haste to assertion without due and mature suspension of judgment. For the two ways of contemplation are not unlike the two ways of action, commonly spoken of by the ancients. The one plain and smooth in the beginning, and in the end impassable; the other rough and troublesome in the entrance, but, after a while, fair and even; so it is in contemplation, if a man will begin with certainties, he shall end in doubts; but if he will be content to begin with doubts, he shall end in certainties.

"Another error is in the manner of the tradition or delivery of knowledge, which is for the most part magistral and peremptory, and not ingenuous and faithful; in a sort, as may be soonest believed, and not easiliest examined. It is true, that in compendious treatises for practice, that form is not to be disallowed. But in the true handling of knowledge, men ought not to fall either on the one side into the vein of Velleius the Epicurean: *nil tam metuens quam ne dubitare aliqua de re videretur;* nor, on the other side, into Socrates his ironical doubting of all things, but to propound things sincerely, with more or less asseveration; as they stand in a man's own judgment, proved more or less."

Lord Bacon in this part declares, "that it is not his purpose to enter into a laudative of learning or to make a hymn to the Muses," yet he has gone near to do this in the following observations on the dignity of knowledge. He says, after speaking of rulers and conquerors:—

"But the commandment of knowledge is yet higher than the commandment over the will: for it is a commandment over the reason, belief, and understanding of man, which is the highest part of the mind, and giveth law to the will itself. For there is no power on earth which setteth a throne or chair of estate in the spirits and souls of men, and in their cogitations, imaginations, opinions, and beliefs, but knowledge and learning. And therefore we see the detestable and extreme pleasure that arch-heretics and false prophets and impostors are transported with, when they once find in themselves that they have a superiority in the faith and conscience of men; so great, as if they have once tasted of it, it is seldom seen that any torture or persecution can make them relinquish or abandon it. But as this is that which the author of the Revelations calls the depth or profoundness of Satan; so by argument of contraries, the just and lawful sovereignty over men's understanding, by force of truth rightly interpreted, is that which approacheth nearest to the similitude of the Divine rule. . . . . Let us conclude with the dignity and excellency of knowledge and learning in that whereunto man's nature doth most aspire, which is immortality or continuance: for to this tendeth generation, and raising of houses and families; to this tendeth buildings, foundations, and monuments; to this tendeth the desire of memory, fame, and celebration, and in effect the strength of all other humane desires; we see then how far the monuments of wit and learning are more durable than the monuments of power or of the hands. For, have not the verses of Homer continued twenty-five hundred years and more, without the loss of a syllable or letter; during which time infinite palaces, temples, castles, cities, have been decayed and demolished? It is not possible to have the true pictures or statues of Cyrus, Alexander, Cæsar, no, nor of the kings or great personages of much later years. For the originals cannot last: and the copies cannot but lose of the life and truth. But the images of men's wits and knowledge remain in books, exempted from the wrong of time, and capable of perpetual renovation. Neither are they fitly to be called images, because they generate still, and cast their seeds in the minds of others, provoking and causing infinite actions and opinions in succeeding ages. So that, if the invention of the ship was thought so noble, which carrieth riches and commodities from place to place, and consociateth the most remote regions in participation of their fruits, how much more are letters to be magnified, which, as ships, pass through the vast seas of time, and make ages so distant to participate of the wisdom, illuminations, and inventions the one of the other?"

Passages of equal force and beauty might be quoted from almost every page of this work and of the Essays.

Sir Thomas Brown and Bishop Taylor were two prose-writers in the succeeding age, who, for pomp and copiousness of style, might be compared to Lord Bacon. In all other respects they were opposed to him and to one another.—As Bacon seemed to bend all his thoughts to the practice of life, and to bring home the light of science to "the bosoms and businesses of men," Sir Thomas Brown seemed to be of opinion that the only business of life was to think, and that the proper object of speculation was, by darkening knowledge, to breed more speculation, and "find no end in wandering mazes lost." He chose the incomprehensible and impracticable as almost the only subjects fit for a lofty and lasting contemplation, or for the exercise of a solid faith. He cried out for an *oh altitudo* beyond the heights of revelation, and posed himself with apocryphal mysteries, as the pastime of his leisure hours. He pushes a question to the utmost verge of conjecture, that he may repose on the certainty of doubt; and he removes an object to the greatest distance from him, that he may take a high and abstracted interest in it, consider it in its relation to the sum of things, not to himself, and bewilder his understanding in the universality of its nature, and the inscrutableness of its origin. His is the sublime of indifference; a passion for the abstruse and imaginary. He turns the world round for his amusement, as if it was a globe of paste-board. He looks down on sublunary affairs as if he had taken his station in one of the planets. The Antipodes are next-door neighbours to him, and Doomsday is not far off. With a thought he embraces both the poles; the march of his pen is over the great divisions of geography and chronology. Nothing touches him nearer than humanity. He feels that he is mortal only in the decay of nature, and the dust of long-forgotten tombs. The finite is lost in the infinite. The orbits of the heavenly bodies or the history of empires are to him but a point in time or a speck in the universe. The great Platonic year revolves in one of his periods. Nature is too little for the grasp of his style. He scoops an antithesis out of fabulous antiquity, and rakes up an epithet from the sweepings of Chaos. It is as if his books had dropt from the clouds, or as if Friar Bacon's head could speak. He stands on the edge of the world of sense and reason, and gains a vertigo by looking down on impossibilities and chimeras. Or he busies himself with the mysteries of the Cabala, or the enclosed secrets of the heavenly quincunxes, as children are amused with tales of the nursery. The passion of curiosity (the only passion of childhood) had in him survived to old age, and had superannuated his other faculties. He moralizes and grows pathetic on a mere idle fancy of his own, as if thought and being were the same, or as if "all this world were one glorious lie." For a thing to have ever had a name is sufficient warrant to entitle it to respectful belief, and to invest it with all the rights of a subject and its predicates. He is superstitious, but not bigoted; to him all religions are much the same, and he says that he should not like to have lived in the time of Christ and the Apostles, as it would have rendered his faith too gross and palpable. His gossiping egotism and personal char acter have been preferred unjustly to Montaigne's. He had no personal character at all but the peculiarity of resolving all the other elements of his being into thought, and of trying experiments on his own nature in an exhausted receiver of idle and unsatisfactory speculations. All that he "differences himself by," to use his own expression, is this moral and physical indifference. In describing himself he deals only in negatives. He says he has neither prejudices nor antipathies to manners, habits, climate, food, to persons or things; they were alike acceptable to him as they afforded new topics for reflection; and he even professes that he could never bring himself heartily to hate the devil. He owns in one place of the *Religio Medici*, that "he could be content if the species were continued like trees," and yet he declares that this was from no aversion to love, or beauty, or harmony; and the reasons he assigns to prove the orthodoxy of his taste in this respect is, that he was an admirer of the music of the spheres! He tells us that he often composed a comedy in his sleep. It would be curious to know the subject or the texture of the plot. It must have been something like Nabbes's "Mask of Microcosmus,' of which the *dramatis personæ* have been already given; or else a misnomer, like Dante's 'Divine Comedy of Heaven, Hell, and Purgatory.' He was twice married, as if to show his disregard even for his own theory; and he had a hand in the execution of some old women for witchcraft, I suppose to keep a decorum in absurdity, and to indulge an agreeable horror at his own fantastical reveries on the occasion. In a word, his mind seemed to converse chiefly with the intelligible forms, the spectral apparitions of things; he delighted in the preternatural and visionary, and he only existed at the circumference of his nature. He had the most intense consciousness of contradictions and non-entities, and he decks them out in the pride and pedantry of words, as if they were the attire of his proper person: the categories hang about hi neck like the gold chain of knighthood, and he "walks gowned' in the intricate folds and swelling drapery of dark sayings and impenetrable riddles!

I will give one gorgeous passage to illustrate all this, from his 'Urn-Burial, or Hydriotaphia.' He digs up the urns of some ancient Druids with the same ceremony and devotion as if they had contained the hallowed relics of his dearest friends; and certainly we feel (as it has been said) the freshness of the mould, and the breath of mortality, in the spirit and force of his style. The conclusion of this singular and unparallelled performance is as follows:

"What song the Syrens sang, or what name Achilles assumed when he hid himself among women, though puzzling questions, are not beyond all conjecture. What time the persons of these Ossuaries entered the famous nations of the dead, and slept with princes and counsellors, might admit a wide solution. But who were the proprietors of these bones, or what bodies these ashes made up, were a question above antiquarianism: not to be resolved by man, nor easily perhaps by spirits, except we consult the provincial guardians, or tutelary observators. Had they made as good provision for their names, as they have done for their reliques, they had not so grossly erred in the art of perpetuation. But to subsist in bones, and be but pyramidally extant, is a fallacy in duration. Vain ashes, which in the oblivion of names, persons, times, and sexes, have found unto themselves a fruitless continuation, and only arise unto late posterity, as emblems of mortal vanities; antidotes against pride, vain-glory, and madding vices. Pagan vain-glories, which thought the world might last for ever, had encouragement for ambition, and finding no Atropos unto the immortality of their names, were never dampt with the necessity of oblivion. Even old ambitions had the advantage of ours, in the attempts of their vain-glories, who, acting early, and before the probable meridian of time, have, by this time, found great accomplishment of their designs, whereby the ancient heroes have already outlasted their monuments and mechanical preservations. But in this latter scene of time we cannot expect such mummies unto our memories, when ambition may fear the prophecy of Elias, and Charles the Fifth can never hope to live within two Methuselahs of Hector.

"And therefore restless inquietude for the diuturnity of our memories unto present considerations, seems a vanity almost out of date, and superannuated pieces of folly. We cannot hope to live so long in our names as some have done in their persons: one face of Janus holds no proportion unto the other. 'Tis too late to be ambitious. The great mutations of the world are acted, or time may be too short for our designs. To extend our memories by monuments, whose death we daily pray for, and whose duration we cannot hope, without injury to our expectations in the advent of the last day, were a contradiction to our beliefs. We, whose generations are ordained in this setting part of time, are providentially taken off from such imaginations. And being necessitated to eye the remaining particle of futurity, are naturally constituted unto thoughts of the next world, and cannot excusably decline the consideration of that duration which maketh pyramids pillars of snow, and all that's past a moment.

"Circles and right lines limit and close all bodies, and the mortal right-lined circle must conclude and shut up all. There is no antidote against the opium of time, which temporarily considereth all things; our fathers find their graves in our short memories, and sadly tell us how we may be buried in our survivors. Grave-stones tell truth scarce forty years: generations pass while some trees stand, and old families last not three oaks. To be read by bare inscriptions like many in Gruter, to hope for eternity by enigmatical epithets, or first letters of our names, to be studied by antiquaries, who we were, and have new names given us like many of the mummies, are cold consolations unto the students of perpetuity, even by everlasting languages.

"To be content that times to come should only know there was such a man, not caring whether they knew more of him, was a frigid ambition in Cardan; disparaging his horoscopal inclination and judgment of himself, who cares to subsist like Hippocrates' patients, or Achilles' horses in Homer, under naked nominations without deserts and noble acts, which are the balsam of our memories, the Entelechia and soul of our subsistences. To be nameless in worthy deeds exceeds an infamous history. The Canaanitish woman lives more happily without a name, than Herodias with one. And who had not rather have been the good thief, than Pilate?

"But the iniquity of oblivion blindly scattereth her poppy, and deals with the memory of men without distinction to merit of perpetuity. Who can but pity the founder of the pyramids? Herostratus lives that burnt the temple of Diana, he is almost lost that built it; time hath spared the epitaph of Adrian's horse, confounded that of himself. In vain we compute our felicities by the advantage of our good names, since bad have equal durations; and Thersites is like to live as long as Agamemnon, without the favour of the everlasting register. Who knows whether the best of men be known? or whether there be not more remarkable persons forgot than any that stand remembered in the known account of time? the first man had been as unknown as the last, and Methuselah's long life had been his only chronicle.

"Oblivion is not to be hired: the greater part must be content to be as though they had not been, to be found in the register of God, not in the record of man. Twenty-seven names make up the first story, and the recorded names ever since contain not one living century. The number of the dead long exceedeth all that shall live. The night of time far surpasseth the day, and who knows when was the equinox? Every hour adds unto that current arithmetic, which scarce stands one moment. And since death must be the Lucina of life, and even Pagans could doubt whether thus to live, were to die; since our longest sun sets at right descensions, and makes but winter arches, and therefore it cannot be long before we lie down in darkness, and have our light in ashes; since the brother of death daily haunts us with dying mementos, and time, that grows old itself, bids us hope no long duration: diuturnity is a dream and folly of expectation.

"Darkness and light divide the course of time, and oblivion shares with memory a great part even of our living beings; we slightly remember our felicities, and the smartest strokes of affliction leave but short smart upon us.

Sense endureth no extremities, and sorrows destroy us or themselves. To weep into stones are fables. Afflictions induce callosities which are slippery, or fall like snow upon us, which, notwithstanding, is no unhappy stupidity. To be ignorant of evils to come, and forgetful of evils past, is a merciful provision in nature, whereby we digest the mixture of our few and evil days, and our delivered senses not relapsing into cutting remembrances, our sorrows are not kept raw by the edge of repetitions. A great part of antiquity contented their hopes of subsistency with a transmigration of their souls. A good way to continue their memories, while having the advantage of plural successions, they could not but act something remarkable in such a variety of beings, and enjoying the fame of their passed selves, make accumulation of glory unto their last durations. Others, rather than be lost in the uncomfortable night of nothing, were content to recede into the common being, and make one particle of the public soul of all things, which was no more than to return into their unknown and divine original again. Egyptian ingenuity was more unsatisfied, conserving their bodies in sweet consistences, to attend the return of their souls. But all was vanity, feeding the wind, and folly. The Egyptian mummies, which Cambyses or time hath spared, avarice now consumeth. Mummy is become merchandize, Mizraim cures wounds, and Pharaoh is sold for balsams.

"In vain do individuals hope for immortality, or any patent from oblivion, in preservations below the moon: men have been deceived even in their flatteries above the sun, and studied conceits to perpetuate their names in heaven. The various cosmography of that part hath already varied the names of contrived constellations; Nimrod is lost in Orion, and Osiris in the Dog-star. While we look for incorruption in the heavens, we find they are but like the earth; durable in their main bodies, alterable in their parts; whereof beside comets and new stars, perspectives begin to tell tales. And the spots that wander about the sun, with Phæton's favour, would make clear conviction.

"There is nothing immortal but immortality; whatever hath no beginning may be confident of no end. All others have a dependent being, and within the reach of destruction, which is the peculiar of that necessary essence that cannot destroy itself; and the highest strain of omnipotency to be so powerfully constituted, as not to suffer even from the power of itself. But the sufficiency of Christian immortality frustrates all earthly glory, and the quality of either state after death makes a folly of posthumous memory. God, who can only destroy our souls, and hath assured our resurrection, either of our bodies or names, hath directly promised no duration. Wherein there is so much of chance, that the boldest expectants have found unhappy frustration; and to hold long subsistence, seems but a scape in oblivion. But man is a noble animal, splendid in ashes, and pompous in the grave, solemnizing Nativities and Deaths with equal lustre, nor omitting ceremonies of bravery, in the infamy of his nature.

"Life is a pure flame, and we live by an invisible sun within us. A small fire sufficeth for life, great flames seemed too little after death, while men vainly affected precious pyres and to burn like Sardanapalus; but the wisdom of funeral laws found the folly of prodigal blazes, and reduced undoing fires unto the rule of sober obsequies, wherein few could be so mean as not to provide wood, pitch, a mourner, and an urn.

"Five languages secured not the epitaph of Gordianus; the man of God lives longer without a tomb than any by one, invisibly interred by angels, and adjudged to obscurity, though not without some marks directing human discovery. Enoch and Elias, without either tomb or burial, in an anomalous state of being, are the great examples of perpetuity, in their long and living memory, in strict account being still on this side death, and having a late part yet to act on this stage of earth. If in the decretory term of the world we shall not all die, but be changed, according to received translation, the last day will make but few graves; at least quick resurrections will anticipate lasting sepultures; some graves will be opened before they be quite closed, and Lazarus be no wonder. When many that feared to die shall groan that they can die but once, the dismal state is the second and living death, when life puts despair on the damned; when men shall wish the covering of mountains, not of monuments, and annihilation shall be courted.

"While some have studied monuments, others have studiously declined them; and some have been so vainly boisterous, that they durst not acknowledge their graves; wherein Alaricus seems most subtle, who had a river turned to hide his bones at the bottom. Even Sylla, that thought himself safe in his urn, could not prevent revenging tongues and stones thrown at his monument. Happy are they whom privacy makes innocent, who deal so with men in this world that they are not afraid to meet them in the next,—who, when they die, make no commotion among the dead, and are not touched with that poetical taunt of Isaiah.

"Pyramids, arches, obelisks, were but the irregularities of vain-glory, and wild enormities of ancient magnanimity. But the most magnanimous resolution rests in the Christian religion, which trampleth upon pride, and sits on the neck of ambition, humbly pursuing that infallible perpetuity, unto which all others must diminish their diameters and be poorly seen in angles of contingency.

"Pious spirits, who passed their days in raptures of futurity, made little more of this world than the world that was before it, while they lay obscure in the chaos of pre-ordination, and night of their fore-beings. And if any have been so happy as truly to understand Christian annihilation, ecstasies, exolution, liquefaction, transformation, the kiss of the spouse, gustation of God, and ingression into the divine shadow, they have already had a handsome anticipation of heaven; the glory of the world is surely over, and the earth in ashes unto them.

"To subsist in lasting monuments, to live in their productions, to exist in their names, and predicament of chimeras, was large satisfaction unto old expectations, and made one part of their Elysiums. But all this is nothing in the metaphysics of true belief To live indeed is to be again ourselves, which being not only a hope but an evidence in noble believers: 'tis all one to lie in St. Innocent's church-yard as in the sands of Egypt; ready to be anything in the ecstacy of being ever, and as content with six foot as the moles of Adrianus."

I subjoin the following account of this extraordinary writer's style, said to be written in a blank leaf of his works by Mr. Coleridge:

"Sir Thomas Brown is among my first favourites. Rich in various knowledge, exuberant in conceptions and conceits; contemplative, imaginative, often truly great and magnificent in his style and diction, though, doubtless, too often big, stiff, and *hyper-latinistic:* thus I might, without admixture of falsehood, describe Sir T. Brown; and my description would have this fault only, that it would be equally, or almost equally, applicable to half a dozen other writers, from the beginning of the reign of Elizabeth to the end of the reign of Charles the Second. He is indeed all this; and what he has more than all this, and peculiar to himself, I seem to convey to my own mind in some measure, by saying that he is a quiet and sublime *enthusiast*, with a strong tinge of the *fantast;* the humourist constantly mingling with, and flashing across the philosopher, as the darting colours in shot-silk play upon the main dye. In short, he has brains in his head, which is all the more interesting for a little twist in the brains. He sometimes reminds the reader of Montaigne; but from no other than the general circumstance of an egotism common to both, which, in Montaigne, is too often a mere amusing gossip, a chit-chat story of whims and peculiarities that lead to nothing; but which, in Sir Thomas Brown, is always the result of a feeling heart, conjoined with a mind of active curiosity, the natural and becoming egotism of a man, who, loving other men as himself, gains the habit and the privilege of talking about himself as familiarly as about other men. Fond of the curious, and a hunter of oddities and strangenesses, while he conceives himself with quaint and humorous gravity, an useful inquirer into physical truths and fundamental science, he loved to contemplate and discuss his own thoughts and feelings, because he found by comparison with other men's, that *they*, too, were curiosities; and so, with a perfectly graceful, interesting ease, he put *them*, too, into his museum and cabinet of rarities. In very truth, he was not mistaken, so completely does he see every thing in a light of his own; reading nature neither by sun, moon, nor candle-light, but by the light of the fairy glory around his own head; that you might say, that nature had granted to *him* in perpetuity, a patent and monopoly for all his thoughts. Read his *Hydriotaphia* above all, and, in addition to the peculiarity, the exclusive *Sir Thomas Browness* of all the fancies and modes of illustration, wonder at, and admire, his *entireness* in every subject which is before him. He is *totus in illo*, he follows it, he never wanders from it, and he has no occasion to wander; for whatever happens to be his subject, he metamorphoses all nature into it. In that 'Hydriotaphia,' or treatise on some urns dug up in Norfolk—how *earthy*, how redolent of graves and sepulchres is every line! You have now dark mould; now a thighbone; now a skull; then a bit of a mouldered coffin; a fragment of an old tombstone, with moss in its *hic jacet*; a ghost, a winding sheet; or the echo of a funeral psalm wafted on a November wind: and the gayest thing you shall meet with shall be a silver nail, or gilt *anno domini*, from a perished coffin top!—The very same remark applies in the same force to the interesting, though far less interesting, treatise on the 'Quincuncial Plantations of the Ancients,' the same *entireness* of subject! Quincunxes in heaven above; quincunxes in earth below; quincunxes in deity; quincunxes in the mind of man; quincunxes in tones, in optic nerves, in roots of trees, in leaves, in every thing! In short, just turn to the last leaf of this volume, and read out aloud to yourself the seven last paragraphs of chapter 5th, beginning with the words, '*More considerable.*' But it is time for me to be in bed. In the words of Sir T. Brown (which will serve as a fine specimen of his manner,) 'But the quincunxes of Heaven (*the hyades, or five stars about the horizon, at midnight at that time*) run low, and it is time we close the five parts of knowledge; we are unwilling to spin out our waking thoughts into the phantoms of sleep, which often continue precogitations, making cables of cobwebs, and wildernesses of handsome groves. To keep our eyes open longer, were to *act* our antipodes? The huntsmen are up in Arabia; and they have already passed their first sleep in Persia.' Think you, that there ever was such a reason given before for going to bed at midnight; to wit, that if we did not, we should be *acting* the part of our antipodes! And then, 'THE HUNTSMEN ARE UP IN ARABIA,'—what life, what fancy! Does the whimsical knight give us thus the *essence* of gunpowder tea, and call it an *opiate*?*

Jeremy Taylor was a writer as different from Sir Thomas Brown as it was possible for one writer to be from another. He was a dignitary of the church, and except in matters of casuistry and controverted points, could not be supposed to enter upon speculative doubts, or give a loose to a sort of dogmatical scepticism. He had less thought, less "stuff of the conscience," less "to give us pause," in his impetuous oratory, but he had equal fancy—not the same vastness and profundity, but more richness and beauty, more warmth and tenderness. He is as rapid, as flowing, and endless, as the other is stately, abrupt, and concentrated. The eloquence of the one is like a river, that of the other is more like an aqueduct. The one is as sanguine, as the other is saturnine in the temper of his mind. Jeremy Taylor took obvious and admitted truths for granted, and illustrated them with an inexhaustible display of new and enchanting imagery. Sir Thomas Brown talks in sum-totals: Jeremy Taylor enumerates all the particulars of a subject. He gives every aspect it will bear, and never "cloys with sameness." His characteristic is enthusiastic and delightful amplification. Sir Thomas Brown

* Sir Thomas Brown has it, "The huntsmen are up in America," but Mr. Coleridge prefers reading Arabia. I do not think his account of the Urn-Burial very happy. Sir Thomas can be said to be "wholly in his subject," only because he is *wholly out of it*. There is not a word in the 'Hydriotaphia' about "a thigh-bone, or a skull, or a bit of mouldered coffin, or a tombstone, or a ghost, or a winding-sheet, or an echo," nor is "a silver nail or a gilt *anno domini* the gayest thing you shall meet with." You do not meet with them at all in the text; nor is it possible, either from the nature of the subject, or of Sir T. Brown's mind, that you should! He chose the subject of Urn-Burial, because it was "one of no mark or likelihood," totally free from the romantic prettinesses and pleasing poetical common-places with which Mr. Coleridge has adorned it, and because, being "without form and void," it gave unlimited scope to his high-raised and shadowy imagination. The motto of this author's compositions might be—"*De apparentibus et non existentibus eadem est ratio.* He created his own materials: or to speak of him in his own language, "he saw nature in the elements of its chaos, and discerned his favourite notions in the great obscurity of nothing!"

gives the beginning and end of things, that you may judge of their place and magnitude: Jeremy Taylor describes their qualities and texture, and enters into all the items of the debtor and creditor account between life and death, grace and nature, faith and good works. He puts his heart into his fancy. He does not pretend to annihilate the passions and pursuits of mankind in the pride of philosophic indifference, but treats them as serious and momentous things, warring with conscience and the soul's health, or furnishing the means of grace and hopes of glory. In his writings, the frail stalk of human life reclines on the bosom of eternity. His 'Holy Living and Dying' is a divine pastoral. He writes to the faithful followers of Christ, as the shepherd pipes to his flock. He introduces touching and heart-felt appeals to familiar life; condescends to men of low estate; and his pious page blushes with modesty and beauty. His style is prismatic. It unfolds the colours of the rainbow; it floats like the bubble through the air; it is like innumerable dew-drops that glitter on the face of morning, and tremble as they glitter. He does not dig his way underground, but slides upon ice, borne on the winged car of fancy. The dancing light he throws upon objects is like an Aurora Borealis, playing betwixt heaven and earth—

> " Where pure Niemi's faery banks arise,
> And fringed with roses Tenglio rolls its stream."

His exhortations to piety and virtue are a gay *memento mori*. He mixes up death's-heads and amaranthine flowers; makes life a procession to the grave, but crowns it with gaudy garlands, and "rains sacrificial roses" on its path. In a word, his writings are more like fine poetry than any other prose whatever; they are a choral song in praise of virtue, and a hymn to the Spirit of the Universe. I shall give a few passages, to show how feeble and inefficient this praise is.

The 'Holy Dying' begins in this manner:—

> " Man is a bubble. He is born in vanity and sin; he comes into the world like morning mushrooms, soon thrusting up their heads into the air, and conversing with their kindred of the same production, and as soon they turn into dust and forgetfulness; some of them without any other interest in the affairs of the world, but that they made their parents a little glad, and very sorrowf'

Others ride longer in the storm it may be until seven years of vanity be expired, and then peradventure the sun shines hot upon their heads, and they fall into the shades below, into the cover of death and darkness of the grave to hide them. But if the bubble stands the shock of a bigger drop, and outlives the chances of a child, of a careless nurse, of drowning in a pail of water, of being overlaid by a sleepy servant, or such little accidents, then the young man dances like a bubble empty and gay, and shines like a dove's neck, or the image of a rainbow, which hath no substance, and whose very imagery and colours are fantastical; and so he dances out the gaiety of his youth, and is all the while in a storm, and endures, only because he is not knocked on the head by a drop of bigger rain, or crushed by the pressure of a load of indigested meat, or quenched by the disorder of an ill-placed humour; and to preserve a man alive in the midst of so many chances and hostilities, is as great a miracle as to create him; to preserve him from rushing into nothing, and at first to draw him up from nothing, were equally the issues of an Almighty power."

Another instance of the same rich continuity of feeling, and transparent brilliancy in working out an idea, is to be found in his description of the dawn and progress of reason :

"Some are called *at age* at fourteen, some at one-and-twenty, some never; but all men late enough; for the life of a man comes upon him slowly and insensiby. But as when the sun approaches towards the gates of the morning, he first opens a little eye of heaven, and sends away the spirits of darkness, and gives light to a cock, and calls up the lark to matins, and by-and-by gilds the fringes of a cloud, and peeps over the eastern hills, thrusting out his golden horns, like those which decked the brows of Moses, when he was forced to wear a veil, because himself had seen the face of God; and still, while a man tells the story, the sun gets up higher, till he shows a fair face and a full light, and then he shines one whole day, under a cloud often, and sometimes weeping great and little showers, and sets quickly; so is a man's reason and his life."

This passage puts one in mind of the rising dawn and kindling skies in one of Claude's landscapes. Sir Thomas Brown has nothing of this rich finishing and exact gradation. The genius of the two men differed, as that of the painter from the mathematician. The one measures objects, the other copies them. The one shows that things are nothing out of themselves, or in relation to the whole: the one, what they are in themselves and in relation to us. Or the one may be said to apply the telescope of the mind to distant bodies; the other looks at nature in its infinite minuteness and glossy splendour through a solar microscope.

In speaking of Death, our author's style assumes the port and withering smile of the King of Terrors. The following are scattered passages on this subject.

"It is the same harmless thing that a poor shepherd suffered yesterday or a maid-servant to-day; and at the same time in which you die, in that very night a thousand creatures die with you, some wise men, and many fools; and the wisdom of the first will not quit him, and the folly of the latter does not make him unable to die." . . . .

"I have read of a fair young German gentleman, who, while living, often refused to be pictured, but put off the importunity of his friends' desire by giving way that after a few days' burial, they might send a painter to his vault, and if they saw cause for it, draw the image of his death *unto the life*. They did so, and found his face half eaten, and his midriff and back-bone full of serpents; and so he stands pictured among his armed ancestors." . . . .

"It is a mighty change that is made by the death of every person, and it is visible to us, who are alive. Reckon but from the sprightfulness of youth and the fair cheeks and full eyes of childhood, from the vigorousness and strong flexure of the joints of five-and-twenty, to the hollowness and dead paleness, to the loathsomeness and horror of a three days' burial, and we shall perceive the distance to be very great and very strange, But so have I seen a rose newly springing from the clefts of its hood, and at first it was fair as the morning, and full with the dew of heaven, as the lamb's fleece; but when a ruder breath had forced open its virgin modesty, and dismantled its too youthful and unripe retirements, it began to put on darkness and to decline to softness and the symptoms of a sickly age, it bowed the head and broke its stalk, and at night, having lost some of its leaves, and all its beauty, it fell into the portion of weeds and out-worn faces. So does the fairest beauty change, and it will be as bad with you and me; and then what servants shall we have to wait upon us in the grave? What friends to visit us? What officious people to cleanse away the moist and unwholesome cloud reflected upon our faces from the sides of the weeping vaults, which are the longest weepers for our funerals?"

"A man may read a sermon, the best and most passionate that ever man preached, if he shall but enter into the sepulchres of kings. In the same Escurial where the Spanish princes live in greatness and power, and decree war or peace, they have wisely placed a cemetery where their ashes and their glory shall sleep till time shall be no more: and where our kings have been crowned, their ancestors lie interred, and they must walk over their grandsires head to take his crown. There is an acre sown with royal seed, the copy of the greatest change from rich to naked, from ceiled roofs to arched coffins, from living like gods to die like men. There is enough to cool the flames of lust, to abate the heights of pride, to appease the itch of covetous desires, to sully and dash out the dissembling colours of a lustful, artificial, and imaginary beauty. There the warlike and the peaceful, the fortunate and the miserable, the beloved and the despised princes mingle their dust, and pay down their symbol of mortality, and tell all the world that when we die, our ashes shall be equal to kings, and our accounts easier, and our pains for our crimes shall be less.* To my apprehension, it is a sad record which is left by Athenæus concerning Ninus the great Assyrian monarch, whose life and death is summed up in these words: 'Ninus the Assyrian had an ocean of gold, and other riches more than the sand in the Caspian sea; he never saw the stars, and perhaps he never desired it; he never stirred up the holy fire among the Magi: nor touched his god with the sacred rod according to the laws: he never offered sacrifice, nor worshipped the deity, nor administered justice, nor spake to the people; nor numbered them: but he was most valiant to eat and drink, and having mingled his wines, he threw the rest upon the stones. This man is dead, behold his sepulchre, and now hear where Ninus is. Sometime I was Ninus, and drew the breath of a living man, but now am nothing but clay. I have nothing but what I did eat, and what I served to myself in lust is all my portion: the wealth with which I was blessed, my enemies meeting together shall carry away, as the mad Thyades carry a raw goat. I am gone to hell: and when I went thither, I neither carried gold, nor horse, nor silver chariot. I that wore a mitre, am now a little heap of dust.' "

He who wrote in this manner also wore a mitre, and is now a heap of dust: but when the name of Jeremy Taylor is no longer remembered with reverence, genius will have become a mockery, and virtue an empty shade!

* The above passage is an inimitably fine paraphrase of some lines on the tombs in Westminster Abbey by F. Beaumont. It shows how near Jeremy Taylor's style was to poetry, and how well it weaves in with it.

" Mortality, behold, and fear,
What a charge of flesh is here!
Think how many royal bones
Sleep within this heap of stones:
Here they lie, had realms and lands,
Who now want strength to stir their hands.
Where from their pulpits, sealed in dust,
They preach 'In greatness is no trust.'
Here's an acre sown indeed
With the richest, royal'st seed
That the earth did e'er suck in,
Since the first man died for sin.
Here the bones of birth have cried,
Though gods they were, as men they died.
Here are sands, ignoble things,
Dropp'd from the ruin'd sides of kings.
Here's a world of pomp and state
Buried in dust, once dead by fate."

LECTURE VIII.

On the Spirit of Ancient and Modern Literature—On the German Drama contrasted with that of the Age of Elizabeth.

Before I proceed to the more immediate subject of the present Lecture, I wish to say a few words of one or two writers in our own time, who have imbibed the spirit and imitated the language of our elder dramatists. Among these I may reckon the ingenious author of 'The Apostate' and 'Evadne,' who, in the last-mentioned play, in particular, has availed himself with much judgment and spirit of the tragedy of 'The Traitor,' by old Shirley. It would be curious to hear the opinion of a professed admirer of the Ancients, and captious despiser of the Moderns, with respect to this production, before he knew it was a copy of an old play. Shirley himself lived in the time of Charles I. and died in the beginning of Charles II.;* but he had formed his style on that of the preceding age, and had written the greatest number of his plays in conjunction with Jonson, Decker, and Massinger. He was "the last of those fair clouds that on the bosom of bright honour sailed in long procession, beautiful and calm." The name of Mr. Tobin is familiar to every lover of the drama. His 'Honey-Moon' is evidently founded on 'The Taming of a Shrew,' and Duke Aranza has been pronounced by a polite critic to be "an elegant Petruchio." The plot is taken from Shakspeare; but the language and sentiments, both of this play and of 'The Curfew,' bear a more direct resemblance to the flowery tenderness of Beaumont and Fletcher, who were, I believe, the favourite study of our author. Mr. Lamb's 'John Woodvil' may be considered as a dramatic fragment, intended for the closet rather than the stage. It would sound oddly in the lobbies of either theatre, amidst the noise and

* He and his wife both died from fright, occasioned by the great fire of London in 1665, and lie buried in St. Giles's churchyard.

glare and bustle of resort; but "there where we have treasured up our hearts," in silence and in solitude, it may claim and find a place for itself. It might be read with advantage in the still retreats of Sherwood Forest, where it would throw a new-born light on the green, sunny glades; the tenderest flower might seem to drink of the poet's spirit, and "the tall deer that paints a dancing shadow of his horns in the swift brook," might seem to do so in mockery of the poet's thought. Mr. Lamb, with a modesty often attendant on fine feeling, has loitered too long in the humbler avenues leading to the temple of ancient genius, instead of marching boldly up to the sanctuary, as many with half his pretensions would have done: "but fools rush in, where angels fear to tread." The defective or objectionable parts of this production are imitations of the defects of the old writers: its beauties are his own, though in their manner. The touches of thought and passion are often as pure and delicate as they are profound; and the character of his heroine Margaret is perhaps the finest and most genuine female character out of Shakspeare. This tragedy was not critic-proof: it had its cracks and flaws and breaches, through which the enemy marched in triumphant. The station which he had chosen was not indeed a walled town, but a straggling village, which the experienced engineers proceeded to lay waste; and he is pinned down in more than one Review of the day, as an exemplary warning to indiscreet writers, who venture beyond the pale of periodical taste and conventional criticism. Mr. Lamb was thus hindered by the taste of the polite vulgar from writing as he wished; his own taste would not allow him to write like them: and he (perhaps wisely) turned critic and prose-writer in his own defence. To say that he has written better about Shakspeare, and about Hogarth, than anybody else, is saying little in his praise. A gentleman of the name of Cornwall, who has lately published a volume of Dramatic Scenes, has met with a very different reception, but I cannot say that he has *deserved* it. He has made no sacrifice at the shrine of fashionable affectation or false glitter. There is nothing common-place in his style to soothe the complacency of dulness, nothing extravagant to startle the grossness of ignorance. He writes with simplicity, delicacy, and fervour;

continues a scene from Shakspeare, or works out a hint from Boccacio, in the spirit of his originals, and though he bows with reverence at the altar of those great masters, he keeps an eye curiously intent on nature, and a mind awake to the admonitions of his own heart. As he has begun, so let him proceed. Any one who will turn to the glowing and richly-coloured conclusion of 'The Falcon,' will, I think, agree with me in this wish!

There are four sorts or schools of tragedy with which I am acquainted. The first is the antique or classical. This consisted, I apprehend, in the introduction of persons on the stage, speaking, feeling, and acting *according to nature*, that is, according to the impression of given circumstances on the passions and mind of man in those circumstances, but limited by the physical conditions of time and place, as to its external form, and to a certain dignity of attitude and expression, selection in the figures, and unity in their grouping, as in a statue or bas-relief. The second is the Gothic or romantic, or, as it might be called, the historical or poetical tragedy, and differs from the former, only in having a larger scope in the design and boldness in the execution; that is, it is the dramatic representation of nature and passion emancipated from the precise imitation of an actual event in place and time, from the same fastidiousness in the choice of the materials, and with the license of the epic and fanciful form added to it in the range of the subject and the decorations of language. This is particularly the style or school of Shakspeare and of the best writers of the age of Elizabeth, and the one immediately following. Of this class, or genus, the *tragédie bourgeoise* is a variety, and the antithesis of the classical form. The third sort is the French or common-place rhetorical style, which is founded on the antique as to its form and subject matter; but instead of individual nature, real passion, or imagination growing out of real passion and the circumstances of the speaker, it deals only in vague, imposing, and laboured declamations, or descriptions of nature, dissertations on the passions, and pompous flourishes which never entered any head but the author's, have no existence in nature which they pretend to identify, and are not dramatic at all, but purely didactic. The fourth and last is the German or paradoxical style, which differs from the others in representing men as acting not from the impulse of feeling, or as debating common-place questions of morality, but as the organs and mouth-pieces (that is, as acting, speaking, and thinking under the sole influence) of certain extravagant speculative opinions, abstracted from all existing customs, prejudices, and institutions. It is my present business to speak chiefly of the first and last of these.

Sophocles differs from Shakspeare as a Doric portico does from Westminster Abbey. The principle of the one is simplicity and harmony, of the other richness and power. The one relies on form or proportion, the other on quantity, and variety, and prominence of parts. The one owes its charm to a certain union and regularity of feeling, the other adds to its effect from complexity and the combination of the greatest extremes. The classical appeals to sense and habit; the Gothic or romantic strikes from novelty, strangeness, and contrast. Both are founded in essential and indestructible principles of human nature. We may prefer the one to the other, as we choose, but to set up an arbitrary and bigotted standard of excellence in consequence of this preference, and to exclude either one or the other from poetry or art, is to deny the existence of the first principles of the human mind, and to war with nature, which is the height of weakness and arrogance at once. There are some observations on this subject in a late number of the 'Edinburgh Review,' from which I shall here make a pretty long extract:

"The most obvious distinction between the two styles, the classical and the romantic, is, that the one is conversant with objects that are grand or beautiful in themselves, or in consequence of obvious and universal associations; the other, with those that are interesting only by the force of circumstances and imagination. A Grecian temple, for instance, is a classical object: it is beautiful in itself, and excites immediate admiration. But the ruins of a Gothic castle have no beauty or symmetry to attract the eye; and yet they excite a more powerful and romantic interest, from the ideas with which they are habitually associated. If, in addition to this, we are told that this is Macbeth's castle, the scene of the murder of Duncan, the interest will be instantly heightened to a sort of pleasing horror. The classical idea or form of any thing, it may also be observed, remains always the same, and suggests nearly the same impressions; but the associations of ideas belonging to the romantic character may vary infinitely, and take in the whole range of nature and accident. Antigone, in Sophocles, waiting near the grove of the Furies—Electra, in Æschylus, offering sacrifice at the tomb of Agamemnon—are classical subjects, because the circumstances and the characters have a correspondent dignity, and an immediate interest, from their mere designation. Florimel, in Spenser, where she is described sitting on the ground in the Witch's hut, is not classical, though in the highest degree poetical and romantic: or the incidents and situation are in themselves mean and disagreeable, till they are redeemed by the genius of the poet, and converted, by the very contrast, into a source of the utmost pathos and elevation of sentiment. Othello's handkerchief is not classical, though "there was magic in the web:"—it is only a powerful instrument of passion and imagination. Even Lear is not classical; for he is a poor crazy old man, who has nothing sublime about him but his afflictions, and who dies of a broken heart.

"Schlegel somewhere compares the Furies of Æschylus to the Witches of Shakspeare—we think without much reason. Perhaps Shakspeare has surrounded the weird sisters with associations as terrible, and even more mysterious, strange and fantastic, than the Furies of Æschylus; but the traditionary beings themselves are not so petrific. These are of marble—their look alone must blast the beholder;—those are of air, bubbles; and though 'so withered and so wild in their attire,' it is their spells alone which are fatal. They owe their power to metaphysical aid: but the others contain all that is dreadful in their corporeal figures. In this we see the distinct spirit of the classical and the romantic mythology. The serpents that twine round the head of the Furies are not to be trifled with, though they implied no preternatural power. The bearded Witches in Macbeth are in themselves grotesque and ludicrous, except as this strange deviation from nature staggers our imagination, and leads us to expect and to believe in all incredible things. They appal the faculties by what they say or do;—the others are intolerable, even to sight.

"Our author is right in affirming, that the true way to understand the plays of Sophocles and Æschylus, is to study them before the groupes of the Niobe or the Laocoon. If we can succeed in explaining this analogy, we shall have solved nearly the whole difficulty. For it is certain, that there are exactly the same powers of mind displayed in the poetry of the Greeks as in their statues. Their poetry is exactly what their sculptors might have written. Both are exquisite imitations of nature; the one in marble, the other in words. It is evident that the Greek poets had the same perfect idea of the subjects they described as the Greek sculptors had of the objects they represented; and they give as much of this absolute truth of imitation as can be given by words. But in this direct and simple imitation of nature, as in describing the form of a beautiful woman, the poet is greatly inferior to the sculptor; it is in the power of illustration, in comparing it to other things, and suggesting other ideas of beauty or love, that he has an entirely new source of imagination opened to him: and of this power the moderns have made at least a bolder and more frequent use than the ancients. The description of Helen in Homer is a description of what might have happened and been seen, as 'that she moved with grace, and that the old men rose up with reverence as she passed;' the description of Belphœbe in Spenser is a description of what was only visible to the eye of the poet:

"Upon her eyelids many graces sat,
Under the shadow of her even brows."

The description of the soldiers going to battle in Shakspeare, 'all plumed like ostriches, like eagles newly baited, wanton as goats, wild as young bulls,' is too bold, figurative, and profuse of dazzling images, for the mild, equable tone of classical poetry, which never loses sight of the object in the illustration. The ideas of the ancients were too exact and definite, too much attached to the material form or vehicle by which they were conveyed, to admit of those rapid combinations, those unrestrained flights of fancy, which, glancing from heaven to earth, unite the most opposite extremes, and draw the happiest illustrations from things the most remote. The two principles of imitation and imagination, indeed, are not only distinct, but almost opposite.

"The great difference, then, which we find between the classical and the romantic style, between ancient and modern poetry, is, that the one more frequently describes things as they are interesting in themselves—the other for the sake of the associations of ideas connected with them; that the one dwells more on the immediate impressions of objects on the senses—the other on the ideas which they suggest to the imagination. The one is the poetry of form, the other of effect. The one gives only what is necessarily implied in the subject, the other all that can possibly arise out of it. The one seeks to identify the imitation with the external object—clings to it—is inseparable from it—is either that or nothing; the other seeks to identify the original impression with whatever else, within the range of thought or feeling, can strengthen, relieve, adorn, or elevate it. Hence the severity and simplicity of the Greek tragedy, which excluded everything foreign or unnecessary to the subject. Hence the Unities: for, in order to identify the imitation as much as possible with the reality, and leave nothing to mere imagination, it was necessary to give the same coherence and consistency to the different parts of a story, as to the different limbs of a statue. Hence the beauty and grandeur of their materials; for, deriving their power over the mind from the truth of the imitation, it was necessary that the subject which they made choice of, and from which they could not depart, should be in itself grand and beautiful. Hence the perfection of their execution; which consisted in giving the utmost harmony, delicacy, and refinement to the details of a given subject. Now, the characteristic excellence of the moderns is the reverse of all this. As, according to our author, the poetry of the Greeks is the same as their sculpture; so, he says, our own more nearly resembles painting—where the artist can relieve and throw back his figures at pleasure—use a greater variety of contrasts—and where light and shade, like the colours of fancy, are reflected on the different objects. The Muse of classical poetry should be represented as a beautiful naked figure; the Muse of modern poetry should be represented clothed, and with wings. The first has the advantage in point of form; the last in colour and motion.

"Perhaps we may trace this difference to something analogous in physical organization, situation, religion, and manners. First, the physical organization of the Greeks seems to have been more perfect, more susceptible of external impressions, and more in harmony with external nature than ours, who have not the same advantages of climate and constitution. Born of a beautiful and vigorous race, with quick senses and a clear understanding, and placed under a mild heaven, they gave the fullest development to their external faculties: and where all is perceived easily, every thing is perceived in harmony and proportion. It is the stern genius of the North which drives men back upon their own resources, which makes them slow to perceive, and averse to feel, and which, by rendering them insensible to the single, successive impressions of things, requires their collective and combined force to rouse the imagination violently and unequally. It should be remarked, however, that the early poetry of some of the Eastern nations has even more of that irregularity, wild enthusiasm, and disproportioned grandeur, which has been considered as the distinguishing character of the Northern nations.

"Again, a good deal may be attributed to the state of manners and political institutions. The ancient Greeks were warlike tribes encamped in cities. They had no other country than that which was enclosed within the walls of the town in which they lived. Each individual belonged, in the first instance, to the state; and his relations to it were so close as to take away, in a great measure, all personal independence and free-will. Every one was mortised to his place in society, and had his station assigned him as part of the political machine, which could only subsist by strict subordination and regularity. Every man was, as it were, perpetually on duty, and his faculties kept constant watch and ward. Energy of purpose and intensity of observation became the necessary characteristics of such a state of society; and the general principle communicated itself from this ruling concern for the public, to morals, to art, to language, to every thing. The tragic poets of Greece were among her best soldiers; and it is no wonder that they were as severe in their poetry as in their discipline. Their swords and their styles carved out their way with equal sharpness. After all, however, the tragedies of Sophocles, which are the perfection of the classical style, are hardly tragedies in our sense of the word.* They do not exhibit the extremity of human passion and suffering. The object of modern tragedy is to represent the soul utterly subdued as it were, or at least convulsed and overthrown, by passion or misfortune. That of the ancients was to show how the greatest crimes could be perpetrated with the least remorse, and the greatest calamities borne with the least emotion. Firmness of purpose and calmness of sentiment are their leading characteristics. Their heroes and heroines act and suffer as if they were always in the presence of a higher power, or as if human life itself were a religious ceremony, performed in honour of the Gods and of the State. The mind is not shaken to its centre; the whole being is not crushed or broken down. Contradictory motives are not accumulated; the utmost force of imagination and passion is not exhausted to overcome the repugnance of the will to crime; the contrast and combination of outward accidents are not called in to overwhelm the mind with the whole weight of unexpected calamity. The dire conflict of the feelings, the desperate struggle with fortune, are seldom there All is conducted with a fatal composure; prepared and submitted to with inflexible constancy, as if Nature were only an instrument in the hands of Fate.

"This state of things was afterwards continued under the Roman empire. In the ages of chivalry and romance, which, after a considerable interval, succeeded its dissolution, and which have stamped their character on modern genius and literature all was reversed. Society was again resolved into its component parts; and the world was, in a manner, to begin anew The ties which bound the citizen and the soldier to the state being loosened, each person was thrown back into the circle of the domestic affections, or left to pursue his doubtful way to fame and fortune alone. This interval of time might be accordingly supposed to give birth to all that was constant in attachment, ad

* The difference in the tone of moral sentiment is the greatest of all others

venturous in action, strange, wild, and extravagant in invention. Human life took the shape of a busy, voluptuous dream, where the imagination was now lost amidst 'antres vast and deserts idle;' or suddenly transported to stately palaces, echoing with dance and song. In this uncertainty of events, this fluctuation of hopes and fears, all objects became dim, confused, and vague. Magicians, dwarfs, giants, followed in the train of romance; and Orlando's enchanted sword, the horn which he carried with him, and which he blew thrice at Roncesvalles, and Rogero's winged horse, were not sufficient to protect them in their unheard-of encounters, or deliver them from their inextricable difficulties. It was a return to the period of the early heroic ages; but tempered by the difference of domestic manners, and the spirit of religion. The marked difference in the relation of the sexes arose from the freedom of choice in women: which, from being the slaves of the will and passions of men, converted them into the arbiters of their fate, which introduced the modern system of gallantry, and first made love a feeling of the heart, founded on mutual affection and esteem. The leading virtues of the Christian religion, self-denial and generosity, assisted in producing the same effect. Hence the spirit of chivalry, of romantic love and honour!

"The mythology of the romantic poetry differed from the received religion: both differed essentially from the classical. The religion or mythology of the Greeks was nearly allied to their poetry: it was material and definite. The Pagan system reduced the gods to the human form, and elevated the powers of inanimate nature to the same standard. Statues carved out of the finest marble, represented the objects of their religious worship in airy porticos, in solemn temples and consecrated groves. Mercury was seen 'new lighted on some heaven-kissing hill;' and the Naiad or Dryad came gracefully forth as the personified genius of the stream or wood. All was subjected to the senses. The Christian religion, on the contrary, is essentially spiritual and abstracted: it is 'the evidence of things unseen.' In the Heathen mythology, form is everywhere predominant; in the Christian, we find only unlimited, undefined power. The imagination alone 'broods over the immense abyss, and makes it pregnant.' There is, in the habitual belief of an universal, invisible principle of all things, a vastness and obscurity which confounds our perceptions, while it exalts our piety. A mysterious awe surrounds the doctrines of the Christian faith: the infinite is everywhere before us, whether we turn to reflect on what is revealed to us of the divine nature or our own.

"History, as well as religion, has contributed to enlarge the bounds of imagination; and both together, by showing past and future objects at an interminable distance, have accustomed the mind to contemplate and take an interest in the obscure and shadowy. The ancients were more circumscribed within 'the ignorant present time'—spoke only their own language—were conversant only with their own customs—were acquainted only with the events of their own history. The mere lapse of time then, aided by the art of printing, has served to accumulate an endless mass of mixed and contradictory materials; and, by extending our knowledge to a greater number of things, has made our particular ideas less perfect and distinct. The constant reference to a former state of manners and literature is a marked feature in modern poetry. We are always talking of the Greeks and Romans:—*they* never said anything of us. This circumstance has tended to give a certain abstract elevation, and ethereal refinement to the mind, without strengthening it. We are lost in wonder at what has been done, and dare not think of emulating it. The earliest modern poets, accordingly, may be conceived to hail the glories of the antique world, dawning through the dark abyss of time; while revelation, on the other hand, opened its path to the skies. So Dante represents himself as conducted by Virgil to the shades below; while Beatrice welcomes him to the abodes of the blest."

The French are the only people in modern Europe who have professedly imitated the ancients; but from their being utterly unlike the Greeks or Romans, they have produced a dramatic style of their own, which is neither classical nor romantic. The same article contains the following censure of this style:

"The true poet identifies the reader with the characters he represents; the French poet only identifies him with himself. There is scarcely a single page of their tragedy which fairly throws nature open to you. It is tragedy in masquerade. We never get beyond conjecture and reasoning—beyond the general impression of the situation of the persons—beyond general reflections on their passions—beyond general descriptions of objects. We never get at that something more, which is what we are in search of, namely, what we ourselves should feel in the same situations. The true poet transports you to the scene—you see and hear what is passing—you catch, from the lips of the persons concerned, what lies nearest to their hearts;—the French poet takes you into his closet, and reads you a lecture upon it. The *chef-d'œuvres* of their stage, then, are, at best, only ingenious paraphrases of nature. The dialogue is a tissue of common-places, of laboured declamations on human life, of learned casuistry on the passions, on virtue and vice, which any one else might make just as well as the person speaking; and yet, what the persons themselves would say, is all we want to know, and all for which the poet puts them into those situations."

After the Restoration, that is, after the return of the exiled family of the Stuarts from France, our writers transplanted this artificial, monotonous, and imposing common-place style into England, by imitations and translations, where it could not be expected to take deep root, and produce wholesome fruits, and where it has indeed given rise to little but turgidity and rant in men of original force of genius, and to insipidity and formality in feebler copyists. Otway is the only writer of this school, who, in the lapse of a century and a half, has produced a tragedy (upon the classic or regular model) of indisputable excellence and lasting interest. The merit of 'Venice Preserved' is not confined to its effect on the stage, or to the opportunity it affords for the display of the powers of the actors in it, of a Jaffier, a Pierre, a Belvidera: it reads as well in the closet, and loses little or none of its power of rivetting breathless attention, and stirring the deepest yearnings of affection. It has passages of great beauty in themselves (detached from the fable) touches of true nature and pathos, though none equal or indeed comparable to what we meet with in Shakspeare and other writers of that day; but the awful suspense of the situations, the conflict of duties and passions, the intimate bonds that unite the characters together, and that are violently rent asunder like the parting of soul and body, the solemn march of the tragical events to the fatal catastrophe that winds up and closes over all, give to this production of Otway's Muse a charm and power that bind it like a spell on the public mind, and have made it a proud and inseparable adjunct of the English stage. Thomson has given it due honour in his feeling verse, when he exclaims:

> "See o'er the stage the Ghost of Hamlet stalks,
> Othelo rages, poor Monimia mourns,
> And Belvidera pours her soul in love."

There is a mixture of effeminacy, of luxurious and cowardly indulgence of his wayward sensibility, in Jaffier's character, which is, however, finely relieved by the bold, intrepid villany and contemptuous irony of Pierre, while it is excused by the difficulties of his situation, and the loveliness of Belvidera; but in the 'Orphan' there is little else but this voluptuous effeminacy of sentiment and mawkish distress, which strikes directly at the root of that mental fortitude and heroic cast of thought which alone makes tragedy endurable—that renders its sufferings pathetic, or its struggles sublime. Yet there are lines and passages in it of extreme tenderness and beauty; and few persons, I conceive (judging from my own experience) will read it at a certain time of life without shedding tears over it as fast as the "Arabian trees their medicinal gums." Otway always touched the reader, for he had himself a heart. We may be sure that he blotted his page often with his tears, on which so many drops have since fallen from glistening eyes, "that sacred pity had engendered there." He had susceptibility of feeling and warmth of genius; but he had not equal depth of thought or loftiness of imagination, and indulged his mere sensibility too much, yielding to the immediate impression or emotion excited in his own mind, and not placing himself enough in the minds and situations of others, or following the workings of nature sufficiently with keenness of eye and strength of will into its heights and depths, its strongholds as well as its weak sides. The 'Orphan' was attempted to be revived some time since, with the advantage of Miss O'Neill playing the part of Monimia. It, however, did not entirely succeed (as it appeared at the time) from the plot turning all on one circumstance, and that hardly of a nature to be obtruded on the public notice. The incidents and characters are taken almost literally from an old play by Robert Tailor, called 'The Hog hath Lost his Pearl.'

Addison's 'Cato,' in spite of Dennis's criticism, still retains possession of the stage with all its unities. My love and admiration for Addison is as great as any person's, let that other person be who he will; but it is not founded on his 'Cato,' in extolling which Whigs and Tories contended in loud applause. The interest of this play (bating that shadowy regret that always clings to and flickers round the form of free antiquity) is confined to the declamation, which is feeble in itself, and not heard on the stage. I have seen Mr. Kemble in this part repeat the 'Soliloquy on Death' without a line being distinctly heard; nothing was observable but the thoughtful motion of his lips, and the occasional extension of his hand in sign of doubts suggested or resolved; yet this beautiful and expressive dumb-show, with the propriety of his costume, and the elegance of his attitude and figure, excited the most lively interest, and kept attention even more on the stretch, to catch every imperfect syllable or speaking gesture. There is nothing, however, in the play to excite ridicule, or shock by absurdity, except the love scenes, which are passed over as what the spectator has no proper concern with; and however feeble or languid the interest produced by a dramatic exhibition, unless there is some positive stumbling-block thrown in the way, or gross offence given to an audience, it is generally suffered to linger on to a *euthanasia*, instead of dying a violent and premature death. If an author (particularly an author of high reputation) can contrive to preserve a uniform degree of insipidity, he is nearly sure of impunity. It is the mixture of great faults with splendid passages (the more striking from the contrast) that it is inevitable damnation. Every one must have seen the audience tired out and watching for an opportunity to wreak their vengeance on the author, and yet not able to accomplish their wish, because no one part seemed more tiresome or worthless than another. The philosophic mantle of Addison's 'Cato,' when it no longer spreads its graceful folds on the shoulders of John Kemble, will I fear fall to the ground; nor do I think Mr. Kean likely to pick it up again, with dauntless ambition or stoic pride, like that of Coriolanus. He could not play Cato (at least I think not) for the same reason that he will play Coriolanus. He can always play a living man; he cannot play a lifeless statue.

Dryden's plays have not come down to us, except in the collection of his printed works. The last of them that was on the list of regular acting plays was 'Don Sebastian.' 'The Mask of Arthur and Emmeline' was the other day revived at one of our theatres without much success. 'Alexander the Great' is by Lee, who wrote some things in conjunction with Dryden, and who had far more power and passion of an irregular and turbulent kind, bordering upon constitutional morbidity, and who might have done better things (as we see from his 'Œdipus') had not his genius been perverted and rendered worse than abortive by carrying the vicious manner of his age to the greatest excess. Dryden's plays are perhaps the fairest specimen of what this manner was. I do not know how to describe it better than by saying that it is one continued and exaggerated common-place. All the characters are put into a swaggering attitude of dignity, and tricked out in the pomp of ostentatious drapery. The images are extravagant, yet not far-fetched; they are outrageous caricatures of obvious thoughts; the language oscillates between bombast and pathos: the characters are noisy pretenders to virtue, and shallow boasters in vice; the versification is laboured and monotonous, quite unlike the admirably free and flowing rhyme of his satires, in which he felt the true inspiration of his subject, and could find modulated sounds to express it. Dryden had no dramatic genius either in tragedy or comedy. In his plays he mistakes blasphemy for sublimity, and ribaldry for wit. He had so little notion of his own powers, that he has put Milton's 'Paradise Lost' into dramatic rhyme to make Adam look like a fine gentleman; and has added a double love-plot to 'The Tempest,' to "relieve the killing languor and over-laboured lassitude" of that solitude of the imagination, in which Shakspeare had left the inhabitants of his Enchanted Island. I will give two passages out of 'Don Sebastian,' in illustration of what I have said above of this mock-heroic style.

Almeyda advising Sebastian to fly from the power of Muley-Moloch, addresses him thus:

"Leave then the luggage of your fate behind;
To make your flight more easy, leave Almeyda.
Nor think me left a base, ignoble prey,
Exposed to this inhuman tyrant's lust.
My virtue is a guard beyond my strength;
And death my last defence within my call."

Sebastian answers very gravely:

"Death may be called in vain, and cannot come:
Tyrants can tie him up from your relief:
Nor has a Christian privilege to die.
Alas, thou art too young in thy new faith:
Brutus and Cato might discharge their souls,
And give them furloughs for another world:
But we, like sentries, are obliged to stand,
In starless nights, and wait the appointed hour."

Sebastian then urging her to prevent the tyrant's designs by an instant marriage, she says:

"'Tis late to join, when we must part so soon.
Sebastian. Nay, rather let us haste it, ere we part:
Our souls, for want of that acquaintance here,
May wander in the starry walks above,
And, forced on worse companions, miss ourselves."

In the scene with Muley-Moloch, where she makes intercession for Sebastian's life, she says:

"My father's, mother's, brother's death I pardon:
That's somewhat sure, a mighty sum of murder,
Of innocent and kindred blood struck off.
My prayers and penance shall discount for these,
And beg of Heaven to charge the bill on me:
Behold what price I offer, and how dear
To buy Sebastian's life.
Emperour. Let after-reckonings trouble fearful fools;
I'll stand the trial of those trivial crimes:
But since thou begg'st me to prescribe my terms,
The only I can offer are thy love;
And this one day of respite to resolve.

Grant or deny, for thy next word is Fate;
And Fate is deaf to prayer.
Almeyda. May heav'n be so
At thy last breath to thine: I curse thee not:
For who can better curse the plague or devil
Than to be what they are? That curse be thine
Now do not speak, Sebastian, for you need not,
But die, for I resign your life: Look, heav'n,
Almeyda dooms her dear Sebastian's death!
But is there heaven, for I begin to doubt?
The skies are hush'd; no grumbling thunders roll:
Now take your swing, ye impious: sin, unpunish'd.
Eternal Providence seems over-watch'd,
And with a slumbering nod assents to murder . . .
Farewell, my lost Sebastian!
I do not beg, I challenge justice now:
O Powers, if Kings be your peculiar care,
Why plays this wretch with your prerogative?
Now flash him dead, now crumble him to ashes:
Or henceforth live confined in your own palace;
And look not idly out upon a world
That is no longer yours."

These passages, with many like them, will be found in the first scene of the third act.

The occasional striking expressions, such as that of souls at the resurrection "fumbling for their limbs," are the language of strong satire and habitual disdain, not proper to tragic or serious poetry.

After Dryden there is no writer that has acquired much reputation as a tragic poet for the next hundred years. In the hands of his successors, the Smiths, the Hughes, the Hills, the Murphys, the Dr. Johnsons, of the reigns of the first Georges, tragedy seemed almost afraid to know itself, and certainly did not stand where it had done a hundred and fifty years before. It had degenerated by regular and studied gradations into the most frigid, insipid, and insignificant of all things. It faded to a shade, it tapered to a point, "fine by degrees, and beautifully less." I do not believe there is a single play of this period which could be read with any degree of interest or even patience, by a modern reader of poetry, if we except the productions of Southern, Lillo and Moore, the authors of 'The Gamester,

'Oroonoko,' and 'Fatal Curiosity,' and who, instead of mounting on classic stilts and making rhetorical flourishes, went out of the established road to seek for truth and nature and effect in the commonest life and lowest situations. In short, the only tragedy of this period is that to which their productions gave a name, and which has been called in contradistinction by the French, and with an express provision for its merits and defects, the '*Tragédie bourgeoise.*' An anecdote is told of the first of these writers by Gray, in one of his letters, dated from Horace Walpole's country-seat, about the year 1740, who says, "Old Mr. Southern is here, who is now above 80; a very agreeable old man, at least I think so when I look in his face, and think of Isabella and Oroonoko." It is pleasant to see these traits of attachment and gratitude kept up in successive generations of poets to one another, and also to find that the same works of genius that have "sent us weeping to our beds," and made us "rise sadder and wiser on the morrow morn," have excited just the same fondness of affection in others before we were born; and it is to be hoped will do so after we are dead. Our best feelings, and those on which we pride ourselves most, and with most reason, are perhaps the commonest of all others.

Up to the present reign, and during the best part of it (with another solitary exception, 'Douglas,' which, with all its feebleness and extravagance, has in its style and sentiments a good deal of poetical and romantic beauty,) Tragedy wore the face of the Goddess of Dulness in the 'Dunciad,' serene, torpid, sickly, lethargic and affected, till it was roused from its trance by the blast of the French Revolution, and by the loud trampling of the German Pegasus on the English stage, which now appeared as pawing to get free from its ancient trammels, and rampant shook off the incumbrance of all former examples, opinions, prejudices, and principles. If we have not been alive and well since this period, at least we have been alive, and it is better to be alive than dead. The German tragedy (and our own, which is only a branch of it,) aims at effect, and produces it often in the highest degree; and it does this by going all the lengths not only of instinctive feeling, but of speculative opinion, and startling the hearer by overturning all the established maxims of society, and setting at nought all the received rules of composition. It cannot be said of this style that in it "decorum is the principal thing." It is the violation of decorum that is its first and last principle, the beginning, middle, and end. It is an insult and defiance to Aristotle's definition of tragedy. The action is not grave, but extravagant: the fable is not probable, but improbable: the favourite characters are not only low, but vicious: the sentiments are such as do not become the person into whose mouth they are put, nor that of any other person: the language is a mixture of metaphysical jargon and flaring prose: the moral is immorality. In spite of all this, a German tragedy is a good thing. It is a fine hallucination: it is a noble madness, and as there is a pleasure in madness which none but madmen know, so there is a pleasure in reading a German play to be found in no other. The world have thought so: they go to see 'The Stranger,' they go to see 'Lovers' Vows,' and 'Pizarro,' they have their eyes wide open all the time, and almost cry them out before they come away, and therefore they go again. There is something in the style that hits the temper of men's minds; that, if it does not hold the mirror up to nature, yet "shows the very age and body of the time, its form and pressure." It embodies, it sets off and aggrandizes in all the pomp of action, in all the vehemence of hyperbolical declamation, in scenery, in dress, in music, in the glare of the senses, and the glow of sympathy, the extreme opinions which are floating in our time, and which have struck their roots deep and wide below the surface of the public mind. We are no longer as formerly, heroes in warlike enterprize; martyrs to religious faith; but we are all the partisans of a political system, and devotees to some theory of moral sentiments. The modern style of tragedy is not assuredly made up of pompous common-place, but it is a tissue of philosophical, political, and moral paradoxes. am not saying whether these paradoxes are true or false: all that I mean to state is, that they are utterly at variance with old opinions, with established rules and existing institutions; that it is this tug of war between the inert prejudice and the startling novelty which is to batter it down (first on the stage of the theatre, and afterwards on the stage of the world,) that gives the excitement and the zest. We see the natural always pitted against the social man; and the majority, who are not of the privileged classes, take part with the former. The hero is a sort of metaphysical Orson, armed not with teeth and a club, but with hard sayings and unanswerable sentences, ticketed and labelled with extracts and mottos from the modern philosophy. This common representative of mankind is a natural son of some feudal lord, or wealthy baron: and he comes to claim, as a matter of course and of simple equity, the rich reversion of the title and estates to which he has a right by the bounty of nature and the privilege of his birth. This produces a very edifying scene, and the proud, unfeeling, unprincipled baron is hooted from the stage. A young woman, a sempstress, or a waiting-maid of much beauty and accomplishment, who would not think of matching with a fellow of low birth or fortune for the world, falls in love with the heir of an immense estate out of pure regard to his mind and person, and thinks it strange that rank and opulence do not follow as natural appendages in the train of sentiment. A lady of fashion, wit, and beauty, forfeits the sanctity of her marriage-vow, but preserves the inviolability of her sentiments and character,

"Pure in the last recesses of the mind"—

and triumphs over false opinion and prejudice, like gold out of the fire, the brighter for the ordeal. A young man turns robber and captain of a gang of banditti; and the wonder is to see the heroic ardour of his sentiments, his aspirations after the most godlike goodness and unsullied reputation, working their way through the repulsiveness of his situation, and making use of fortune only as a foil to nature. The principle of contrast and contradiction is here made use of, and no other. All qualities are reversed: virtue is always at odds with vice, "which shall be which:" the internal character and external situation, the actions and the sentiments, are never in accord: you are to judge of every thing by contraries: those that exalt themselves are abased, and those that should be humbled are exalted: the high places and strongholds of power and greatness are crumbled in the dust; opinions totter, feelings are brought into question, and the world is turned upside down, with all things in it! "There is some soul of goodness in things evil"—and there is some soul of goodness in all this. The world and every thing in it is not just what it ought to be, or what it pretends to be; or such extravagant and prodigious paradoxes would be driven from the stage—would meet with sympathy in no human breast, high or low, young or old. "*There's something rotten in the state of Denmark.*" Opinion is not truth: appearance is not reality: power is not beneficence: rank is not wisdom: nobility is not the only virtue: riches are not happiness: desert and success are different things: actions do not always speak the character any more than words. We feel this, and do justice to the romantic extravagance of the German Muse.

In Germany, where this *outré* style of treating every thing established and adventitious was carried to its height, there were, as we learn from 'The Sorrows of Werter,' seven-and-twenty ranks in society, each raised above the other, and of which the one above did not speak to the one below it. Is it wonderful that the poets and philosophers of Germany, the discontented men of talent, who thought and mourned for themselves and their fellows, the Goëthes, the Lessings, the Schillers, the Kotzebues, felt a sudden and irresistible impulse by a convulsive effort to tear aside this factitious drapery of society, and to throw off that load of bloated prejudice, of maddening pride and superannuated folly, that pressed down every energy of their nature and stifled the breath of liberty, of truth and genius, in their bosoms? These Titans of our days tried to throw off the dead weight that encumbered them, and in so doing, warred not against heaven, but against earth. The same writers (as far as I have seen) have made the only incorrigible Jacobins, and their school of poetry is the only real school of Radical Reform.

In reasoning, truth and soberness may prevail, on which side soever they meet: but in works of imagination novelty has the advantage over prejudice; that which is striking and unheard-of over that which is trite and known before, and that which gives unlimited scope to the indulgence of the feelings and the passions (whether erroneous or not) over that which imposes a restraint upon them.

I have half trifled with this subject; and I believe I have done so because I despaired of finding language for some old rooted feelings I have about it, which a theory could neither give nor can it take away. 'The Robbers' was the first play I ever read· and the effect it produced upon me was the greatest. It stunned me like a blow, and I have not recovered enough from it to describe how it was. There are impressions which neither time nor circumstances can efface. Were I to live much longer than I have any chance of doing, the books which I read when I was young I can never forget. Five-and-twenty years have elapsed since I first read the translation of 'The Robbers,' but they have not blotted the impression from my mind: it is here still, an old dweller in the chambers of the brain. The scene in particular in which Moor looks through his tears at the evening sun from the mountain' brow, and says in his despair, "It was my wish like him to live, like him to die: it was an idle thought, a boy's conceit," took fast hold of my imagination, and that sun has to me never set! The last interview in 'Don Carlos' between the two lovers, in which the injured bride struggles to burst the prison-house of her destiny, in which her hopes and youth lie coffined, and buried, as it were, alive, under the oppression of unspeakable anguish, I remember gave me a deep sense of suffering and a strong desire after good, which has haunted me ever since. I do not like Schiller's later style so well. His 'Wallenstein,' which is admirably and almost literally translated by Mr. Coleridge, is stately, thoughtful, and imaginative: but where is the enthusiasm, the throbbing of hope and fear, the mortal struggle between the passions; as if all the happiness or misery of a life were crowded into a moment, and the die was to be cast that instant? Kotzebue's best work I read first in Cumberland's imitation of it in 'The Wheel of Fortune;' and I confess that that style of sentiment which seems to make of life itself a long-drawn endless sigh, has something in it that pleases me, in spite of rules and criticism. Goëthe's tragedies are (those that I have seen of them, his 'Count Egmont,' 'Stella,' &c.) constructed upon the second or inverted manner of the German stage, with a deliberate design to avoid all possible effect and interest, and this object is completely accomplished. He is however spoken of with enthusiasm almost amounting to idolatry by his countrymen, and those among ourselves who import heavy German criticism into this country in shallow, flat-bottomed unwieldly intellects. Madame de Stael speaks of one passage in his 'Iphigenia,' where he introduces a fragment of an old song, which the Furies are supposed to sing to Tantalus in Hell, reproaching him with the times when he sat with the Gods at their golden tables, and with his after-crimes that hurled him from heaven, at which he turns his eyes from his children and hangs his head in mournful silence. This is the true sublime. Of all his works I like his 'Werter' best, nor would I part with it at a venture, even for the 'Memoirs of Anastasius the Greek,' whoever is the author; nor ever cease to think of the times, "when in the fine summer evenings they saw the frank, noble-minded enthusiast coming up from the valley," nor of "the high grass that by the light of the departing sun waved in the breeze over his grave."

But I have said enough to give an idea of this modern style, compared with our own early Dramatic Literature, of which I had to treat. I have done: and if I have done no better, the fault has been in me, not in the subject. My liking to this grew with my knowledge of it: but so did my anxiety to do it justice. I somehow felt it as a point of honour not to make my hearers think less highly of some of these old writers than I myself did of them. If I have praised an author, it was because I liked him: if I have quoted a passage, it was because it pleased me in the reading: if I have spoken contemptuously of any one, it has been reluctantly. It is no easy task, that a writer, even in so humble a class as myself, takes upon him; he is scouted and ridiculed if he fails; and if he succeeds, the enmity and cavils and malice with which he is assailed, are just in proportion to his success. The coldness and jealousy of his friends not unfrequently keep pace with the rancour of his enemies. They do not like you a bit the better for fulfilling the good opinion they always entertained of you. They would wish you to be always promising a great deal, and doing nothing, that they may answer for the performance. That shows their sagacity, and does not hurt their vanity. An author wastes his time in painful study and obscure researches, to gain a little breath of popularity, meets with nothing but vexation and disappointment in ninety-nine instances out of a hundred; or when he thinks to grasp the luckless prize, finds it not worth the trouble—the perfume of a minute, fleeting as a shadow, hollow as a sound: "as often got without merit as lost without deserving." He thinks that the attainment of acknowledged excellence will secure him the expression of those feelings in others, which the image and hope of it had excited in his own breast, but instead of that he meets with nothing (or scarcely nothing) but squint-eyed suspicion, idiot wonder, and grinning scorn. It seems hardly worth while to have taken all the pains he has been at for this!

In youth we borrow patience from our future years: the spring of hope gives us courage to act and suffer. A cloud is upon our onward path, and we fancy that all is sunshine beyond it. The prospect seems endless, because we do not know the end of it. We think that life is long, because art is so, and that, because we have much to do, it is well worth doing: or that no exertions can be too great, no sacrifices too painful, to overcome the difficulties we have to encounter. Life is a continued struggle to be what we are not, and to do what we cannot. But as we approach the goal, we draw in the reins; the impulse is less, as we have not so far to go; as we see objects nearer, we become less sanguine in the pursuit: it is not the despair of not attaining, so much as knowing that there is nothing worth obtaining, and the fear of having nothing left even to wish for, that damps our ardour and relaxes our efforts; and if the mechanical habit did not increase the facility, would, I believe, take away all inclination or power to do anything. We stagger on the few remaining paces to the end of our journey; make perhaps one final effort; and are glad when our task is done!

BOOKS FOR THE YOUNG.

ANIMALS, THEIR HOMES AND THEIR HABITS.

A Book for Young People. By UNCLE WARREN. With 24 full-page Illustrations. Small folio. Cloth, full gilt, and gilt edges. $2.00.

This volume, like Uncle Warren's about Birds, is especially written for the young, and has a fund of information which will be highly enjoyed by them.

BIRDS, THEIR HOMES AND THEIR HAUNTS.

A Book for Young People. By UNCLE WARREN. With 24 full-page Illustrations. Small folio. Cloth, full gilt, and gilt edges. $2.00.

This work, carefully prepared for the young, contains an account of upward of a hundred of the most popular birds. It is crowded with instruction and entertainment, and well adapted to the taste of the children of the present generation.

RED BEAUTY.

A STORY OF THE PAWNEE TRAIL. By WILLIAM O. STODDARD. With Frontispiece. 12mo. Extra cloth. $1.25.

A thrilling tale of pioneer life in the far West, written in Mr. Stoddard's happiest vein. It is full of adventure and stirring incidents, and graphically depicting the dangers surrounding first settlers in that region.

CHARLEY LUCKEN AT SCHOOL AND COLLEGE

By the Rev. H. C. ADAMS, M.A., author of "For James or George," "School-Boy Honor," etc. With Illustrations by J. FINNEMORE. 12mo. Extra cloth. $1.50.

THE PRINCESS AND THE GOBLIN.

By GEORGE MACDONALD. With Thirty Illustrations. 12mo. Extra cloth. $1.25.

BY THE SAME AUTHOR:

THE PRINCESS AND CURDIE.

A New Juvenile. Companion volume to "The Princess and the Goblin." With numerous full-page Illustrations. 12mo. Extra cloth. $1.25.

RANALD BANNERMAN'S BOYHOOD.

With numerous Illustrations. 12mo. Extra cloth. $1.25.

AT THE BACK OF THE NORTH WIND.

With 76 Illustrations. 12mo. Extra cloth. $1.25.

THE FOUR VOLUMES IN A BOX, $5.00.

www.ingramcontent.com/pod-product-compliance
Lightning Source LLC
LaVergne TN
LVHW050528100826
845148LV00002B/475